The Boeing 787
DREAMLINER

Claude G. Luisada
& Steven D. Kimmell

Schiffer Publishing Ltd

4880 Lower Valley Road • Atglen, PA 19310

Dedication

This book is respectfully dedicated to Michael "Mike" Bair, Boeing Commercial Airplanes Company, Vice-President and General Manager on the 787 Program, who provided leadership for the design and development of the Dreamliner with his vision, skills, and understanding; Steven D. Kimmell, 1938-2012, co-author and director of illustrations for this book – a man of tremendous integrity and intellect and the truest of friends; and Andrea R. Luisada, my daughter. May the sun always shine on you.

Title Page: One of the Boeing 787 Dreamliner test aircraft flies near Mt. Ranier, Washington.

Acknowledgments

The author wants to acknowledge the various organizations and people who made it possible to write this book. First of all, the Boeing Company and Boeing Commercial Airplanes, a division of the Boeing Company. At Boeing Commercial Airplanes, the following people were instrumental in helping me obtain the necessary information. Prior to starting this project, I am grateful to Yvonne Leach, then head of 787 Communications, who with great patience got me started and who pointed out that to write this book would involve a process. She has since moved on to greater responsibilities. Within 787 Communications, I am indebted to the following individuals: Jennifer Cram, Scott Lefeber, and Deborah Heathers. Of the three, I worked the longest with Scott Lefeber and he was instrumental in arranging a number of visits to Boeing facilities.

All illustration credits are Boeing Commercial Airplanes except where otherwise shown.

Copyright © 2014 by Claude G. Luisada

Library of Congress Control Number: 2014932628

Type set in Helvetica & Times

ISBN: 978-0-7643-4637-8
Printed in China

Published by Schiffer Publishing, Ltd.
4880 Lower Valley Road
Atglen, PA 19310
Phone: (610) 593-1777 Fax: (610) 593-2002
E-mail: Info@schifferbooks.com

For our complete selection of fine books on this and related subjects, please visit our website at www.schifferbooks.com. You may also write for a free catalog.

This book may be purchased from the publisher. Please try your bookstore first.

We are always looking for people to write books on new and related subjects. If you have an idea for a book, please contact us at proposals@schifferbooks.com

Schiffer Publishing's titles are available at special discounts for bulk purchases for sales promotions or premiums. Special editions, including personalized covers, corporate imprints, and excerpts can be created in large quantities for special needs. For more information, contact the publisher.

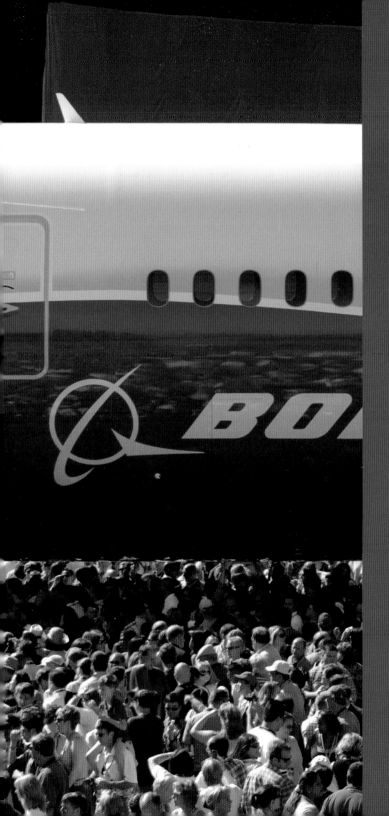

Contents

Prologue

Tuesday, December 15, 2009
Paine Field, Everett, Washington

The weather outside is typical of the Seattle Metropolitan Area in winter. It is cloudy, drizzling, cold, and rather windy. And yet, a crowd estimated at over 12,000 people is huddling in a group at one side of the field. Nearby sits a beautiful, large twin-jet commercial transport painted in blue and white and carrying in bold letters the word BOEING. This is Boeing's latest airplane design, the 787 Dreamliner, and today is the moment of truth, for today, this airplane is expected to leave the ground on its very first flight.

One of the 787 test aircraft in flight.

The people, standing and shuffling around trying to stay warm, are mostly Boeing employees who have come outside for this historic moment, the first first flight of the first totally new airplane design for Boeing in almost a decade. Included in the throng are some 200 or more media people from many parts of the world. There is still a question as to whether the weather will permit this first flight to take place today. Earlier in the morning, the ceiling was around 1,500 feet above ground, considered to be VFR (Visual Flight Rules) weather and thus legal for flying without resorting to instruments. But, for such an important flight as this, a 1,500-foot ceiling is really too low. Now, it is announced that the ceiling has lifted to between 2,500 and 3,500 feet, and it becomes obvious that the decision has been made to go ahead and fly the airplane!

Now the two-man crew can be seen boarding the airplane. The crew is made up of Chief Pilot Mike Carriker and Captain Randy Neville, both former military pilots with thousands of hours of flight experience. Shortly, the increasing whine of the two Rolls-Royce Trent jet engines is heard, and after a few minutes the 787 begins to taxi very slowly. It follows a long taxi route around the perimeter of Paine Field until it finally reaches the beginning of Runway 34L. After a few short minutes, the landing lights flash on and the whine of the engines is heard increasing to take-off power.

The big, shiny airplane begins to roll and quickly picks up speed. At 10:27 local time and 140 knots Indicated Air Speed (IAS), the airplane rotates and lifts off the runway accompanied by loud cheers and yells from the large crowd; after all, this is *their* airplane. It climbs slowly and gradually disappears into the mist that covers the entire area.

Three hours and six minutes later, the 787 is brought to a safe landing at Boeing Field, south of Seattle. Despite the inclement weather, the flight has been a total success. The 787 was taken to an altitude of 15,000 feet and a speed of 180 knots,

No. 1 787 (ZA001) lifting off from Paine Field on the first ever flight, December 15, 2009.

the landing gear was cycled, and the airplane was tested in a variety of ways.

For the Boeing Commercial Airplane Company and for commercial aviation, it is truly the beginning of a new era. The Dreamliner represents a new generation of jet transport, with new materials, aerodynamics, engine design, increased electronic architecture, and passenger-oriented interiors. It also represents a very significant reduction in both operating and maintenance costs to the airlines that buy it. So, jump aboard and let us together begin this voyage of discovery to learn how and why Boeing developed, built, and sold the exciting 787 Dreamliner.

CHAPTER 1

From Whence it Came

Commercial airplanes are not usually just the result of a designer's dream at three in the morning after a hard night, although sometimes they are the result of a far-reaching vision. Generally speaking, modern jet transports are the incarnation of various forces and opportunities that combine to produce a final result. These various forces have to be balanced carefully for the final product to be worth the tremendous research, development, and manufacturing costs that are involved. Furthermore, modern airplanes are the result of a large number of compromises.

The origin of the 787 *Dreamliner* dates back to 1997, when Boeing began a quiet internal company design study called Project 20XX. This was a double-headed effort made up of Project Glacier, which was later named the Sonic Cruiser, and Project Yellowstone, which had three components identified as Y1, Y2, and Y3. The second component, Y2, was a replacement study for the 757 and 767, and was first known as the 7E7, then the 787.

Components Y1 and Y3 were less clearly identified, but Y1 was meant to study an aircraft design to replace the 737, while Y3 was meant to study a replacement for the 777 and even the 747 long-range models.

There were various reasons for Boeing to initiate Project 20XX at this particular time. One reason was that Boeing felt sales of the 767 were beginning to slow down. A second reason was that the sales numbers of the competing Airbus A330 and A340 were selling better than the 767. The Airbus models had 295 to 335 seats, versus 181 to 255 for the 767-200ER, while the 767 had greater range. The later 767-300ER and 400ER carried more passengers than the A330 or A340, but the range was roughly the same. Additionally, the A340, having four engines versus the two of the 767, was less economical. Interestingly enough, the sales for the A330 and the A340 for this period were almost identical. The Boeing 767-300ER greatly outsold the 767-200, which was probably an indication that airlines were seeking greater range versus more seats.

The chart below shows a comparison of sales for the two airplanes over the period 1981 through 1997, when Project 20XX was initiated.

Year	767	A330/A340
1981	5	-
1982	2	-
1983	20	-
1984	15	-
1985	38	-
1986	23	-
1987	57	-
1988	83	6
1989	100	188
1990	52	33
1991	65	31
1992	21	23
1993	54	16

1994	17	30
1995	22	19
1996	43	76
1997	79	89
Total	697	511

The chart shows how the sales for the 767 and the A330/A340 moved up and down, almost in lockstep year by year. This can be interpreted as demonstrating that both Boeing and Airbus were susceptible to the same economic trends that affected airlines around the world.

Meanwhile, the 777 was being upgraded with such meaningful changes as greater range, and by the end of 1997, it had outsold the competing Airbus A340 by a considerable margin. The 777 sales were due in part to increases in gross weight and range extensions. But the 777 was really too big for some of the applications that the airlines were considering, as will explained later in this chapter. Boeing worked the two branches of Project 20XX while keeping an eye on both the airline situation and competition from Airbus.

Boeing was also conscious of the fact that in the 767-size category, it should start looking at an aircraft that could incorporate new technology. The 767 design used 1970s technology, and it was now time to take advantage of advances, such as a higher level of electronic integration and sophistication and a possible increase in the use of composites.

Another reason for this dual project was undoubtedly the fact that Boeing had not fielded

A Boeing 767-300 ER twin-aisle, wide-body transport with extended range.

The Boeing Sonic Cruiser, a highly advanced design originally conceived as a replacement for the 767.

any new designs since the 777 in 1990. Before that was the successful double program of the 757 and 767. The 757 line was shut down in 2005 after delivering 1,049 airplanes. The 767 production line, which had delivered 682 airplanes by the end of 1997, was still functioning, but at a far slower rate. What Boeing was looking at conceptually was a replacement for the 767, which, after all, embodied technology that dated back to the late 1970s. While the 777 was a newer design that continued to sell well, it was also a larger airplane that seated more passengers and was not truly a replacement for the 767. In fact, as it turned out, the 777 and 787 complemented each other and led to several airlines ordering both models – a happy circumstance for

the company. Boeing was also keeping an eye on the Airbus 330 and 340 models, which were in the same size and range category as the 767.

The basic premise that Boeing made back in 1997 was that the 767 was unlikely to garner many new sales; this was largely correct, although it did continue to sell at a rate that enabled Boeing to keep the production line open while making a profit.

The table below shows 767 sales from 1998 through 2010 and reflects a stronger-than-expected sales quantity.

Year	Sales
1998	38
1999	30
2000	9
2001	40
2002	8
2003	11
2004	8
2005	19
2006	10
2007	36
2008	24
2009	7
2010	3

Initially, the main attraction of Project 20XX was the Sonic Cruiser. This was an airplane of truly advanced design, with canards near the nose, a delta wing, and double horizontal fins located just above the rear-mounted twin engines. It was designed primarily to fly between city pairs. The Sonic Cruiser would have been an airplane similar in size and operating cost to the 767-300, but able to operate at Mach 0.95 to 0.98 – right in the transonic range. With such a cruising speed, a minimum of one hour could be cut from a transcontinental flight and two hours from a trans-Pacific flight. Thus, the proposed design would have had a 15 to 20 percent speed advantage over other commercial jets. Moreover, in spite of the increase in cruising speeds, the Sonic Cruiser was expected to use the same amount of fuel as other commercial transports of comparable size. This was to be attained by jet engines of improved design, which would also be quieter and produce lower nitrogen oxide emissions.

Part of the initial excitement over the Sonic Cruiser came from the commercial air carriers, and for good reason. Certain airlines make a large percentage of their profit on long flights with business and first-class passengers. With the speed advantage provided by the Sonic Cruiser, these airlines saw the airplane as a tremendous drawing card for such passengers, for whom time was money.

The two design projects had moved forward concurrently from the beginning, and much of the technology being considered, particularly the use of composites, was shared between the two. But the Sonic Cruiser first ran into the problem of finding a suitable engine with the right combination of power and economy. What is more, the Sonic Cruiser carried the same number of passengers at a higher speed, but also at a higher operating cost, while the 7E7 traded off the higher speed for lower operating costs.

By September 2001, the terrorist attack on the World Trade Center buildings and the Pentagon finally spelled the end of that project. This was the case because the downward economic spiral that was already under way by that date had picked up speed, and the airlines, now fighting for their economic survival, could see no real advantage in the purchase of the Sonic Cruiser.

Thus, while early on there was much talk in the aviation press about this advanced design, in time, the airlines' enthusiasm died down as fuel prices rose. Some environmentalists mistakenly thought the airplane would use more fuel than other models and the economics for operating the Sonic Cruiser no longer appeared quite so advantageous to the airlines. In essence, the airlines decided to trade the 20 percent speed advantage of the Sonic Cruiser for the 20 percent cost advantage of the 7E7. It was at that point that the 7E7 design came to the forefront, as the airlines became more concerned with operating costs and efficiency than speed. The Sonic Cruiser project was finally terminated in December 2002, and the entire focus was then put on the 7E7 project.

Together with other factors, this downward economic spiral was what really helped to spur the design of the 7E7. In the final analysis, modern airplanes are the result of many compromises. In the commercial jet transport field, they are also an attempt by airplane manufacturers to respond to customer needs. Only when such needs are met can a new design be reasonably assured of commercial success.

The 7E7 Comes to the Fore

Various factors eventually led to the 7E7 design, later to become known as the 787 *Dreamliner*:

1. A general point-to-point philosophy that travelers want to go where they want to go when they want to go
2. The needs expressed by potential customer airlines
3. The competition from Airbus that spurred Boeing to seriously consider a new design. This was particularly true in the case of the A330 versus the 767
4. The availability of new or improved technologies

Let's take a look at these four areas in detail.

General Point-to-Point Philosophy

Travelers in general, and business passengers, in particular, want to go where they want to go when they want to go there. This runs counter to the philosophy prevalent among airline operators that try to siphon flights through hubs, where passengers must then change planes. As explained later in this chapter, hubs not only create passenger dissatisfaction and frustration, they also contribute to other problems that result in excessive financial costs to the airlines. Thus, during Boeing's planning phase for the 7E7, the airlines were beginning to look more favorably at an airplane that could fly point to point with a moderate number of passengers. They also realized that point-to-point operations save time and fuel, as compared with operating through hubs. It has been estimated that, on both domestic and international flights, flying point to point can save an average of more than two and a half hours in total travel time. This estimate is based on there being no delays at the hub.

This translates into a far better and stress-free flight for passengers and a savings for the carrier. In fact, one aviation consultant has estimated that flying passengers on a hub-and-spoke system can cost as much as 45 percent more than flying them point to point.

Airline Needs

The acceptance of a new design by potential customers is what finally determines the success or failure of an airplane design. Historically, numerous excellent airplanes did not sell well, in large part because the airlines either knew or believed that those designs did not meet their needs in terms of customer requirements.

For example, in the 1950s, Boeing's model 377 Stratocruiser and Lockheed's model 1649A Jetstream both failed to sell and lost money for their companies. The Boeing Stratocruiser lost out because it debuted somewhat later than the competing Lockheed Constellation and Super Constellation and the Douglas DC-6 and DC-7 models, owing in part to a 1948 labor strike at Boeing.

The airlines, for the most part, had already committed to other airplanes and Boeing was disadvantaged, although the company did well, selling 888 of the military/cargo tanker version similar to the model 377. In the 1960s, Convair introduced the model 880, a design espoused by Howard Hughes of TWA, and the model 990.

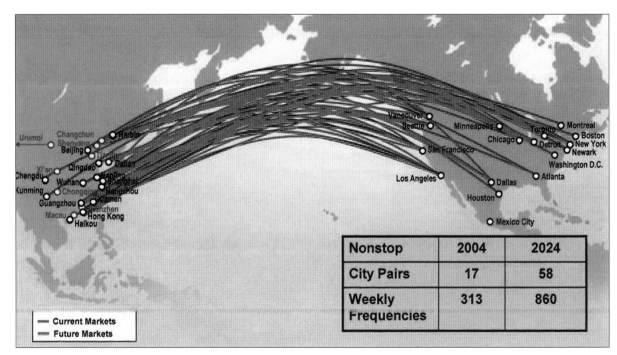

Nonstop	2004	2024
City Pairs	17	58
Weekly Frequencies	313	860

A projection of the huge increase in point-to-point routes across the Pacific Ocean forecast by 2024.

Both were faster than other jet transports, but had less seating capacity and greater fuel consumption; the combination pretty much scared away most of the airlines. Convair lost so much money on these two models that its parent company, General Dynamics, almost went bankrupt. Yet, all these airplanes were good, solid performers. In all cases, either the timing was wrong or the airplanes mentioned were not what the airlines believed they needed to serve their customers and be competitive.

By the early 2000s, the airlines were facing a number of corporate life-threatening problems in addition to the terrorist threat, with its ensuing fear among passengers, and the general downturn in the economy. These problems were:

1. Costly flight delays at major hub airports
2. Passenger dislike of changing airplanes one or more times per trip
3. The opening of new markets, particularly in Pacific Rim countries
4. Steadily increasing fuel prices

Over the past ten to fifteen years, the major hubs became a source of congestion, delays, higher costs, and considerable frustration for passengers. During periods of severe weather, such as thunderstorm activity, heavy snow, and poor visibility, the hubs generated disastrous multi-hour delays, cancellations, and a need to reroute passengers, as well as to deadhead empty airplanes and their crews

The Boeing Model 377 Stratocruiser, a luxury transport of the early 1950s which never sold well.

The Convair CV-880, a jet transport of the early 1960s and the fastest at the time.

The Lockheed Model L-1649A transport of the late 1950s. This aircraft had the longest range of any transport up to that time, but also did not sell well.

The Convair CV-990, a follow-up to the CV-880, which was even faster.

so as to relocate them to the proper airports. All this meant increased costs for airlines that could ill-afford them.

These factors coalesced into the desire by the airlines for an airplane that could service the so-called *long*, *thin routes*. The term is a way of describing routes that are generally 3,000 to 8,000 miles long and connect both large- and medium-sized cities. It also means that loads on such routes would not, and could not warrant the use of large airplanes seating 400 to 550 passengers. Several Pacific Rim countries (Australia, China, India, Japan, and Singapore) had cities that fit this category and lacked direct service to international markets.

The concept of long, thin routes constituted a fundamental change in the thinking of the world's major airlines, most of which had heretofore relied heavily on the hub concept. Yet, the hub concept had become its own worst enemy, with such large numbers of flights congregating at a few large airports to create almost insurmountable air traffic

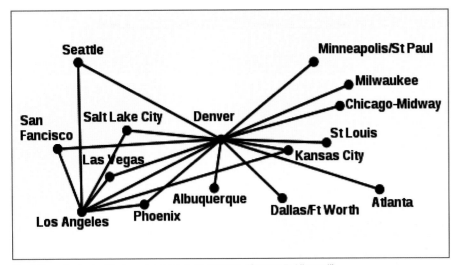

Depiction of a typical hub-and-spoke route pattern. (Steven D. Kimmell)

An Airbus A380 at the Paris Air Show. This is the largest passenger transport to date.

control (ATC) problems. If nothing were changed and the number of flights at these hubs continued to increase, then only a few possible solutions existed. One was to build more expensive runways, which the surrounding communities might object to. Another was to spread out the timing of the flights, which would cancel the purpose of the hubs, namely for passengers to be able to switch flights with minimum delay. This is why the 7E7 came to be called the *hub buster* by the aviation press. If the 7E7 could bring about a quantum increase in direct city-to-city routes, then a number of important results could be expected.

Here is a summary of the expected benefits resulting from the introduction of the 7E7:

1. A reduction in congestion on airways leading to major hubs as well as *at* the major hubs
2. Fewer flight delays caused by bad weather, since many flights would avoid hubs where weather delays might be occurring
3. Fewer transfers for passengers, as well as shorter overall flight times as a result of the removal of an intermediate transfer stop
4. Improvement in aircraft utilization
5. General greater efficiency and lower costs for the airlines

To better visualize the fundamental difference of flying between cities point to point or with a transfer at a hub, consider the following:

- Routing by way of a hub adds a minimum of 60 to 90 minutes flying time, plus the additional cost.
- Point-to-point travel eliminates an additional landing fee, plus an extra climb to altitude, which uses more fuel.
- Hub transfers can add a minimum of 1 to 1½ hours of travel time for the passenger, plus the added stress and possibility of lost baggage.

- Hub operations in themselves result in greater costs for the airlines.

In addition to these considerations, the constantly rising price of fuel was causing a serious threat to airline finances, so the need for greater operating efficiency and lower seat-mile costs became a major priority. Furthermore, passengers were rebelling at the lack of comfort in economy class, especially on trips that lasted up to twenty hours.

During this period, as Boeing's sales staff met with airlines, it became clear that the emphasis by the airlines had gradually shifted from the Sonic Cruiser to the 7E7. Boeing had to consider these market forces if it expected to produce a new transport design that would be a financial success.

As expressed by the airlines, here is a summary of what they needed:

1. An airplane seating 200 to 300 passengers in a three-class configuration

2. A range capability from 3,000 to 8,000 nautical miles, the latter to service long, thin routes
3. An airplane with considerably improved operating costs and lower fuel usage per passenger
4. Greater passenger comfort, especially on long flights, and an improved passenger environment

If Boeing were to bring forth a new design that had the potential to sell for many years, it would have to go a long way toward meeting these needs.

The Airbus Competition

The competition from Airbus had to be a real consideration for Boeing in the planning of any future commercial airplane. Airbus was created as a multinational consortium, and over a period of some twenty years had grown to the point where it was considered to be in a virtual tie with Boeing as the world's leading manufacturer of large commercial airplanes, in terms of the number of airplanes delivered per year. Boeing did, however, appear to have an advantage in the category of large, wide-body, twin-aisle airplanes.

Airbus competition had become an increasing factor for Boeing and the two companies were virtually tied in total airplane sales. Boeing was able to garner more wide-body airplane orders, while the Airbus A380, which inspired a great deal of conversation initially, was beginning to look like a design that had jumped too far in terms of size and might not be as useful as a smaller design. Besides, over the years, some of the Airbus design concepts had come under fire by both engineers and flight crews. The entire Airbus-Boeing rivalry also may well have been overblown by the media.

There had been much controversy over the allegation that Airbus was able to sell its airplanes more cheaply because it was subsidized by a consortium of participating governments. This argument became so heated that the U.S. government and the European Union began trading accusations. In May 2011, the World Trade Organization, after a very long investigation, affirmed a landmark decision that Airbus had, in fact, received subsidies of $18 billion, all considered illegal. The outcome of this issue will not be known for many months, nor its effect on Boeing.

In any case, Boeing knew it needed a new model that would interest the airlines and could compete effectively with Airbus. Airbus had announced in December 2000 that it was designing and would produce the world's largest commercial airplane, the A380. This two-story behemoth was to carry 555 passengers in a three-class configuration.

In some markets, the A380 could prove to be ideal. Yet, it was an expensive plane to buy and could only fly into a few major airports because of its size. Even those airports would require costly modifications to their terminals, taxiways, and runways.

The biggest problem for the A380 was that it appeared to be the opposite of what Boeing's staff was hearing from the airlines. The A380, with its combination of huge size and large passenger-carrying capacity, could be used profitably only between large cities, which in most cases were also hubs. This severely limited its potential use and thus its attractiveness to airlines. In addition, the A380 had a high acquisition cost. Airbus decided to hedge its bets and announced first a smaller version of its model A330-200 and later introduced

the model A350XWB. This airplane was partially a competitor to the 787. The A350XWB, in its various models, would have a seating range from 270 to 350 seats. That put it in the higher seating range of the 787, but also the lower seating range of the 777. With this design, Airbus seemed to be attempting to create a family of airplanes to meet different customer needs. The Airbus 350XWB is scheduled first flew in June 2013 and first deliveries are 3rd quarter 2014. Since the A350XWB will not be available to airlines until some years later than the 787, it will give Boeing a real sales advantage.

New Technologies

Various technological advances came to the forefront at this time. Among them were:

1. Advanced composite materials
2. More efficient jet engines
3. Aerodynamic improvements
4. Improved airplane systems

In the interim period between the 777 and the 787, advances had taken place in applicable technology. The principal advance was the increased use of composites in airframes, as designers became more familiar with these materials and manufacturing technologies were developed that made the fabrication of large composite structures not only more feasible, but also less expensive. Computer programs for designing and refining airframe aerodynamics were further improved. Bypass fan jets were also somewhat improved in efficiency and reliability. As well, advanced aircraft systems were now available. These and other factors coalesced to enable Boeing to create an airplane that would cost less to operate and maintain, and consume less fuel. Some of the details of these new technologies are discussed here in chapters 5, 6, 7, and 8.

The Need for a New Product

Boeing's last new airplane was the 777 – a successful airplane, but with technology that dated back to the mid-1990s. The 757 and 767 designs dated back even further, to the late 1970s. The various 767 models could carry anywhere from 185 to 245 passengers, but were limited in range to around 6,600 nautical miles or less, depending on the particular model. The 777 models could carry 301 to 368 passengers in various configurations, with the latest version able to fly more than 9,400 nautical miles. What is more, in the period 2002-2005, in part as a result of the 9/11 terrorist attacks, orders for the 767 slumped badly to where a shutdown of the assembly line was contemplated. On the other hand, 777 sales during the same period were brisk. This seemed to be a strong indication that a new design was indeed needed.

Of equal importance was the fact that these two airplanes (757 and 767) were able to carry considerably more passengers than the airlines had been forecasting for their long, thin routes. To stay competitive with Airbus, as well as have the ability to meet the airlines' changing needs, the time had come to design a new and different airplane. The 7E7 was viewed by Boeing as a replacement for both the 757 and the 767. This was a tall order, since those two models were quite different in terms of size and mission capabilities.

By the early 2000s, Boeing executives were already forecasting the phaseout of the 757, and eventually even the 767. By offering a family of airplanes with considerably improved economics and various mission capabilities from the very beginning, Boeing also felt that the 787 would replace not only the 757 and 767, but also possibly the lower end of the 777. It further believed that it would be a feasible, marketable product family for many years to come.

As a testament to Boeing's commitment to remain highly competitive in the commercial jet transport market, the 787 family is the eleventh new-airplane family introduced since the 707 first flew in 1954. Thus, over a period of exactly fifty years, Boeing has introduced a new airplane design approximately every thirteen years, keeping in mind that the 757/767 duo came out simultaneously. Considering the amount of design and development effort required to create a new and competitive design, this is indeed an amazing track record.

The Global Environment

Above and beyond all the various considerations listed, there was another overriding factor: the continual growth and changing nature of air transportation throughout the world. Companies like Boeing and Airbus depend on the world's airlines for airplane sales, and these airlines, in turn, depend totally on the acceptance and growth of air transportation everywhere.

Air transportation grew steadily from its inception back in the 1920s. The 1930s showed a modest yet continuing growth. World War II interrupted this, although the technological advances in aircraft design and operation that occurred during that period did much to advance the reliability of passenger airplanes. After World War II, recovery took a number of years, but from 1949 on air transport, particularly in the United States and across the North Atlantic, grew at a satisfactory rate.

With the large-scale introduction of jet transports, led by Boeing's own 707, the number of air passengers grew at a much faster rate because of four factors:
1. Larger and faster airplanes
2. Lower fares
3. More routes to cities of different sizes
4. A quantum jump in air safety

In the early years of the jet age, the growth was concentrated mainly in the United States, with Europe as a healthy second player. All this was to change by the 1990s.

The following statistics for worldwide passengers carried present a clear picture of the tremendous growth of air transportation.

Year	Air Passengers Carried (millions)	Average Trip Length (millions) (miles)
1946	18	560
1950	31	565
1960	106	640
1970	312	760
1980	645	900
1990	1,029	1,000
2000	1,632	1,120

In 2002, the number of passengers carried in airplanes fell to 1,615 million as a result of the terrorist attacks of 9/11, as well as the economic downturn everywhere. By 2004, however, the number had increased robustly to 1,887 million passengers. Yet another change in the general picture of international air transportation was the tremendous increase in ridership in Asia, namely China, India, and Japan.

The above statistics, generated by the International Council of Airline Organizations (ICAO), show how from 1980 to 2000 the number of air passengers almost tripled, while the average trip length increased by only 25 percent. In that same period, the number of city pairs served by scheduled airline service nearly doubled to 10,500. All these data points clearly show *the market need for an airplane able to carry a moderate number of passengers over long distances on direct routes.*

The Big Gamble

Note that the decision to go ahead with the 787 project constituted a huge gamble for Boeing. Why a gamble? Consider the following:

- The decision to build the 787 gambled that the Airbus 380 was, in fact, too big and expensive for many airlines.
- By deciding to build the 787 instead of the Sonic Cruiser, Boeing made a major decision in terms of the basic airplane type it would develop.

- Boeing needed to alter and improve its manufacturing processes and productivity drastically in order to price the airplane competitively and make it affordable.
- The prevalent financial situation of the airlines in the early 2000s could have meant that the airlines in general might not be willing or able to renew their fleets in subsequent years.
- Designing and committing to a family of four related, but still differing models, required increasing the size of the gamble even further from the very beginning.
- The 787 was to be the first large commercial airplane ever produced with 50 percent of its airframe (by weight) made of composites. While the material was proven, new manufacturing methods for building large composite structures had to be developed.
- Initiating the 787 meant committing to large contracts with aerospace partners all over the world in order to spread the risk.

Granted, Boeing had gambled the business before. Its original jetliner, the 707, was a $16 million gamble taken with Boeing's own funds and built before either the airlines or the military had ordered a single airplane. The company then followed this up with the trijet 727, another gamble that paid off handsomely. Then followed the 737 airplane, which has been built continuously for 40 years and which Boeing has delivered in the amazing quantity of more than 5,000 units. In 1968,

Boeing introduced the huge 747 – another gamble. Yet the 747 is still in production and still selling, and the next three models (757/767/777) have all sold well, with the 777 still a strong performer. All of which seems to indicate that while Boeing has in fact taken some enormous risks, it has done so on the basis of extensive market and airline research and through the execution of a solid business plan.

This then was the genesis of the 787: a combination of challenges and opportunities that resulted in its superb design. These factors were the major considerations that went into the decision to develop and market a new airplane. They were also the driving forces that helped determine the design and operating parameters of the 787. Now let us examine the design process that resulted in the *Dreamliner*.

CHAPTER 2
Birth Pangs

The life of the 787 began in 1997 as a product-development study. Five years elapsed before the project became Boeing's next new airplane design, in December 2002. During that evaluation period, Boeing continued to analyze the pros and cons of a 787-type airplane versus the new and exciting Sonic Cruiser concept. In the meantime, Boeing's sales personnel maintained a constant dialogue with its customer airlines and came to realize that the initial interest for the speed associated with the Sonic Cruiser was being gradually replaced by an overriding need by the airlines for a more efficient airplane. The reason was the painful realization by those airlines that they needed an airplane with substantially lower operating costs, while simultaneously being able to carry 200 to 300 passengers over routes as long as 8,800 nautical miles and as short as 3,500 nautical miles or less. This was the bottom line that delineated the parameters of the 787 design. In December 2002, Boeing began moving ahead quickly to create the airplane that was to become so important to its future.

So how does a company like Boeing go about creating a brand new airplane design and then building it in quantity? It does not start with a blank sheet of paper or a blank computer screen. The company needs to have a broad set of parameters that describe the airplane; it needs a time line to facilitate moving the project forward; it needs to commit necessary funds; and lastly, it needs to create an organization to carry out the project.

The Critical Dates
In the fall of 2002, Boeing began taking the necessary steps to make the initial corporate decisions that would eventually result in the creation and production of a new model. Still identified as the 7E7 at that time, Boeing formally announced the beginning of the program December 10, 2002.

During the following seventeen months, the company made a number of major decisions:

January 2003
• Leadership was selected for the program
May 2003
• A worldwide search was begun for a name for the proposed airplane
June 2003
• Composites were chosen as the primary airframe material
• Worldwide, 500,000 votes decided *"Dreamliner"* as the airplane name
November 2003
• Airlines were invited to receive a briefing and view the interior mock-up
• Partner companies for the airframe work were chosen
December 2003
• Boeing board of directors authorized the 7E7 to be offered to customers

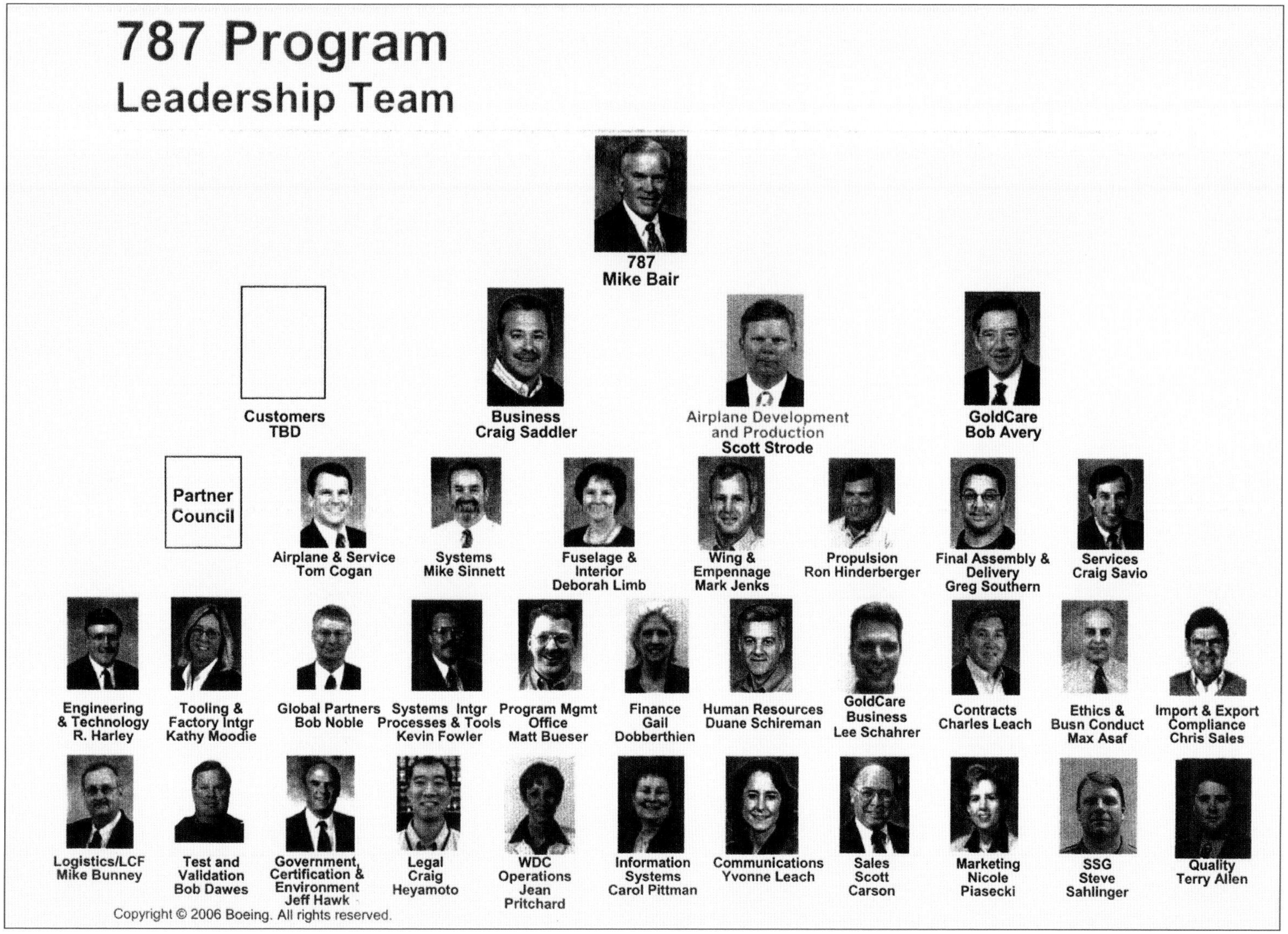

787 Program
Leadership Team
787
Mike Bair
Customers
TBD
Business
Craig Saddler
Airplane Development
and Production
Scott Strode
GoldCare
Bob Avery
Partner
Council
Airplane & Service
Tom Cogan
Systems
Mike Sinnett
Fuselage &
Interior
Deborah Limb
Wing &
Empennage
Mark Jenks
Propulsion
Ron Hinderberger
Final Assembly &
Delivery
Greg Southern
Services
Craig Savio
Engineering
& Technology
R. Harley
Tooling &
Factory Intgr
Kathy Moodie
Global Partners
Bob Noble
Systems Intgr
Processes & Tools
Kevin Fowler
Program Mgmt
Office
Matt Bueser
Finance
Gail
Dobberthien
Human Resources
Duane Schireman
GoldCare
Business
Lee Schahrer
Contracts
Charles Leach
Ethics &
Busn Conduct
Max Asaf
Import & Export
Compliance
Chris Sales
Logistics/LCF
Mike Bunney
Test and
Validation
Bob Dawes
Government,
Certification &
Environment
Jeff Hawk
Legal
Craig
Heyamoto
WDC
Operations
Jean
Pritchard
Information
Systems
Carol Pittman
Communications
Yvonne Leach
Sales
Scott
Carson
Marketing
Nicole
Piasecki
SSG
Steve
Sahlinger
Quality
Terry Allen
Copyright © 2006 Boeing. All rights reserved.

The 787 Leadership Team as of January 2003, when the project was first created at Boeing.

April 2004

- The selection of General Electric (GE) and Rolls-Royce as engine manufacturers
- Primary suppliers for the 7E7 are announced
- All Nippon Airlines (ANA) of Japan announces a firm order for fifty 7E7 airplanes
- The Boeing board of directors approves formal launch of the 7E7 program

These dates clearly show the deliberate yet steady progress of the 787 program during its initial years. Boeing was now ready to move ahead with the critical steps relating to the design and manufacture of this new airplane. The first step was to create the team that would lead the effort.

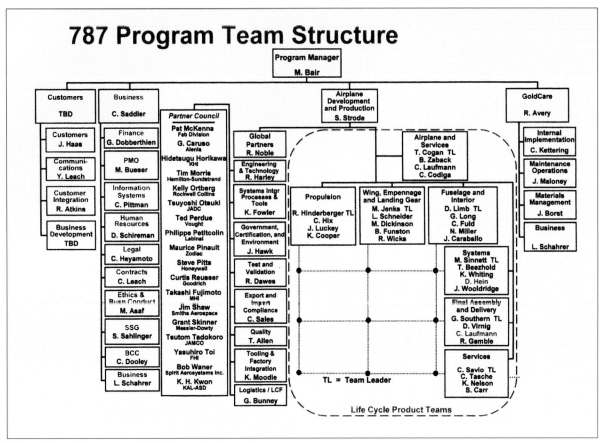

787 Program Team Structure

Program Manager
M. Bair

Customers
TBD

Customers
J. Haas

Communications
Y. Leach

Customer Integration
R. Atkins

Business Development
TBD

Business
C. Saddler

Finance
G. Dobberthien

PMO
M. Bueser

Information Systems
C. Pittman

Human Resources
D. Schireman

Legal
C. Heyamoto

Contracts
C. Leach

Ethics & Business Conduct
M. Asaf

SSG
S. Sahlinger

BCC
C. Dooley

Business
L. Schahrer

Partner Council
Pat McKenna *Fab Division*
G. Caruso *Alenia*
Hidetsugu Horikawa *KHI*
Tim Morris *Hamilton-Sundstrand*
Kelly Ortberg *Rockwell Collins*
Tsuyoshi Otsuki *JADC*
Ted Perdue *Vought*
Philippe Petitcolin *Labinal*
Maurice Pinault *Zodiac*
Steve Pitts *Honeywell*
Curtis Reusser *Goodrich*
Takashi Fujimoto *MHI*
Jim Shaw *Smiths Aerospace*
Grant Skinner *Messier-Dowty*
Tsutom Tadokoro *JAMCO*
Yasuhiro Toi *FHI*
Bob Waner *Spirit Aerosystems Inc.*
K. H. Kwon *KAL-ASD*

Global Partners
R. Noble

Engineering & Technology
R. Harley

Systems Integr Processes & Tools
K. Fowler

Government, Certification, and Environment
J. Hawk

Test and Validation
R. Dawes

Export and Import Compliance
C. Sales

Quality
T. Allen

Tooling & Factory Integration
K. Moodie

Logistics / LCF
G. Bunney

Airplane Development and Production
S. Strode

Airplane and Services
T. Cogan TL
B. Zaback
C. Laufmann
C. Codiga

Propulsion
R. Hinderberger TL
C. Hix
J. Luckey
K. Cooper

Wing, Empennage and Landing Gear
M. Jenks TL
L. Schneider
M. Dickinson
B. Funston
R. Wicks

Fuselage and Interior
D. Limb TL
G. Long
C. Fuld
N. Miller
J. Caraballo

Systems
M. Sinnett TL
T. Beezhold
K. Whiting
D. Hein
J. Wooldridge

Final Assembly and Delivery
G. Southern TL
D. Virnig
C. Laufmann
R. Gamble

Services
C. Savio TL
C. Tasche
K. Nelson
S. Carr

TL = Team Leader

Life Cycle Product Teams

GoldCare
R. Avery

Internal Implementation
C. Kettering

Maintenance Operations
J. Maloney

Materials Management
J. Borst

Business
L. Schahrer

The 787 Team Structure as originally conceived.

The 787 Team

In January 2003, Boeing's top management began to form the 787 team that would lead the entire design, including functions such as production, financing, sales, marketing, and in-service support. They chose Mike Bair, a 24-year veteran of Boeing, to be the vice president and general manager of the 787 program. Bair holds a Bachelor of Science degree, degrees in physics, and two masters degrees. At Boeing, he had worked in sales and as the chief project engineer and director of engineering on the 777, among other assignments. He had also served as the general manager and vice president on the 757 program. Altogether, Bair had worked in engineering, sales, marketing, and management before being assigned to head the 787 program. Thus, he came to the 787 program highly qualified. In addition to his education and experience, Bair also had a reputation for being approachable, a trait that greatly facilitated communication within the 787 staff.

Under Bair were several major divisions, including Engineering, Manufacturing, Partner Alignment, Finance, Business Operations, Sales, Marketing, and In-Service Support.

Engineering, Manufacturing, and Partner Alignment, initially under Walter Gillette, defined, developed, and designed the airplane. In addition, the division developed and implemented the production of the 787. This included the 747 Large Cargo Freighter, later named the *Dreamlifter*, which is used to deliver major 787 subassemblies. Gillette was a longtime employee of Boeing, having joined the company in 1966. An aerospace engineer by training, Gillette worked on virtually all the Boeing jet transport programs. He had a worldwide reputation as someone able to integrate large scale systems and was the head of a team that researched the development of the Sonic Cruiser and later integrated those concepts into the 7E7 program. Walter Gillette retired May 31, 2006, but there is no question that his contributions fundamentally affected the program.

Finance and business operations initially fell under the supervision of Craig Saddler, who was responsible for developing the business case and business model for the 787. That arm of the project included responsibility for estimating, contracts, and cost management pertaining to the 787 program. Saddler originally trained in engineering and engineering management. Saddler's career in aerospace began with McDonnell Douglas in 1981. He then moved to Boeing when the two companies merged. Over the years, he held increasingly responsible positions involving finance. Saddler left the program in February 2007 to become the president of Boeing Australia.

Finally, Sales, Marketing, and In-Service Support were originally led by John Feren, who worked with the potential customer base, shaped the marketplace and defined and developed the associated services for the 787. Feren joined Boeing Commercial Airplanes in 1997. Before that time, Feren was with McDonnell Douglas and had been the program manager on the MD-90/MD-80 program, as well as the vice president of Commercial Marketing. At Boeing, Feren worked in sales and leasing for North America and Latin America. Subsequently, he worked for more than two years as the vice president of Sales, Marketing, and In-Service Support for the 787 program. Feren has since moved on to become a vice president of sales for Boeing Commercial Airplanes.

Thomas Cogan was the original 787 Chief Project Engineer. He was responsible for the definition and product integrity of the airplane. Cogan also led a team responsible for integrating the airplane and achieving the program's technical and business goals. Cogan, an aerospace engineer, joined Boeing in 1977. He worked in aerodynamics for twelve years, then became the marketing manager for the 757 and 737 models. He also filled other management positions in the 737 and 757 programs, including chief project engineer of the 757. Before the 787 program, he worked on the Sonic Cruiser. Cogan took on a new assignment at Boeing in July 2008.

The 787 Comes to Life

The conceptual design of the 787 was an amalgamation of the needs of the airlines and the availability of new technology. As of December 2002, when Boeing announced it would focus its commercial product development efforts on the 7E7, the broad design parameters had already been determined. They were based on the feedback that the sales people had received from the airlines (see Chapter 4) and included range and passenger capacity requirements. These parameters were gradually determined over the five-year period between the inception of Project Yellowstone (the theoretical paper airplane) and the initiation of the 7E7 program in December 2002. At that point, Boeing concluded that the airlines wanted an airplane that could seat between 200 and 300 passengers and had a range capability that varied from 3,500 to 8,800 miles. The spread of the seat requirements, plus the really large variation in range, were such that a single aircraft model could not meet all the requirements. Thus, it became obvious that more than one airplane model would be needed if the program were to be a true commercial success. Boeing decided to move ahead with a three-airplane family that would give the airlines the flexibility of choice that the market seemed to require.

Major decisions made at that time were that most of the airframe would be made from composite materials and that the airplanes would operate at a considerably lower cost per mile. These, together with other new technology, would make the 787 attractive to prospective customers for many years to come. The decision to incorporate more composite materials than ever before on an airplane of this size was a natural progression because of Boeing's significant use of composites in the 777, which began in 1993.

In January 2005, the airplane was formally given the designation the Boeing 787 *Dreamliner*. During the span of time from April 2004 to November 2005, 304 firm orders and commitments for the 787 were received. Simultaneously, Boeing completed designs for the airframe, flight deck, and the interior.

The 787-8 and 787-3, launched in April 2004 by All Nippon Airlines (ANA), and the 787-9, launched in May 2006 by Air New Zealand, are identical in some aspects and different in others. The 787 family of airplanes are all twin-engine and twin-aisle planes with identical fuselage diameters, cruise altitude ceilings, and cruise speeds, but differ considerably in wingspan, fuselage length, range, gross takeoff weight, and passenger capacity. These differences translate into a range of options that airlines can choose from and fit their individual needs far more closely than ever before. (See "Specifications of All 787 Models" in Appendix I.)

All 787s fall into the official "heavy" jet category, as defined by the Federal Aviation Administration (FAA). That definition states that any aircraft with a maximum gross takeoff weight of 300,000 pounds or more is to be considered a heavy jet. In fact, such aircraft are required to identify themselves with the word *heavy* in all radio transmissions to Air Traffic Control (ATC) facilities. For example, a Qantas 787 Flight 150 would call in to an air traffic control facility and say, "Center: Qantas 150 heavy is with you at flight level 350."

The Shape of it All

One of the driving forces in the design of the 787 was the need to make the airplane more efficient, and therefore cheaper to operate. Part of that efficiency had to be realized from aerodynamic improvements to the airframe. In this area, a new tool, known as *computational fluid dynamics*, had become available. Through the use of highly advanced and sophisticated equations, computational fluid dynamics predict the flow of air over the airframe, and in particular over the wing. By taking advantage of this tool, in addition to greatly improved and more powerful computers, aerodynamic engineers are now able to predict with accuracy the airflow characteristics of a particular design. This in turn dictates the efficiency of the airframe.

As an indication of the great strides taken in this area, design development of the 767 required more than 50 wing designs to be wind tunnel tested. By the time the design of the 777 was under way, approximately 18 wing designs had been tested. With the 787, using the powerful new design tools, fewer than 12 wing designs reached the wind tunnel stage. The upshot was greatly reduced wind tunnel testing and the ability to forecast the effect of any small change in design better.

The goal Boeing set for itself was to improve the efficiency of the 787 by 20 percent. In Chapter five, the writer explains precisely how this efficiency, which is accomplished in the increments listed below, was achieved:

1. Engine improvements equal 8%
2. Aerodynamics add 3%
3. Composite materials add 3%
4. Systems contribute 3%
5. Additional savings from system interaction add 3 percent

Total: 20% efficiency improvement

Another significant improvement was the large reduction in maintenance costs resulting from the use of composites for such a major portion of the airframe. Most of this benefit comes from longer intervals between scheduled maintenance events, more system reliability, and the elimination of the nonroutine maintenance of the airframe from corrosion and fatigue (*see* Chapter 6).

The Basic Design Process

Boeing and the airlines continued to be in constant communication throughout this design process. That input in turn was used in various design decisions. Because of the airlines' desire for a range of variation in passenger capacities and trip lengths, it became clear early on that the 787 would necessarily become a *family* of airplanes. This resulted in the initial offering of three models. The original base model was the 787-8; the 787-9 was the second model designed, followed by the 787-3 (the 787-3 was later replaced by the 787-10). Yet by March 2006, customers began to express an interest in a fourth model.

During the initial design steps, certain basic parameters were set. Since the airlines did not wish to achieve higher speeds at the expense of higher operating costs, Boeing decided that all 787 models would have a basic cruise speed of Mach 0.85, and that they be certified for a maximum cruise altitude of 43,000 feet. The latter condition would enable the *Dreamliner* to operate at altitudes above even more weather conditions than other transports. It would also allow the 787 to use its higher cruise speed as it bypassed slower airplanes, instead of flying at their lower altitudes and having to fly more slowly in trail. Note that most jet transports today operate at cruise speeds of Mach 0.80 or slower. Boeing further decided that the -8 model would carry 210 to 250 passengers in a typical three-class configuration and have a maximum range of 8,500 nautical miles. The maximum gross takeoff weight (MTOW) for such a configuration was 484,000 pounds. The table below shows the major parameters for the three 787 models.

The extent of variation between the three models clearly shows the large flexibility of the basic design, as well as the goal achieved by Boeing in meeting the different needs as expressed by the airlines.

Determining these parameters constituted the conceptual development phase, at the end of which, in September 2005, Boeing had a firm configuration. This configuration constituted a critical decision point, since the airplane's structural, propulsion, and system architectures were made final at this point in the process, thus enabling the program to proceed to a detailed design. Keep in mind that

Model	Fuselage Length (feet)	Wing Span (feet)	Range (nm)	Passenger Capacity	Maximum Gross Takeoff Weight (pounds)
787–8	186	197	8,000–8,500	210–250	502,500
787–9	206	203	8,600–8.800	250–290	553,000
787–10	224	197	7,000	323	553,000

these various parameters had to be balanced against one another throughout the process. Designing the entire airframe involved more than a thousand major trade-off studies, which truly illustrates how an airplane design results from many compromises.

The basic design of all the 787 models is as follows:

1. An airplane that has an appearance generally similar to other Boeing transports, although critical differences exist both internally and externally.
2. The 787 has a swept-wing, twin-aisle, twin-engine configuration.
3. The nose has a four-pane windshield and is more streamlined than previous Boeing designs.
4. The fuselage has a double bubble cross section shaped like a figure eight, with a larger diameter than most wide-body airplanes.
5. The wing is of relatively conventional design, with a sweepback of 32.4 degrees.
6. The tail assembly is also of conventional appearance, with the vertical fin having a sweepback of 36 degrees.

The design of the *Dreamliner* airframe was accomplished using sophisticated analytical tools. Chief among these was computational fluid dynamics (previously mentioned), which is a formidable computer program that shows the engineer how an airframe, or some component therein, interacts with the air molecules it flies through. The formulas in this program are standard and can be applied to different aircraft.

The airframe component that received the most design analysis was the wing. This was critical in arriving at an efficient and economical airplane design, something clearly requested by the airlines. An additional design tool was CATIA, a five-design suite of computer tools. The sweepback of the wing was a function of many parameters, including drag versus lift – a critical part of any wing design.

On the one hand, reducing drag is a constant goal of aerodynamic engineers, since it reduces fuel burn. On the other hand, sufficient lift is necessary in order for the airplane to function properly. The final wing design for the 787 represents a compromise, with drag somewhat improved over that of previous airplanes, while the lift is sufficient to meet the projected maximum takeoff weight.

In addition, jet transports, for many years, have been designed to operate safely from runways that are no longer than 10,000 feet. That limitation has built-in variables. The length of runway that any airplane requires to lift off depends on the elevation of the airport above sea level, outside air temperature and ambient humidity at that specific time, wind velocity and direction, and the weight of the airplane. The FAA certifies that a commercial transport can take off safely from a 10,000-foot runway at its maximum gross weight on a day when the temperature is 59 degrees Fahrenheit. But change any one of the variables, such as temperature, and on a hot day, a fully loaded airplane could easily require far more runway length. Thus, having the ability to lift off quickly gives a commercial transport far more flexibility in its operation.

A particularly interesting aspect of the design process – one that most air travelers are probably unaware of – is that safety considerations take up more design time than anything else, yet are integral to the reputation of an airplane over the decades it remains in operation.

The Design Partnership

When Boeing decided to move ahead with the 7E7 project, it embraced a business plan that was innovative and unusual. First of all, the 787's design and manufacturing were accomplished by a team of companies collaborating with Boeing. Known as the Global Collaborative Environment, this collaboration continued a tradition of partnership established during World War II. The design and manufacture of the 787 required partners to both design and build entire assemblies. Boeing contracted that work to various major aerospace companies throughout the world. In doing so, it spread the workload and was able to carry out the 787 design more efficiently. Contracting also enabled Boeing to tap into the technical resources of its partners. Such a manufacturing approach is not new. In fact, Boeing used it in the development of the 747 in 1967, but never before did completed portions of the airplane arrive at the Everett, Washington, plant ready to be assembled.

Boeing's partners were also involved from the beginning in the development of the conceptual design, and each was responsible for the detailed design of the assembly it manufactured. Yet all such design work, done on computers, is part of a worldwide computer network that leads back to Boeing. In this way, Boeing is able to monitor and approve all such designs at all times. (See chapter 9 for the names of the major contractors and their areas of responsibility.)

Kevin Fowler, formerly Boeing's vice president of Systems Integration Processes and Tools, explained how this approach differs in one important aspect from the previous 777 project. For the first time, the partners were responsible for both the total design and for manufacturing the plane. By combining both functions, it became far easier for a partner to incorporate design changes as the process unfolded.

For Boeing to maintain control over the entire process, new communication tools were required. By 2001, the World Wide Web and other e-enabled tools made collaboration with Boeing much easier, simplifying communication between partners. In addition, the Dassault Systèmes Corp. of France developed its Product Lifestyle Management tools to help this collaboration further. Its "V5" suite of tools included CATIA®, DELMIA®, and ENOVIA®. Each of these software management tools is used for a different application.

CATIA is used for designing the virtual product, enabling users to simulate the entire range of industrial design processes, from initial concept to product design, analysis, and assembly.

ENOVIA enables Boeing to operate a global collaborative lifecycle management system crucial to coordinating the designs of the various companies involved.

DELMIA enables companies to plan, create, monitor, and control production and maintenance processes digitally.

Together, these Dassault Systèmes products have been key to Boeing's approach to designing and producing the 787, since they coordinated the contractors' designs and allowed Boeing to monitor those same contractors. To facilitate further the working relationships between Boeing and companies in other countries with different languages and cultures, Boeing employees spent considerable time at the locations of the various contractors. Inversely, employees from those companies spent time at Boeing's Everett plant. This exchange of personnel greatly enhanced working relationships and was all part of the general business plan.

Another major change in the design process, first introduced in the 777 program, was designing the airplane systems simultaneously with the structural design. This approach saved time, reducing the need to later adapt the structural design to new systems.

Wind Tunnel Testing

The wind tunnel testing of models of a new aircraft design constitutes a major step in the development of a new airplane. It proves how the new design works in high- and low-speed airflows, and it may indicate a hereto-unforeseen design problem that can be corrected before manufacture. In fact, the results of wind tunnel testing can and do result in changes in design that make the ultimate configuration a better airplane.

The wind tunnel testing of the various airframe designs and configurations was critically important in determining the final design of the 787 models. To maximize the benefits of wind tunnel testing, Boeing used several different and highly specialized wind tunnels around the world. Among these were testing facilities in Seattle, Washington; Mountain View, California; Minneapolis, Minnesota; Philadelphia, Pennsylvania; Hampton, Virginia; Farnborough, United Kingdom; Cologne, Germany; Le Fauga, France; and Gifu, Japan. In each case, scale models of either the full 787 airframe or a specific portion (such as an engine nozzle) were tested.

Two of the wind tunnels were used more extensively than others. Most of the high-speed wing development and validation testing was done at the Boeing Transonic Wind Tunnel in Seattle. Most of the high-lift aerodynamic development and validation were accomplished at the QinetiQ 5-Metre wind tunnel in Farnborough, United Kingdom.

Among other conditions, wind tunnel testing checks the way the wing functions at high Mach numbers and Reynolds numbers. The Mach number is a measure of the speed of the airplane as compared with the speed of sound. All the 787 airplanes are designed to operate effectively at a speed of 0.85 Mach, or 85 percent of the speed of sound. This is somewhat faster than the speed of many other jet transports.

The other condition that is carefully measured is the Reynolds number of the airplane at the nominal cruising speed. Simply put, the Reynolds number is a measure of how the air – a viscous fluid – behaves over models of various sizes. Ideally, the Mach and Reynolds numbers should match flight conditions as closely as possible.

Other items validated in the wind tunnel include nacelle inlet, engine nozzle, and thrust reverser designs. The acoustic signature of the airplane (that is, the level of sound at various distances created by a particular airplane configuration) is measured through wind tunnel testing. The flutter characteristics of the airplane at various speeds are also tested, as is the ice protection system.

The 787 wind tunnel testing program used far fewer wind tunnel hours, thanks in large part to the use of computational fluid dynamics. To demonstrate this point, note that in 1990, the wind tunnel testing for the 777-200 took 25 percent fewer hours than for the 767 in 1980, while in 2005, the 787 program took 30 percent fewer hours than the 777-200.

Ergonomics and the 787 Design

Ergonomics is often defined as the proper matching of people to work environments so as to produce maximum safety, efficiency, and quality. In the case of the 787, the introduction of ergonomics *during*, instead of after, the design phase was a breakthrough in aerospace design.

This effort was led by Boeing team leader Richard Gardner. As an ergonomics engineer, he was able to influence the design of various aircraft parts while the 787 was being developed. Using the same computer aided design software as the design engineers, Gardner and his team conducted detailed human modeling studies and communicated results directly to design personnel. Their efforts not only affected the design of parts, but also manufacturing processes. This fundamental change was accomplished by introducing design requirements early in product development that placed focus on the workers who would have to build the 787 in production. The net result was that the design engineers had to consider how their designs impacted manufacturing personnel from an ergonomics perspective.

One example of this approach is the placement of a removable wing panel that provides better access and a safer installation process for the 787's main landing gear actuators. Another example is the integration of lifting points designed into interior commodities, such as galleys, passenger seats, and lavatories, which enable use of material handling equipment to assist workers during the installation processes. Additionally, the ergonomics team created a process to review and approve all factory tooling designs prior to use, ensuring safe and functional operation for manufacturing personnel.

Gardner himself applied many other innovations to impact manufacturing ergonomics for the 787 program. For instance, he introduced the use of virtual reality technology to simulate assembly processes in real-time, using 3D stereo display systems. Additionally, he was the principal inventor of a patented process to systematically evaluate thousands of manufacturing work instructions for ergonomic risks. As a result of his pioneering work, Gardner was the first Boeing employee to be presented the Ergonomic Professional of the Year award by the Puget Sound Human Factors and Ergonomic Society.

The Final Product

The 787 program is a family of airplanes with two distinct models that have already been designed or are currently being designed and a third that is being considered for the near future. While a quick look at a 787 may, to the casual observer, look much the same as many other Boeing jets, the 787 is considerably different. The development described up to this point, however, covers only the basic airframe. More details, as well as a description of the interior of the 787, reveal many innovations and surprises, as the writer describes in Chapter 7. At this point, the reader may wonder why the Boeing Company in particular should have been the one to bring forth an airplane that was, in many ways, ahead of all other jet transports. In the next chapter is an outline of many of the reasons for this.

(Flight International Magazine)

CHAPTER 3
Who Else But Boeing?

There are not many airplane manufacturers in the world that could have been the creators of an airplane like the *Dreamliner*. In reality, who else but Boeing could be the one? A quick look back at Boeing's history clearly shows why the company was the logical choice for a new-generation jet transport. To better understand why this chapter is titled "Who Else But Boeing?," it is worthwhile to take a closer look at the company's history. The history of Boeing falls neatly into three distinct phases that make it easy to follow the growth and expansion of the firm.

Phase 1:
Boeing's Early Years

The Boeing Company, founded in July 1916 as Pacific Aero Products, was created and owned by a lumber merchant named William E. Boeing. In May 1917, the company name was changed to the Boeing Airplane Company.

Boeing began making planes in 1916, and by 1923, was already building a U.S. Army pursuit plane in quantity. During the 1920s the company manufactured other models, but none in large quantities. This focused production generally

A rendering of the 1928 Boeing fighter known as the U.S. Army P-12. (Steven D. Kimmell)

reflected the small, tentative steps that aviation was taking at that time.

In 1928, the company came out with its first true commercial passenger transport, the model 80, a trimotor, twelve-passenger plane. A later version, the model 80A, carried eighteen passengers, but only sixteen 80A airplanes were built between 1928 and 1930. All were operated by Boeing Air Transport – a subsidiary operation – which explains why so few were built.

Also in 1928, Boeing began production of a single-seat biplane fighter that was offered in various configurations and with differing model numbers. All were similar in design, however, and were generally known as the U.S. Army P-12

pursuit plane / U.S. Navy F4B. Between 1928 and 1933, a total of 578 were delivered – a breakthrough for Boeing, since it represented a large quantity for that time.

Beginning in 1930, Boeing introduced an all-metal, single-wing aircraft, the forerunner of the modern airplane. Several models were produced, all in small quantities, but all were highly successful and promising. Among these was the model 247, a ten-passenger transport that preceded concurrent

products from Douglas and Lockheed. With a cruising speed in excess of 180 miles per hour, the model 247 began to show the promise of future air transportation.

In 1934, a major program came to Boeing. The company acquired the Stearman Aircraft Company of Wichita, Kansas, and with it, a biplane trainer called the Kaydet. Known variously as models 70, 75, and 76, this military trainer was built continuously from 1935 to 1945, and during that

A rendering of the 1934 Kaydet trainer built from 1935 to 1945. (Steven D. Kimmell)

period no fewer than 10,346 aircraft were delivered to the military. This impressive total meant that Boeing was beginning to spread its wings and getting into large-scale aircraft production.

While the above-mentioned models were not the only ones designed and built by Boeing during this period, they constitute the most important airplanes from this phase, which then led to a second phase.

Phase 2:
The Big Plane
and World War II

The year 1934 was a turning point for Boeing for several reasons. One was increasing world tension caused by the rearming of Germany and Japan, a factor carefully noticed by the U.S. War Department, which later became part of the Department of Defense.

A second reason was the increasing acceptance and use of commercial air travel by the general public, especially business travelers. These factors came together in the period 1934-1940 to create an opportunity for Boeing. In mid-1934, the War Department authorized the design and construction of a massive experimental bomber.

Identified at Boeing as model 294 and by the military as model XB–15, the bomber was a 70,000-pound maximum gross weight, four-engine airplane capable of carrying four tons of bombs and having a cruising speed of 152 miles per hour. For its time, the B-15 was a truly gigantic aircraft that forever changed Boeing's vision by moving the company into the arena of big planes.

While this was merely a one-aircraft order, it meant that Boeing's designers and engineers had to deal with the challenge of creating a mammoth aircraft with a wingspan of nearly 150 feet. The technology developed for this project was of real value in the design of three distinct projects that came about shortly thereafter: two of the projects were for commercial application, while the third was for military use.

A few months after beginning the XB-15 design phase, Boeing won a contract to develop a multi-engine, long-range heavy bomber. Identified as model 299 at Boeing and B-17 by the military, this heavy bomber was the famous *Flying Fortress*, possibly the best-known airplane to fight in World War II. The prototype was designed and built in the amazingly short time of only twelve months and it first flew in July 1935.

The story of the B-17 stretches over a full decade and through many model configurations. The many

A rendering of the Boeing Model 294 heavy bomber. Identified as the B-15 by the U.S. Army, it was the largest bomber of that time. Note the P-12s crossing overhead. (Steven D. Kimmell)

A B-17G Flying Fortress World War II heavy bomber. It was probably the most famous airplane of that era. (Steven D. Kimmell)

changes were caused by the wartime experiences encountered, and also by the availability of engines with ever-increasing horsepower. These circumstances led to the rather astonishing growth of the takeoff gross weight of the B-17, from 32,000 pounds for the prototype to more than 65,000 pounds for the *G* model by 1943, representing a growth of more than 100 percent!

During the decade of its production, Boeing built 6,981 B-17s, with another 5,750 manufactured by Douglas and Vega under license. The true impact of this production was huge growth in the production capability of Boeing, a factor that would play an important role years later in the company's future plans.

In 1934-1935, Boeing, anxious to make inroads to the growing commercial aviation field and spurred by the success of the Martin flying boats in service with Pan American World Airways (Pan Am), designed a large flying boat. Known as the model 314, it incorporated some of the design features of the B-15 and, while able to cruise at only 190 miles per hour, it nevertheless had an impressive range of 5,000 miles. This meant that, for the first time, a commercial aircraft could fly safely across the North Atlantic in regular service year-round. Pan Am studied the design and, in June 1936, ordered six of the giant aircraft. Later, six more were built for Pan Am and, with the onset of World War II, three of the Clippers were sold to British Overseas Airways Corporation. Able to carry 77 passengers and with a gross takeoff weight of 84,000 pounds, this aircraft was truly a giant in the skies of that period.

Shortly after the start of the model 314 design cycle, Boeing initiated the design of its model 307. This airplane incorporated a new concept of pressurizing the fuselage so that passengers would be safe and comfortable at higher altitudes. This resulted in higher cruising speeds and smoother flights above much of the weather. With a perfectly circular fuselage cross section, model 307 proved capable of meeting its goal.

Only ten model 307s were built, including the prototype, which was lost during testing: five for TWA, three for Pan Am, and one for Howard Hughes. Yet, while the aircraft showed real promise, the advent of World War II cut short any possibility of further orders and production. The design and production techniques learned in producing the

A Pan American Boeing Model 314 Clipper taking off at sunset. This airplane established the first regular tran-Atlantic passenger service. (Steven D. Kimmell)

The Boeing Model 307 passenger transport boasted the first pressurized cabin.

An illustration of the Boeing U.S. Army B-29 flying near Mt. Fujiyama, Japan. (Steven D. Kimmell)

B-307 would shortly become important to Boeing, as military needs became their top priority.

During World War II, Boeing was involved in B-17 production, but more work was on the way. In 1938, military planners indicated the potential need for a bomber having a longer range than the B-17. No federal funds were available at that time, but Boeing executives decided to initiate a new design on their own, which became model 345, eventually to be known as the B-29 Superfortress. By mid-1940, Boeing's early design work paid off and an initial order for two XB-29 prototypes was placed by the government. The plane first flew in September 1942 and was an aerodynamic success. Yet, many technical problems surfaced, in particular the Curtiss-Wright R-3350 engines, which boasted 2,200 horsepower.

While of magnificent design, the engines had flaws that led to an early spate of engine fires. One, in early 1943, caused the crash of one of the prototypes and killed Boeing's chief test pilot, Eddie Allen. Eventually, these and other problems were solved and the B-29 went into large-scale production. During the period mid-1944 through August 1945, the B-29 built an enviable reputation as the best long-range, heavy bomber in the world.

Between its inception and the end of production, 2,766 B-29s were built by Boeing, with 1,204 more manufactured by Bell and Martin. Boeing converted some existing B-29s for other duties, such as air-to-air refueling. The impact on Boeing created by the B-29 program was twofold: not only did the company have to expand further to produce both the B-17 and B-29 models, but it also had to deal with the fact that the B-29 was a much more sophisticated aircraft. Its electronics alone constituted a new field, and its wing boasted a new airfoil of advanced design. With the end of the war, production slowed dramatically. The last B-50, an improved version of the B-29, was built in 1953, and if it had not been for the Korean War, production might have ended even sooner. In fact, only 371 B-50s were produced in all.

An offshoot of the B-29 program was the model 367 Stratofreighter, labeled the C-97/KC-97 by the U.S. Air Force (USAF). This was a large aircraft that used the B-29/B-50 wings, tail, and engines, but had a totally new fuselage design. Model 367 had a figure-eight cross section, a blunt nose, and somewhat resembled a whale. After the prototype first flew in 1944, an initial order for 10 YC-97s was placed by the USAF in 1945. Eventually, seventy-seven C-97s were delivered. Of far greater importance to Boeing, however, was that the USAF determined a need for a large air-to-air refueling aircraft. A version of the C-97 called the KC-97 was ordered. Between 1951 and 1956, 811 KC-97 tankers were delivered. This program helped Boeing survive during the immediate postwar period, when airplane production fell to a fraction of what it had been.

Not long after the successful start of the C-97 program, Boeing developed a commercial transport version of the model 367 known as the model 377 Stratocruiser, which boasted high speed and great passenger comfort. Pan Am bought twenty of these and other airlines also ordered a few, but only a total of fifty-six Stratocruisers were ever built. If it had not been for the C-97/KC-97 program, the Stratocruiser alone would have represented a substantial financial loss for Boeing.

In any case, the entire model 367/377 program signaled the end of the reciprocating engine propeller airplane era for Boeing. Far bigger events awaited them, and Boeing was geared up for an almost unbelievable string of successes.

Phase 3:
Boeing and the
Big Jets

Shortly after the end of World War II in 1945, it became apparent that worldwide peace had not arrived, as had been fervently hoped. Communism, as espoused by the Soviet Union, was hard at work to expand its boundaries and, by 1948, a period that came to be known as the Cold War had begun.

During the three intervening years, U.S. military planners and strategists, particularly in the U.S. Air Force, strove mightily to convince a peace-minded Congress that a strong air force was necessary. This led first to the creation of a separate U.S. Air Force in 1947, and within that branch of the military the creation of the Strategic Air Command (SAC). SAC concentrated on having all bombers and associated support units under one authority. A direct result of this was orders for the KC-97 tankers used to refuel the B-29/B-50 bomber force. The creation of SAC would shortly affect the destiny of Boeing.

With the advent of the jet engine and the introduction, by Germany, of the swept-wing concept, major strides became possible in aircraft design. Boeing's engineers had begun working on a jet bomber during World War II. After a major design change caused by the discovery of the German swept-wing concept, model 448 was finished and presented to the Pentagon in 1946. The military wanted a few more alterations and the final design became the model 450 (USAF designation B-47). An initial order for twelve airplanes was placed and in December 1947, the first B–47 was flown. The design proved to be extremely successful and multiple orders followed.

By 1956, Boeing had produced 1,373 B-47s, with Douglas and Lockheed building an additional 659 under license. This made for a powerful force of 2,032 bombers. It also brought Boeing firmly into the camp of a company that could build large numbers of sophisticated jet aircraft of large size, since the B-47, for all its beautiful streamlining, was a large jet aircraft – one that was heavier than anything that had flown previously.

Not long after initiating the B-47 design, however, Boeing was asked to submit a design for an even larger bomber with a greatly extended range and bomb-carrying capacity. This became the model 464, generally known as the B-52 – the consequence of previously designed models, all of which the military had turned down. In April 1952, the first B-52 took flight and the aircraft proved to be everything that SAC could have hoped for. Here was the largest jet airplane flying; it had a top speed of almost 600 miles per hour and a range of close to twice that of the B-47. Eventually, the Air Force ordered a grand total of 744 of the giant aircraft first built in 1952, with the last one rolling off the assembly line in 1962. Fifty-nine years after its initial flight, B-52s are still in active service with the U. S. Air Force.

During this period, two important circumstances occurred. The Air Force was finding out that refueling its jet bombers by the much slower KC-97s presented a continuing problem. Boeing, which had not generated much commercial success with its Stratocruiser design, was looking with increasing interest at the future of commercial jet transports. This latter interest was stimulated by the advent of such airliners as the *De Havilland Comet* jet transport, as well as the *Vickers Viscount* and *Bristol Britannia* turboprop transports. Aside from these two circumstances, it was obvious to Bill Allen, Boeing's president, that the end of the KC-97 production was looming and Boeing had no other large commercial type aircraft in the works.

The two circumstances came together in the early 1950s, when Boeing decided it really needed to produce a design for a new airplane, one that might be used as both a commercial passenger transport and a military tanker. In 1952, design work was begun on a model 367-80, which was commonly referred to as the Dash 80. It was a secret project, funded entirely by Boeing to the tune of $16 million, a great sum for that time (this translates to $114 million or more in today's money).

The airplane was to be a demonstrator, and when it began flying, it accomplished its assignment far beyond anyone's expectations. To understand clearly the extent of Boeing's gamble, consider that in the early 1950s, the airlines were buying new and improved reciprocating-engine transports from Douglas and Lockheed. Transports powered by turboprop engines were coming online, and the first commercial jet transport, the *De Haviland Comet*, suffered two disastrous crashes in 1954 that grounded the airplane.

A rendering of a Boeing/U.S. Air Force B-47 jet medium bomber. Note how the aircraft is toss-bombing a nuclear device. (Steven D. Kimmell)

The Dash 80 first flew in July 1954, and its proving flights, followed by demonstration flights all over the world, created a great deal of interest. Yet Boeing still needed orders from either the airlines or the military. What eventually ensued was that Boeing brought forth two new designs: a 16-inch-wider fuselage for the commercial model, known as the 707, and a 12-inch wider fuselage for the military tanker version, known as the KC-135. In the summer of 1954, the gamble began to pay

off, as the USAF ordered 117 KC-135s (Boeing model 717), and in October Pan American ordered twenty model 707s. While neither order was particularly large, the Pan Am order was a wake-up call for the airlines of the world that the Jet Age had truly arrived.

Eventually, the Air Force would order a total of 732 KC-135 Stratotankers, plus another 88 C-135 Stratolifter passenger/cargo aircraft. In addition, the USAF and the air forces of other nations procured 129 model 707s for a variety of uses.

The huge Boeing U.S. Air Force B-52 heavy bomber, still in service 50 years after its initial introduction. (Steven D. Kimmell)

On the commercial side, the world's airlines would eventually order a total of 856 model 707s in various configurations, plus another 154 model 720s, a shortened version of the 707 designed in part to compete with the then-proposed Convair 880. The 720 was slightly faster than the 707, carried fewer passengers, could operate from shorter runways, and had lower fuel consumption.

The commercial 707 line, with 1,010 total sales, competed well with the Douglas DC-8, which accumulated a total of only 556 sales. Of course, if one adds the military sales of both the 707 and the C/KC-135, it was by far a colossal success.

The program for the 707, 717, and 720 not only accumulated a bountiful number of sales, but in effect set the pattern for Boeing for the forty years to follow. It also accomplished something else entirely. By virtue of its sales, as well as the physical size of the 707 family, Boeing gave the world's airlines the impetus to lower fares substantially,

which in turn increased passenger boardings by multiples over what they had been only a few years previously.

Boeing followed its early commercial successes with a string of new aircraft designs, all of which sold well. First was the medium-sized B-727 trijet, an airplane notable for its many moving wing surfaces, that enabled it to perform safe short-field takeoffs and landings. The decision to design and market the 727 represented another gamble by Boeing, inasmuch as for decades tri-engine airplanes had been shunned by airlines. Furthermore, the short-field performance of the 727 was an innovation and required the careful training of crews transitioning into the airplane. The 727 line accumulated 1,831 sales, very possibly more than the Boeing sales force had ever expected. Their production ran from 1962 to 1984.

The Boeing 737 single-aisle short-range jet. This airplane holds the record for the most orders of any commercial transport to date. This photo is of a late model 737. (Steven D. Kimmell)

Boeing also saw the need for an even smaller aircraft, the twin-engine 737. The word *small* is deceptive, however, because in time, some of the 737 models carried as many or more passengers as the 727, or the original 707. Over the years, jet engines grew progressively more powerful, enabling twin-engine aircraft to carry as many passengers as the four-engine jets had carried a few years earlier. The 737 was first produced in 1967, and it is still being produced to this day, with 11,545 B-737s ordered as of December 31, 2013 – a truly amazing total.

In 1968, Boeing went from its smallest airplane to its largest with the introduction of the B-747. This behemoth was the largest and heaviest commercial plane built at the time, and only the USAF Lockheed C-5 *Galaxy* weighed more. By the time 747 production ended in 2010 Boeing had built 1,418 B-747s.

The production periods for the 737 and 747 constitute record years in production and attest to the ability of Boeing to design airplanes that are attractive to the markets decade after decade.

For a number of years after the 747 was introduced, Boeing, to some extent, rested on its laurels, content to build the designs on hand, along with various large modifications. By the late 1970s, fresh designs were needed to remain competitive. Moreover, ever-increasing passenger loads had to be accommodated and more powerful jet engines were the key to doing so economically.

In 1982, the company introduced two new designs simultaneously. One was the twin-engine, single-aisle, medium- range 757. The other was the considerably bigger twin-engine, twin-aisle, long-range 767. Introducing two designs simultaneously was a gutsy move by Boeing.

Boeing developed a new wrinkle with the 757 and 767. The models had almost identical cockpits and commonality of many components of the models. The 757 was produced from 1982 to 2005, and in that time 1,049 were delivered. The 767 is still being built, and as of December 31, 2013, 1,110 have been sold and 1,061 delivered, plus 179 KC-46A tankers for the U.S. Air Force, which will use the 767 airframe.

Boeing decided to bring out another wide-body design to satisfy the growing long-range market. This was the model 777, which had its first delivery in 1995. Still being manufactured today, 1,544 model 777s have been sold (1,164 delivered) as of December 31, 2013. Built in various configurations, the 777 can carry up to 368 passengers on flights as long as 9,420 nautical miles.

Boeing Grows

In late 1996, Boeing expanded its overall size by acquiring Rockwell International's aerospace divisions, which, prior to 1967, had been known as North American Aviation. Rockwell International

A Boeing 747 twin-aisle long-range jet transport, the largest of its time. (Steven D. Kimmell)

A Boeing 757 single-aisle medium-range jet transport.

A Boeing 767 twin-aisle long-range jet transport.

was formed in 1967 by the merging of North American Aviation and Rockwell Standard. In August 1997, Boeing then followed this move by merging with McDonnell Douglas, a company formed when Douglas Aviation and McDonnell Aviation merged in 1967. Boeing also acquired Vertol in 1960 and Hughes Aviation in 2000.

While these various airplane manufacturers are now part of Boeing, this writer does not consider their histories here or any contribution to the ranks of Boeing's Commercial Airplane Division to be a part of the story of that division. However, engineers from the various aviation companies that joined Boeing have been transferred to Boeing Commercial, in Everett, and may, as a consequence, have influenced the ultimate design of the 787. Since the end of World War II, the corporation expanded generally, so that now Boeing Commercial Airplane Co., a division of The Boeing Company, represents only a portion of the entire corporation.

This litany of Boeing's design and manufacturing history is recounted because it shows why the company was the perfect choice to begin the *Dreamliner* project. Over a period of 70 years, Boeing became the leader in large, innovative airplanes, for both military and commercial use. It accumulated tremendous wealth of both technical and manufacturing experience, and also developed a sales force that, over the years, seemed to have the pulse of the commercial market firmly in hand. How else can you explain the continuous string of successful airplanes sold throughout the world?

In retrospect, the four most important aircraft designs, among those listed, were the B-15, B-17, B-47, and the 707. The B-15 forced Boeing's technical staff to come to grips with an airplane that was many times larger than anything the company had worked on before. The B-17 was the catalyst that created large Boeing assembly lines and enabled it to master large-scale production. The B-47 introduced the jet engine, swept wing, and other aerodynamic advances later used on all subsequent Boeing aircraft. And the 707 was the lever that brought Boeing to the forefront in world commercial plane sales. For these reasons, these four models are seen as the ones that brought the greatest changes in Boeing's ability to design and manufacture large jet aircraft.

One might ask whether there were not other aerospace companies that might have brought forth an aircraft similar to the 787. In reality, the answer is no. Both Douglas and McDonnell had been acquired by Boeing. Convair, Grumman, Lockheed, Martin, and Northrop had all built excellent airplanes, but none in the large commercial category for decades. Plus, none of these companies had a sales force with the experience and contacts within the commercial airline industry that Boeing had developed over a period of fifty years.

Thus, the combination of experience, technical know-how, manufacturing facilities, and a potent sales force really made Boeing the only aerospace company in the United States that was in a position to bring forth such a new and innovative design. In Chapter 4, the reader will see how the 787 design was clearly a function of the needs of the world's airlines. Yes, indeed, who else but Boeing!

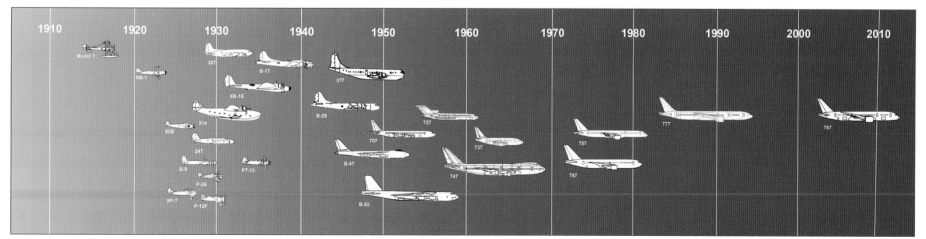

A time line chart of Boeing commercial airplane production. (Steven D. Kimmell)

CHAPTER 4
Marketing the 787

Selling $150 million airplanes is a far different proposition than selling $25 widgets. Thus, when one compares the 787 *Dreamliner* sales record with the records of other airplanes, it becomes clear that this is truly a success story. Never before, in the history of commercial aviation, has a brand new design garnered so many orders before its first flight. It is a testimony to the excellence of their marketing, sales, and engineering staffs, and to the quality of the 787 design. Still, certain other factors also played a part in this success.

To begin with, Boeing's leadership position for fifty years in the sale of many classes of commercial transports – all technically successful – gave it a tremendous advantage. Further, Boeing had long established close communication ties with the world's airlines. These ties proved invaluable during the gestation period of Project Yellowstone and the design phases that followed, for it was the airlines that were able to verbalize successfully to Boeing what their future needs were. And these needs directly shaped the parameters of the 787 family of airplanes and later design decisions. Boeing, throughout this process, was guided by the maxim that it wanted to give the airlines the best possible value for their money. That led to the use of the latest available proven technologies.

Still, selling the 787 brought strong challenges. First, Boeing faced competition from Airbus. This European multinational airplane manufacturer was a private-public entity. Starting in 1970, it grew constantly until 1999, when Airbus outsold Boeing in airframes delivered during a calendar year. However, while Airbus delivered more narrow-body airplanes, Boeing received more wide-body orders, which meant greater revenues for Boeing.

Another problem facing Boeing was the perennial issue of airlines wanting deliveries by a certain date. As 787 sales increased, new orders called for deliveries further into the future. In the past, in order to remain competitive with the latest designs, this schedule had led airlines to order airplanes from different manufacturers. This practice gave Airbus an excellent opportunity to take advantage of Boeing's filled production slots and garner many orders. But, this did not happen to the extent expected. An interesting side story is why, since it provides an opportunity to obtain a good look at the intricacies of determining what goals a new airplane design should achieve.

What Drives the Industry?

To fully understand what led to the success of the 787, it is necessary to examine in detail the major and dramatic changes that took place in commercial aviation in the period 1980-2000. Four main forces caused these changes in those 20 years:

- Airline liberalization
- Increases in airplane and aerospace capabilities
- Changing airline strategies
- Market needs

Airline Liberalization

Since 1976, deregulation has enabled airlines to expand their route structures greatly, as well as to be more flexible in their fares. The result of this change in regulations has been the following:

- Greatly increased competition between air carriers
- The availability of more flights
- The ability of start-up, low-cost carriers to grow and thrive, which created even more competition

Increased Technical Capabilities

Advances in technical capabilities available in the last twenty years of the past century helped to make the 787 more attractive to customers than previous designs. Among these were the following:

- Engines with increased efficiencies and reduced fuel usage
- Better manufacturing methods for working with composites
- Improved computer design programs
- Better electrical systems

All these went into making the 787 an airplane considerably improved over what had been available ten to twelve years earlier.

Changing Airline Strategies

The intense competition that exists in the airline industry forced airlines to take a serious look at the entire concept of increasing point-to-point service and reducing connecting flights through hubs. As delineated below, hubs present ever-increasing problems and costs. In addition, passengers are becoming ever more resistant to passing through hubs and having to make connections to reach their destinations. Also having a significant impact on the airlines are the following situations:

- Steadily increasing passenger traffic
- The impressive expansion of services in China, India, the Pacific Rim, and Russia
- The constant growth of air cargo shipments

To remain competitive – in fact, to remain in business at all – airline strategies are largely driven by passenger needs and wishes. To that end, the airlines pay close attention to three items:

- The availability of safe, reliable service
- The shortest trip times. This means nonstop, point-to-point flights with a greater choice of flights
- Low fares in comfortable surroundings

Airline safety during the current decade has reached an all-time peak. On the other hand, on-time arrivals, particularly at major hubs, have not been realized often enough.

The wish to have more direct, nonstop flights has been clearly demonstrated by the low-cost carriers, both in the United States and in Europe, which have attracted large numbers of passengers by providing passengers with just such services.

Lower fares introduced by the low-cost carriers with spectacular results have obviously shown that passengers respond positively when airfares are in a range they consider to be equitable.

A factor that has influenced long over-water flights is the widespread acceptance of extended range two-engine operations (ETOPS), which have permitted twin-engine wide-body jets to fly long routes across oceans. Interestingly, Airbus has retained the four-engine philosophy on some of its mid-size, twin-aisle transports, which means higher operating and maintenance costs as occur with the A340 airplane.

Market Needs

The three main forces described above all result in market needs. The needs are developed and considered by airlines as they plan their fleet purchases for coming years. The needs also are passed along to marketing representatives of companies such as Boeing and Airbus, who visit the corporate offices of airlines on a regular basis. Based on the information airlines are passing along, marketing departments, in conjunction with other corporate offices, seek the best solutions to meet current and future market needs.

In addition, Boeing developed traffic projections well into the future. These projections, based on many factors – some historical and some economic – are used in developing future airplane designs, whether they be development of an existing airplane or, as in the case of the 787, a brand-new design.

Once the projections and initial design concepts are complete, the manufacturer presents the entire package to its past and future potential customers.

Thus, Boeing believed that all the elements described here would translate into the kind of airplane represented by the 787 family which would be well received by the airline community.

The Growth of Air Travel

The continued growth of air travel, despite such specific negative influences as the fear of terrorism, has clearly demonstrated a need for more total capacity. Air carriers can meet this need by acquiring larger airplanes for their existing route structures, or they can add more midsize airplanes that will permit more point-to-point nonstop routes and greater frequencies. The latter strategy is known as fragmentation.

Studies of this growth in air traffic show that most of the growth has come through additional direct flights (city or airport pairs), as well as greater frequencies, rather than from substituting larger airplanes on existing flights. In fact, since 1995, all air travel growth has been generated by new nonstop flights and greater flight frequencies. During the period from 1995 to date, the average airplane size has gone down slightly, while frequency growth, air travel growth, and nonstop markets have all increased by 60 percent.

Additional proof of this can be seen in the air traffic data across the North Atlantic since 1985. That was the year that Boeing introduced the 767 to that market. The 767 was an airplane that quickly began replacing the larger 747. Average airplane size went down as nonstop markets and flight frequencies grew at an astonishing rate. By 2006,

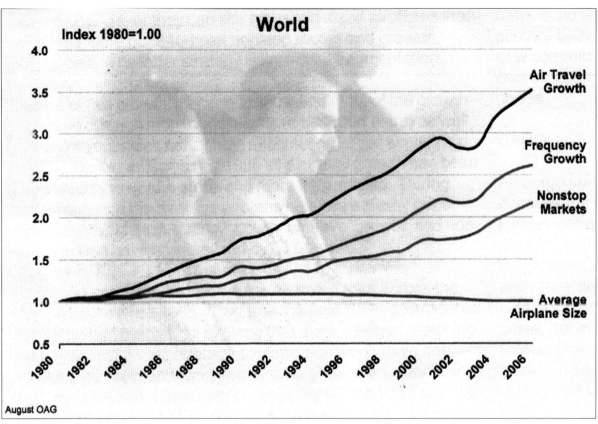

This chart shows the growth of world air travel, 1980-2006.

only 13 percent of the flights used 747s on North Atlantic routes. This fact makes a strong case for using midsize airplanes and for further fragmenting markets. As well, 1998 saw the same trends across the Pacific Ocean as 1995 had seen across the Atlantic Ocean, with the longer-range 777 able to serve those Pacific markets.

The China, India, the Pacific Rim, and Russia Markets

China, India, the Pacific Rim, and Russia represent vast potential markets for the 787 for two reasons: first, they all have huge populations; and second,

all these travel markets have shown a tremendous increase in air travel in recent years. China alone is expected to have travel growth that is twice the predicted world average.

This growth prediction is reflected on Boeing's study of the airplane markets over the next twenty years (also known as their Current Market Outlook). China is expected to need 2,880 new airplanes, of which 25 percent will be twin-aisle aircraft. India is expected to need 860 new airplanes, with 15 percent being twin-aisle planes. Russia will also be acquiring many new commercial airplanes, but may decide to develop its own aircraft manufacturing and thus partly supply its own needs.

Cargo Services

Air cargo shipments are nothing new, but over the past few decades, the level of shipments has grown almost nonstop. Passenger airlines have carried more cargo on passenger flights, and in some instances have begun operating freighters. Cargo-only airlines have mushroomed in number, and many are using 747s to meet their needs. Increases in the cost of jet fuel have slowed the growth of cargo shipments at times, but even then, some growth has occurred. Boeing's forecast for cargo traffic in the next two decades is that it will grow at an average yearly rate of six percent worldwide, or tripling during that time. China's domestic needs and Asian cargo traffic are expected to lead that growth.

Cargo airlines are currently meeting this growth by switching to wide-body freighters, rather than adding airplanes to their fleets. This strategy, however, can work for only so long. This is reflected in Boeing's forecasts that the total freighter fleet will double in the next 20 years. A corollary to this expansion is that the 787 will be able to carry more cargo pallets in the passenger versions than similarly-sized transports.

The Airbus Philosophy

Across the Atlantic, Boeing's main – and basically only – competitor in the manufacture of large commercial airplanes, Airbus, chose to follow a different philosophy. Airbus initially opted to put most of its financial resources into a project to design and build the world's largest commercial transport. Known as the A380, this giant can carry 555 passengers in a three-class configuration. But this size airplane is also the most expensive on the market and is designed to operate out of large airports that double as hubs. This, of course, counters the Boeing philosophy of point-to-point air travel.

The A380 may ultimately find its proper niche, but as shown by comparing the 259 orders booked as of November 2013 (116 delivered), the A380 appears to be much more limited in its ability to service the needs of the airlines than the 787. Furthermore, as of that date, 90 of those orders were from the ambitious Emirates, and one has to wonder whether it can, in fact, make use of and pay for such a major order. Another troubling factor in the short history of the A380 is that since its first flight in 2005, only 30 have been delivered over the intervening five years.

Meanwhile, in December 2006, Airbus launched the A350XWB model, which will compete directly with Boeing's 787. This could prove to be a risky move, since first deliveries will be a minimum of three years after the debut of the 787. This airplane is roughly the same size as the 787-9 and the 777, with the same speed and range, but it is planned to have an airframe made of composite panels connected by metal components. This planned combination of materials is proving to be controversial among aerospace engineers and is felt to be weaker than the Boeing approach. The A350XWB will come in three sizes, all long range, and seat between 270 and 350 passengers, thus straddling the upper end of the 787 and the lower end of the 777 families. By doing this, it eliminates the shorter length trips and may be trying to do too much with a single basic design. In any case, the A350XWB had received 814 orders by November 30, 2013. Yet, with first deliveries now projected to begin two to four years after the 787 appears, if that schedule is not met, Boeing will obviously have a real head start.

Hubs and Their Limitations

Indisputably, many large air carriers committed to using major hubs many years ago. But as air traffic has continued to grow, passengers are finding hubs more and more distasteful. There are valid reasons why hubs may be outliving their usefulness. Among these reasons are:

1. The large capital expense to both communities and airlines required for building and operating major hubs
2. The traffic backups in bad weather that tend to be generated at hubs by their very nature, because flights are scheduled close together to allow for quick transfers
3. That hubs generate a certain percentage of short-haul flights that are the least profitable for airlines
4. The long distances that passengers and crews frequently have to walk within enormous terminals in a short span of time to make connections
5. That the delays of a few flights can lead to additional delays in other connecting flights in a snowball effect
6. That total travel times for passengers who transfer are considerably longer and generally considerably more tiring, stressful, and frustrating than direct, point-to-point flights
7. That air carriers incur greater expenses because of additional flight hours, greater fuel usage, and the need to have additional employees to service customers and transfer luggage between flights

The lower percentage of on time arrivals at major hubs has been a continuing problem for both airlines and passengers. Major weather disturbances can cause havoc with schedules at these hubs, with the delays and cancellations affecting destinations throughout the country and beyond. As well, to provide necessary connecting flights, the major airlines have instituted the use of large fleets of small transports. These smaller airplanes, with their lower departure and arrival speeds, and the need for greater separation from wide-body "heavy" jets have contributed considerably to the delays at hubs.

Chicago's O'Hare Airport, which competes yearly with Atlanta for the title of "World's Busiest Airport," has as many as 25 percent of its total flights handled by small regional aircraft. The distance these flights serve appears to be growing. A meaningful growth in point-to-point direct flights could result in a reduction in flight delays and congestion at these hubs.

With more larger cities demanding flights to additional destinations and with greater frequency, the entire hub approach becomes increasingly complex, unwieldy, and expensive. Thus, air carriers are starting to move slowly away from hubs, partly in response to passenger discontent with the system. As just one example, U.S. Southwest Airlines, which has shown strong growth, operates many of its flights point-to-point, although it too uses some hubs.

Another example of the inefficiency of using hubs is provided by Boeing. A study done by the company shows a comparison of flying direct from Narita, Japan, to Vienna, Austria, versus going through the hub at Frankfurt, Germany. By flying direct using a 787, flight time is reduced by 1.3 hours, fuel by 25 percent, and the passenger saves 2.8 hours of travel time. These are meaningful numbers in terms of both flight costs and total passenger travel time.

The 787 is capable of opening point-to-point routes as a result of its combination of mid-size, lower operating costs, and long range. In fact, a transition to more direct point-to-point flights can occur only if the airlines can justify changing their operational strategy. This is particularly true when considering U.S. airlines serving domestic markets. It is possible that in the near future, increasing traffic and costs associated with hubs may influence all carriers, and particularly the heritage airlines, to begin a slow but steady movement away from using such hubs.

The Demand for Direct Service

Direct point-to-point flights appear to be far more prevalent in areas where new services are being instituted than where hubs have existed for a long time. The United States is probably the best example

An artist's rendering of the new Airbus A350XWB transport cabin.

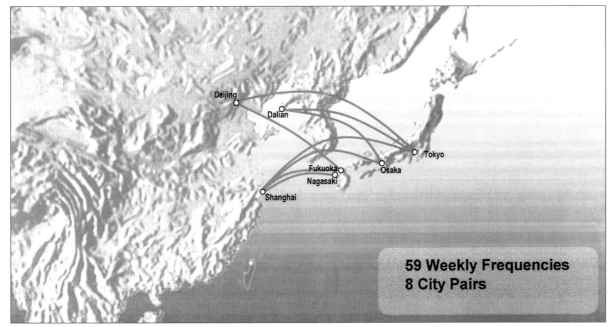

**59 Weekly Frequencies
8 City Pairs**

The weekly air frequencies between Japan and China in 1990.

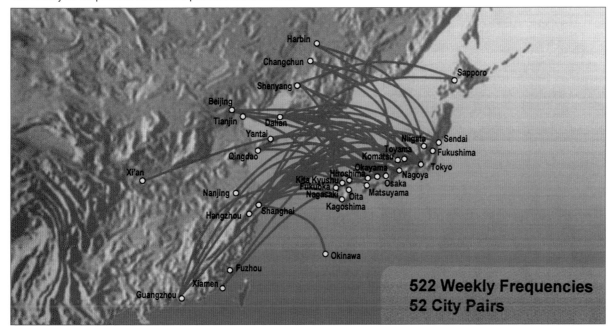

**522 Weekly Frequencies
52 City Pairs**

The weekly air frequencies between Japan and China in 2006.

of a country where hubs are the norm and have been for some decades. In response to this type of route structure, extremely large and expensive terminals have been developed at the largest hubs. Europe's airlines use hubs somewhat less, but they are nevertheless quite prevalent.

If one closely examines the Far East, it is illuminating to see how services for city pairs between China and Japan have grown from eight city pairs and 59 weekly frequencies in 1990 to 52 city pairs and 522 weekly frequencies in 2006. This sixfold growth in the space of 16 years clearly shows the trend being followed by these airlines. Still, this additional service is being handled by airplanes of the same size as before the service expansion took place. Among the reasons for using more mid-size aircraft, rather than fewer larger airplanes, is that larger aircraft cost considerably more to acquire and operate and because larger aircraft that are not filled with passengers incur greater losses.

Domestic service in China since 1990 showed a frequency growth of 13 times what it had been, while city pairs quadrupled. Likewise, domestic services in India are beginning to show healthy growth.

When one considers the age of many airplanes in the U.S. airline fleets combined with increased worldwide air travel, it becomes obvious that the market for the 787 family could in fact be larger than originally envisioned.

As world markets evolve, along with new recreational destinations, the airlines will continue to feel pressured to increase city-pair services while lowering fares. One indication of this trend is that by September 2013, Boeing had already received

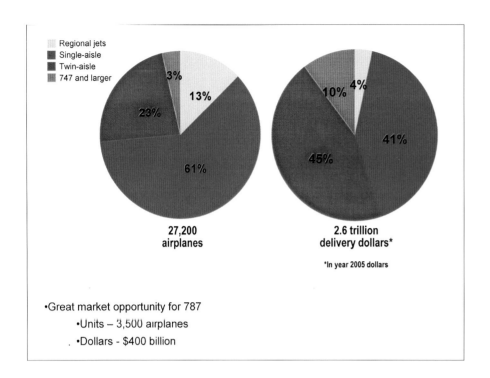

Boeing's projection for world transport sales by 2024.

Legend:
- Regional jets
- Single-aisle
- Twin-aisle
- 747 and larger

27,200 airplanes
- 3%
- 13%
- 23%
- 61%

2.6 trillion delivery dollars*
- 10%
- 4%
- 41%
- 45%

*In year 2005 dollars

•Great market opportunity for 787
- •Units – 3,500 airplanes
- •Dollars - $400 billion

a stunning total of 982 firm orders from 60 cutomers for all its various 787 models.

The Future Outlook

Looking into the future is always a chancy business, but by assessing the recent past and extrapolating the near-term outlook of aviation markets, we can see that Boeing has developed a theoretical picture of the next 15 to 20 years with which it is comfortable.

Boeing sees two major forces developing in this period. One is the gradual but continuing increase of point-to-point direct flights between large and mid-size cities everywhere. The other is the phenomenal economic growth of the Pacific Rim countries, particularly China, with India ranking second.

Boeing's forecast for the year 2024 shows that for nonstop traffic between North America and various Chinese cities, the number of city pairs will more than triple, and the weekly frequencies will grow by 250 percent. Boeing expects this traffic to be handled mainly by 777- and 787-size airplanes. This projection obviously translates into a large market for long-range, medium-size aircraft, such as the 787.

Similar growth is anticipated in markets all over the world, which in part explains the success of the 787 sales. Additionally, there is the age factor of the existing fleets, as well as the higher fuel costs of older airplanes. All these factors were taken into account when the basic parameters of the 787 were first laid out.

The one additional factor that appears to be working very much in Boeing's favor is the attraction for the airlines of combining the 787 and the larger 777 into fleets that can service a variety of routes and varying passenger loads. The table below shows the orders for the 777 and 787 during the period 2004 through 2013:

Year	777	787
2004	53	36
2005	235	40
2006	157	65
2007	369	83
2008	93	61
2009	-59	88
2010	-4	74
2011	72	45
2012	75	50
2013	121	81
TOTALS	644	1,113

During the period 2004 through 2006, thirteen customers ordered both 777 and 787 airplanes. This report appears to buttress the conclusion that the 777 and 787 airplanes do indeed complement each other in the mid-size long-range category, with the 777 offering larger passenger capacity.

Conclusion

These various factors were all part of the mix that was carefully considered and analyzed by Boeing as it determined the basic parameters of the 787. To date, the basic analysis and assumptions arrived at by Boeing appear to be entirely correct, as borne out not only by the 787 sales, but also by the continuing strong sales of the 777.

Sales of the 787 up to September 2013, which total 930 firm orders, commitments, options, and purchase rights, constitute the largest number of commercial airplanes ever sold before the first flight of an airplane. In an interview by *Aviation Week and Space Technology* editors with Scott Carson, chief executive officer of Boeing Commercial Airplanes, published December 18, 2006, this assertion was borne out. Carson, who had previously headed the sales team, said that he felt that if orders for the 787 had reached 300-350 by the end of 2006, it would be a tremendous success. The actual firm total of orders far exceeded everyone's expectations.

Few of those sales have been to U.S. airlines, which are currently facing difficult financial times. In the interview with Carson, he commented that he believed by late 2007 or 2008, U.S. vintage airlines might be in a position to begin ordering the 787. Unfortunately, the rapid rise in fuel costs that began mid-2007 created serious, and in some cases fatal financial problems for airlines worldwide. By the same token, this very rise in fuel costs may turn out to be the precise circumstance needed to motivate airlines to begin ordering 787s to take advantage of the airplane's lower fuel usage.

Thus, it is obvious that a number of trends and circumstances are at play in the continuing saga of sales of the 787. It is impossible to predict accurately such items as the growth of worldwide commerce, the various problems associated with hubs, and the future financial health of the world's major airlines. Ultimately, if the various forces that shape an airplane model's sales are reasonably correct, then it seems safe to predict the 787 family will have a long and highly profitable future.

Now it is time to examine in some detail how Boeing made good on its promise of creating an airplane that would be 20 percent more efficient than any other jet transport of comparable size.

CHAPTER 5
Let's Improve Efficiency by 20 Percent!

When Boeing decided to move ahead with the 7E7 program in late 2002, the basic parameters for the airplane had already been set. One of these was that the new airplane should operate at 20 percent greater efficiency compared with similarly-sized airplanes. This was no small task, considering that airplanes of the previous generation, such as the 767 and 777, were already considered to be highly efficient airplanes. Aside from that, a 20-percent greater overall efficiency in and of itself is a giant step forward and requires various elements working together to accomplish this truly ambitious goal. In fact, there is no documented instance of such an improvement between two succeeding generations of airplanes.

The general approach for reaching this goal breaks down into five distinct areas. These areas and their individual contributions are:

1. Engine improvements, 8 percent
2. Aerodynamics, 3 percent
3. System design and integration, 3 percent
4. The use of composite materials, 3 percent
5. Systems interaction and cycling, 3 percent

Cycling, a Boeing term and number five on the list, accrues from introducing area numbers one through four on a brand new airplane. It refers to the ability to let one improvement reduce requirements elsewhere. For example, more efficient engines use less fuel, which in turn results in the planes being able to carry less fuel, which then allows for a smaller wing size.

A 20 percent overall operating improvement at a single stroke was unprecedented, and was possibly the biggest single reason for the early sales success of the 787. In this chapter, we look at four of these five areas in some detail. Inasmuch as composites (are number 4) form such a large part of the 787 airframe and are so important to the end product, they are covered separately in Chapter six.

Engines

The engine of any airplane is the heart of that machine, and the engine of the 787 was designed to deliver the necessary power at a considerable increase in efficiency.

From the time the 7E7 program was formally announced in December 2002, three aircraft jet engine companies showed interest in supplying the new power plants. Two (General Electric and Pratt and Whitney) are American firms, while the third (Rolls-Royce) is a British company. Of the three competitors, only Pratt and Whitney proposed a brand new design, while the other two brought forth improved versions of previously introduced and highly successful engines.

In April 2004, Boeing announced that GE and Rolls-Royce had been chosen to develop the engines for the 787. Further, Boeing said it intended to offer both engines to each customer from which to choose. Both companies clearly understood that they would have to develop engines with better fuel efficiency and lower operating and maintenance costs.

The GE engine is identified as the GEnx, for Next Generation, while Rolls-Royce calls its engine the Trent 1000. Boeing specified that these engines had to be rated at 74,000-pound thrust and they would be used initially on the 787-8 and later on the heavier 787-9 models. While the requirements for both engines are identical, the two differ markedly in their design and achieve the required power ratings and fuel efficiencies in different ways. The engine thrust requirements for each 787 model are:

787-8	70,000 pounds of thrust
787-9	74,000 pounds of thrust

These numbers give some idea of the range of power needed from the same basic engine as required by the two 787 models. For GE and Rolls-Royce to meet the aggressive fuel efficiencies demanded by Boeing, they had to do a number of things. They had to come up with innovations while maintaining their proven technology frameworks. Further, to meet the NO_x and CO_2 20 percent emission improvements stipulated by Boeing, they had to achieve certain technologies by 2008 that were originally expected to come online by 2010 or later. A major change introduced in the 787 was the GEnx engine.

The GEnx Engine

The GEnx is a fifth-generation version of GE's GE90, with the previous generation, called the CF6, having successfully powered both the Boeing 767 and Airbus 330.

The GEnx is designed to operate at 15 percent better specific fuel consumption as compared with previous engines of comparable thrust, remain in service 30 percent longer between major overhauls, and use 30 percent fewer life-limited parts.

The GEnx is a high bypass fan jet engine with a large percentage of the total air entering the engine passing through the bypass duct. Inside the fan case is the fan itself. When GE first built the original GE90, it employed composite fan blades for the first time. This was an engine that had been used on the 777 beginning in the 1990s. In designing this new engine, GE introduced several innovations. The fan blades, as in the GE90, are made of composite material. The number of fan blades was reduced from 22 on the GE90 to just 18 in this engine. The fan case is also made of composite material, rather than the titanium used previously. To better grasp this concept, a brief description of how a jet engine operates is useful.

The original jet engines were based on a turbine that sucked in air and passed it to a so-called *hot section*, or combustion chamber, where the ambient air was mixed with fuel. The mixture was then ignited. The resulting reaction as the exhaust exited from the rear created forward thrust. In later years, engineers discovered that by installing a large rotating ducted fan in the front of the engine, driven by the turbine, massive amounts of air would be moved to the rear around the turbine, resulting in far greater thrust. Furthermore, this ambient air moving outside the turbine itself provided a cushion between the hot exhaust and the surrounding cold atmosphere. This in turn resulted in far quieter engines.

As shown in Figure A (*see* p 48), the outside air is drawn into the engine by the fan at ambient pressure. The GEnx has a bypass ratio of 9:1. With this 9:1 ratio, 90 percent of the total engine thrust is the result of the bypass air passing through the ducted fan and then accelerated by the core exhaust, while only 10 percent of the thrust results from the air passing through the core or turbine sections. The sequence of steps in the operation of this engine are as follows:

1. The front-mounted fan draws outside air in.
2. Ninety percent of the air goes through the bypass duct.
3. Ten percent of the air flows through the low-pressure compression stage.
4. The air that exits from the low-pressure compression stage then passes through to the high-pressure compression stage.
5. The air then passes through the Twin-Annular Premixing Swirler (TAPS) combustor, where air and fuel are premixed.
6. The fuel-air mixture is ignited, expands rapidly, and escapes through the high-pressure turbine, hence driving it, then through the low-pressure turbine, also driving it, and finally exiting from the core nozzle.

The high-pressure turbine extracts energy from combustion and drives the high-pressure compressor via a shaft that passes through the center of the engine. Similarly, the low-pressure turbine also extracts energy from combustion, which in turn drives the low-pressure turbine, as well as the fan itself through a second shaft. This second shaft is longer, has a smaller diameter, and rotates inside the high-pressure turbine shaft.

There are other new or improved technologies introduced on this engine, the TAPS combustor being one. Fuel is introduced into the engine through twenty-two fuel nozzles at the combustor. The combustor then achieves this mixing of air and fuel by using two, high-energy swirlers located adjacent to the fuel nozzles. The result is a more

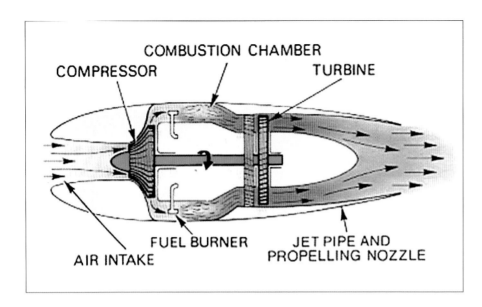

Figure A: Cross-section of a typical turbo-jet engine.

COMBUSTION CHAMBER

COMPRESSOR

TURBINE

AIR INTAKE

FUEL BURNER

JET PIPE AND PROPELLING NOZZLE

The extra time that became available when the 787 program ran into delays enabled GE to accomplish two important items: first, it worked hand-in-hand with its suppliers to ensure that its higher rate of production could be supported on a continuing basis by the supply chain. Second, the extra time allowed GE to fine-tune the propulsor portion of the GEnx engine and to squeeze more efficiency from it.

The Rolls-Royce Trent 1000 Engine

The Rolls-Royce Trent 1000 (*see* p 50) grew out of the Trent 700 engine, which powers the Airbus 330, and the later Trent 800 used on the original Boeing 777. Rolls-Royce, however, has designed the Trent 1000 with significant differences from the GEnx. The Trent 1000 does not use composites for the fan blades or fan case; rather, they are all metal. Moreover, the Trent 1000 uses a three-shaft design as opposed to the two-shaft GEnx.

The three-shaft design employs a separate shaft for each of its low, intermediate, and high-pressure systems, with each system having its own compressor and turbine stages. Rolls-Royce believes that since the optimum operating speeds of the three stages differ greatly, using individual drive shafts for each stage results in a more efficient engine. This three-stage design allows for more flexibility in reaching optimum efficiency over the large power range of 53,000- to 74,000-pound thrust required to power the three 787 models.

The three-shaft engine is also shorter and more rigid compared with the two shaft engines. This results in less flexing in flight, which in turn means less wear. This design is also lighter than the GEnx.

homogenous fuel-air mixture that is leaner, resulting in lower fuel usage and reduced temperatures. Furthermore, the combustor, by reducing those temperatures, also reduces the level of nitrous oxide (NO_2) emissions by as much as 50 percent when compared with the emissions of the popular CF6 engine that powers many of today's commercial jet aircraft.

The TAPS combustor is new to GE engines, and the 787 will be the first aircraft to put its benefits to use. Combustor development began in the 1990s as part of the National Aeronautics and Space Administration (NASA) Advanced Subsonic Development Program. It was first demonstrated and tested on a CFM56–7 engine produced by CFM International, a company owned equally by GE and Snecma.

The core of the GEnx, called the propulsor, is assembled at GE's Durham, North Carolina, plant.

This propulsor includes a high-pressure compressor, combustor, and a high-pressure turbine. The propulsor is assembled vertically, then rotated to a horizontal position, where the low-pressure compressor assembly and the low-pressure turbine are installed. Assembly takes about fifteen days. The completed propulsor is then shipped to the Peebles, Ohio, GE Test Operation for final assembly. Here, the fan case assembly received from GE's Batesville, MS, plant, together with fan blades and spinner, are installed. This latter step requires an additional two days.

General Electric has had to reconfigure itself, owing to the ever-increasing number of jet engine orders. The company's total engine orders have nearly doubled in a five-year span. Much of the increase has been for the large fan jets that power wide-body airplanes. The unexpected speed with which the 787 garnered orders put real pressure on GE to ramp up its production rate.

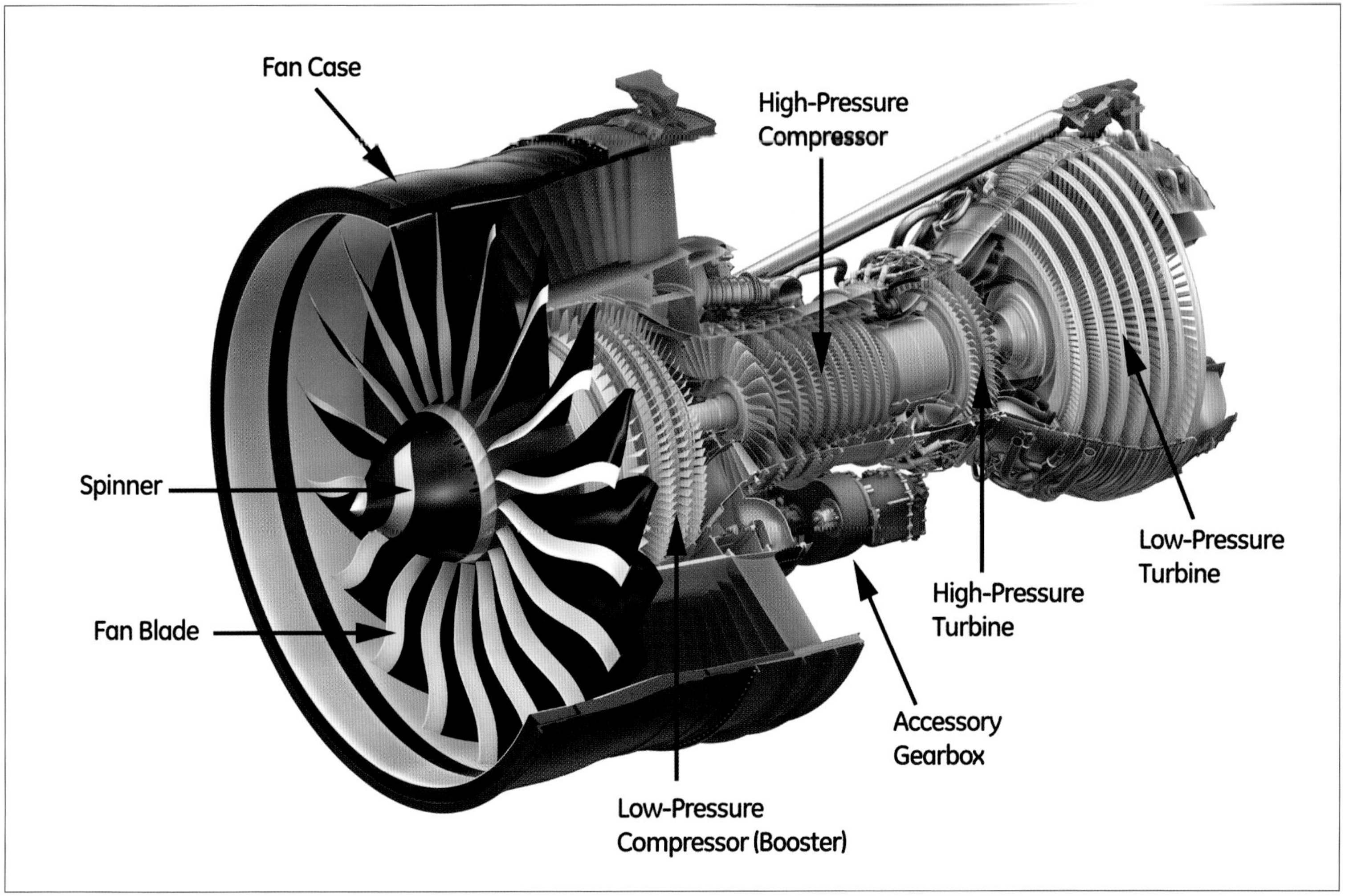

Fan Case

High-Pressure Compressor

Spinner

Fan Blade

Low-Pressure Turbine

High-Pressure Turbine

Accessory Gearbox

Low-Pressure Compressor (Booster)

The General Electric GEnx fan-jet engine, one of two that power the 787. (General Electric)

The temperature and pressure of the engine at its core is the key to the optimum efficiency of the unit. In the case of the Trent, the maximum temperature is greater than 2,912 degrees Fahrenheit and the pressure is 40 atmospheres.

Rolls-Royce pioneered the hollow, titanium, wide-chord fan blades used in the Trent engine and introduced them in airline service in the 1980s.

These blades were designed specifically for high-bypass turbofan engines, and the width of the blades set them apart from other designs. Each wide-chord blade is fabricated from three layers of titanium that are bonded together after being heated to a super-plastic state. The blade is then filled with gas.

Although the Trent 1000 was originally slated to be manufactured at Rolls-Royce's primary large

civil engine plant in Derby, United Kingdom, a new site was recently announced. The new plant will be located on the city/island of Singapore. There, on the island's north side at an industrial site called Seletar, a new factory is under construction. The plant will be fully operational for Trent 1000 production and test by early 2013. This plant will be the first one outside the United Kingdom for

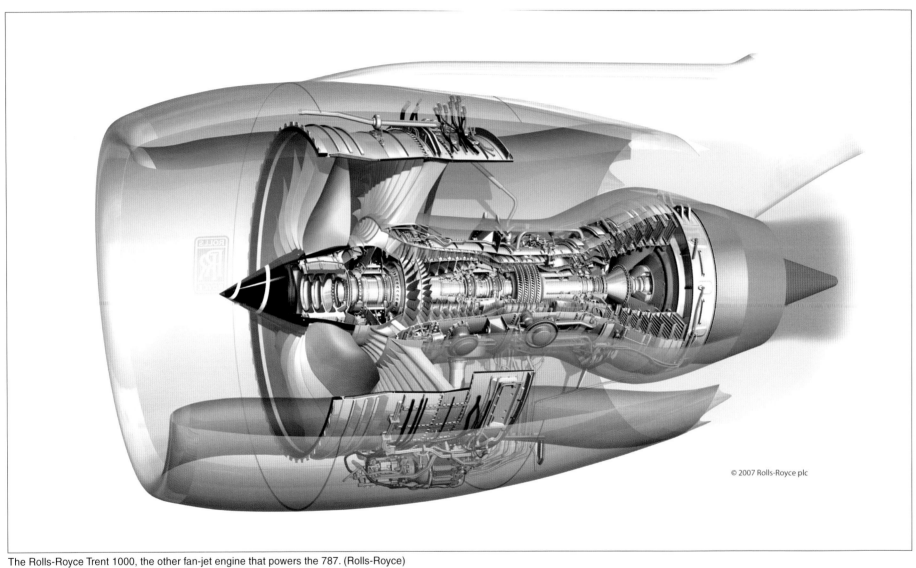

The Rolls-Royce Trent 1000, the other fan-jet engine that powers the 787. (Rolls-Royce)

Rolls-Royce. It was designed to operate using a moving assembly line, as well as cross-functional teams to allow mechanics to operate more closely with engineering and logistical support.

Engine Noise Reduction

Both Boeing and the two engine manufacturers were interested in achieving considerable reductions in engine noise. To that end, a maximum of 85 decibels in external noise levels was set for airports and surrounding areas. To reach this low level of engine noise, various design features were employed. The engine nacelles were given chevrons, or serrated edges, at the rear of the engines. The engine inlets were acoustically treated and other noise-reducing measures were applied to both the engines and the engine casings. The following table compares the two power plants.

	GEnx	Trent 1000
Number of shafts	2	3
Maximum length (inches)	182	160
Bare engine weight (pounds)	12,904	12,808
Fan diameter (inches)	111	112
Fan speed (rpm)	2,476	2,683
High-pressure system speed (rpm)	12,701	13,391
Maximum operating temperature (°F)	3,040	2,912
Total pressure ratio	42	40

The two engine manufacturers took different paths to reach the same fundamental result.

A 787 engine nacelle showing the noise reducing chevrons mounted on the rear.

Later Engine Updates

The 27-month delay of the first flight of the 787 had at least one positive result: it gave the two engine suppliers time to develop and introduce improvements in their respective power plants.

For Rolls-Royce, improvements were made to its turbine aerodynamics, cooling flow, and cooling air. The result was the thrust reached for the 787-9 is the required 74,000 pounds, while for the 787-8 it is 70,000 pounds.

General Electric likewise used the extra time to make improvements. About one-third of its GEnx-

1B has been redesigned, and as a result is also expected to produce improved performance.

Aerodynamics

The aerodynamics of the 787 play a part in improving the efficiency of the airplane. The all-composite fuselage and wings present a smoother surface to the airstream, thus reducing drag. The wing is designed for optimum efficiency, and here composites played an important part. The thinner

a wing, the more efficient it is, but thinner wings require a stronger and heavier structure. Yet with composites, the same strength is retained in spite of the thinner wing, thus making for a win-win situation. In addition, because the wing is made largely of composites that allow for more complex curvatures, the various wing curvatures could be optimized for the best aerodynamic flow.

System Design and Integration

Power Generation

The system design of the 787 incorporates a major and truly revolutionary change, the use of electrical power to drive almost everything in the airplane. This feature is contrary to all earlier designs, where hydraulic and pneumatic power played a large part. The clearest example of this change is a comparison of what drives various systems in the 777-200—previously the highest technology airplane built by Boeing—and the 787.

Function	777-200	787
Engine start	Pneumatic	Electric
Cabin pressure heat	Pneumatic	Electric
Wing de-icing	Pneumatic	Electric
High-demand hydraulic power	Pneumatic	Electric
Hydraulic pressure (psi)	3,000	5,000
Braking	Hydraulic	Electric
Flight control power	Hydraulic	Hydraulic and electric
In-flight entertainment systems	Electric	Electric

There are two reasons for Boeing's move to a basically all-electric airplane: first, power electronics are much smaller and lighter than they were ten years ago; second, it was felt that hydraulic or pneumatic efficiencies had reached their optimum levels, while electrical systems would continue to improve.

By moving to an all-electric airplane, Boeing was able to abolish using engine-bleed air to drive any system. Bleed air is hot compressed air taken directly from the engine and used to drive various systems. Total reliance on the electrical power system helped reduce fuel burn, reduced emissions, and lowered long-term maintenance costs. Interestingly, both the GE and Rolls-Royce engines can be used with or without a bleed air system. In fact, on the new Boeing 747-8 airplane, bleed air systems are being retained.

The 787 generates at least four times the electrical power used in other airplanes. To generate that much electrical power, a radical change in design was the only answer. In the 787, each jet engine is equipped with two 250-kilowatt generators, plus two additional 225-kilowatt generators functioning as auxiliary power units (APU), for a total of 1,450 kilowatts. The generators are manufactured by Hamilton Sunstrand, located in Rockford, Illinois. By comparison, the Airbus A380, which uses more conventional systems such as bleed air and pneumatics and weighs two and a half times as much, generates only 840 kilowatts.

As a further example of how advanced these power generators are, and of how small and lightweight they have become, the two 250 kVA generators take up only slightly more room than a single 120 kVA generator used on the 767 fifteen

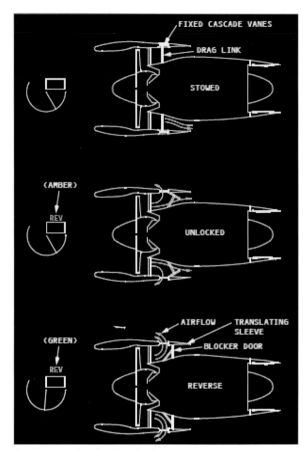

A schematic showing how jet thrust reversers operate.

years earlier. This is truly a stupendous advance in power generating technology.

These generators do double duty, operating as engine starters. To accomplish this, they have to operate briefly at overload, but are considered totally capable of accepting that load. During engine start-ups, if both generators are used, the engines will start in less than 40 seconds, while if one generator is used, the engines will start in less than 70 seconds. The 787 also carries a small gas turbine APU in the unlikely event that total electrical failure occurs.

Electronic Systems

The electronic systems of the 787 are integrated to a far greater extent than any previous commercial airplane design. The point is demonstrated by the fact that the Boeing 777 has 80 separate computer systems with about 100 different devices, while the 787 has only 30 computer systems. The secret to this massive integration is the Common Core System (CCS) developed by Smith Aerospace Division of General Electric. The CCS combines the processing functions of many separate systems, thus saving weight, power, and cost. The CCS is modular in design, which allows future additions and changes to be made easily without major system redesigns.

The Common Core System had its foundation in the Lockheed C-130 Hercules Aircraft Modernization Program—managed by Boeing—and the Boeing 777 Aircraft Information Management System concept. The CCS comprises three major elements:

1. A common computing resource (CCR), which is a cabinet containing general processing and application specific modules
2. A common data network developed by Rockwell Collins that employs the deterministic Ethernet 664/AFDX (Avionics Full Duplex) standard
3. A series of 21 GE remote data concentrators

The complete Common Core System is made up of two CCR cabinets, eight general processing modules, network switches, and two fiber-optic translator modules in each CCR cabinet. This entire system integrates a large number of functional items, including the following:

- Cabin services
- Crew alerting
- Displays
- Electrical system
- Environmental system
- Fire protection equipment
- Flight management
- Fuel management
- Health management
- Hydraulic system
- Maintenance
- Mechanical system
- Navigation

From this brief description of the electronic data system, it can easily be seen how Boeing and its main partners have managed to integrate many functions into one electronic system. Some of the by-products of this system integration process are:

1. A reduction in the amount of equipment and its total weight
2. Ease of maintenance
3. The ability to expand the system easily
4. Greater efficiency and reduced fuel usage
5. System improvements for the flight deck
6. Integrated health management

System Integration

Designing and proving the systems that operate the 787 required a major effort. Boeing employed approximately 1,500 engineers working in labs to complete the effort. One of the challenges of an airplane having the complexity and sophistication of the 787 *Dreamliner* lies in integrating the various systems. Unless and until that is accomplished, the airplane is neither ready nor safe to fly.

A major task that had to be completed was the checking out of more than six million lines of software codes used by the various onboard computers. This particular job turned out to require considerably more time than had originally been contemplated.

One of the most critical systems is the flight control system. To test this system in real time, Boeing built what it calls the Iron Bird, which is a real flight control hardware built inside a lab and connected to a simulated control system. Using the Iron Bird, engineers tested all the functions of the system and corrected any issues that arose.

In Cedar Rapids, Iowa, Rockwell Collins built an avionics lab for the specific purpose of testing and checking out the complex electronic systems that fly the 787. There, the systems are tested as though in flight, and part of the testing relates to the successful integration of the electronic systems. The Common Core and Flight Management Systems are both tested here. Boeing also has five similar avionics labs in Seattle to test how these systems interact with the airframe. Boeing previously carried out this type of integration and testing for other airplanes, but this is the first time Rockwell Collins has built its own lab to test a Boeing airplane.

Maintenance Cost Reductions

One additional component adds materially to the ability of the 787 to operate at 20 percent greater efficiency. It is not a particularly glamorous area, but is extremely important, and that is the general maintenance cost over the life cycle of the airplane. Boeing estimates that when the 787-8 is twelve years old, the cost of its maintenance will be 30 percent lower than a comparable 767-300 of the same age. Beyond that point, the cost difference becomes even greater, with the maintenance cost savings realized when the airplane is between 12 and 24 years old growing gradually to as much as 60 percent. This is a truly phenomenal improvement. The way the savings are achieved is worth examining.

Possibly the largest contributing factor to this large cost saving is the airframe itself. The all-composite structure is known to be far more resistant to both corrosion and fatigue than an aluminum structure. Additionally, the composite skin will suffer much less damage from minor impacts and scratches while on the ground, and those that do occur can be repaired more quickly at a fraction of the cost of repairing a metal structure. Thus, non-routine maintenance occurs far less frequently. This is significant, because such maintenance during a scheduled maintenance check will double or triple the person-hours expended. In addition, Boeing has developed a means of repairing minor external airframe damage within one hour.

Boeing has also shown that composite structures require less scheduled maintenance, which is a big-ticket item. An example of this is the 777 composite tail assembly, which is 25 percent larger than the all-metal tail of a 767, but requires 35 percent less scheduled maintenance. These numbers are not theoretical, but rather empirical, and are based on real maintenance records.

Another cost savings results from the use of composite floor beams. The 777, which has been in service since 1995, has an all-composite floor, and during its entire lifetime not a single floor beam has had to be replaced owing to corrosion.

The change from hydraulic to electrical brakes is another example of reduced maintenance. This change has not only reduced the mechanical complexity of the braking system, but also has eliminated hydraulic failures, such as leaking hydraulic fluid, leaking valves, and other common hydraulic problems.

As previously noted, the 787 has done away with the bleed-air system for powering onboard systems, as well as any pneumatic systems, in favor of all-electrical systems. This change in the airplane architecture has materially simplified the onboard systems and done away with much of the mechanical complexity formerly found on large airplanes. Once again, the result is reduced maintenance and more cost savings.

The dependence on electrical rather than hydraulic and pneumatic systems has reduced the mechanical complexity of the airplane by 50 percent as compared with a 767, with the elimination of the pneumatic systems being the major contributor.

Some other innovations that positively affect this drive for lower maintenance costs include the following:

1. Greatly expanded and improved maintenance monitoring computer systems, including ground-based monitoring capability
2. Selective paint stripping using a stripping chemical that works in three hours
3. Electrochromatic dimmable windows, which replace mechanical window shades and have a 20-year life
4. The ability to change engines of different manufacturers on the same pylons quickly
5. High-intensity discharge and light emitting diode lighting with a much greater operational life
6. Improved dispatch reliability, with the 787's component reliability estimated to be 15 percent greater than on the 767

Conclusion

Considering all these items, it becomes obvious that Boeing's engineers made major strides in greatly improving the 787's reliability and reducing maintenance costs over the life of the airplane.

The description of these advances gives an indication how Boeing went about meeting the challenge of making the 787 more efficient than any previous large commercial jet by 20 percent. The reader, though, will remember that the writer has said nothing about the fifth and last item on the original list of the methods Boeing used to meet its stated goal: the introduction of an all-composite airframe. Owing to its importance and complexity, this subject is covered separately in the following chapter.

CHAPTER 6
The Composite Story

Critical to the 787 design process was the early decision to use composite materials for the airframe. This was a truly major decision, since no commercial aircraft before the 787 had used that much composite material. One reason was the cost, and another was

A 1916 photo of Boeing employees assembling an early aircraft using cloth and varnish, which was an early composite.

the learning curve in terms of how to use the material economically in the manufacture of airplanes. In fact, no one had ever attempted to mass produce such large carbon-reinforced plastic structures. The tooling for such large sections was still being developed and was another potential hurdle. Furthermore, new coatings had to be developed to deal with the issue of crack propagation in these composite structures.

What exactly are composite materials? They are two or more materials combined to perform a useful purpose. Steel-reinforced concrete qualifies as a composite. In the case of the aerospace industry, composites are made up of nonmetallic plastic fibers embedded in an epoxy resin matrix.

Boeing's earliest airplanes, built in 1916, had wings made of cloth and varnish. By today's definition, these wings were made of composites.

The use of composites in general is relatively new. Statistics show that in 1975, less than 100 tons

of composites were used worldwide, whereas by 2005, the demand had grown to 25,000 tons.

The use of composites in airplanes is hardly new for Boeing. In the mid-1960s, Boeing used composites in the then-new 747 for control surfaces, fairings, and wing trailing edge panels. In the 1970s, composites were used for Boeing 727 elevators and 737 stabilizers. Proof of their strength can be seen in two 737 horizontal stabilizers originally manufactured and installed in 1984 that are still flying today, after accumulating more than 55,000 flight hours each.

In the 1980s, composites were used in applications on both the 757 and 767. In the 1990s, composites were used in the 777 on the tail assembly, as well as other locations. The manufacturing process of composites by Boeing in its jet transports is most clearly demonstrated in the following table:

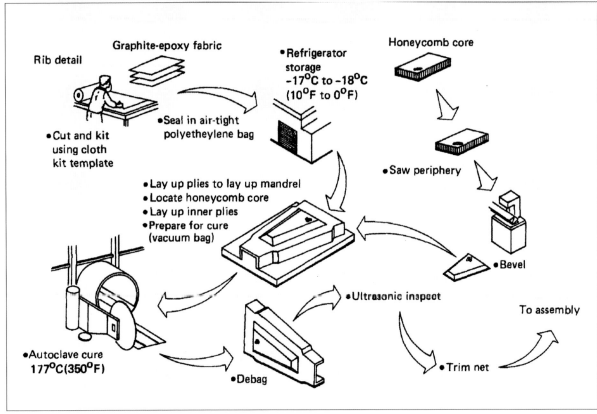

The typical sequence of steps in creating structures from advanced composites. (Steven D. Kimmell)

Model	Composite Percentage by Weight
747	1
757/767	3
777	11
787	50

Among all of today's large jet transports, the 787 is the only airplane with virtually its entire airframe made from composites and constituting 50 percent of the total airplane weight. This statement is somewhat misleading, inasmuch as it is true that only 50 percent of the total weight comprises composites, but that is true only because the composites used in the 787 airframe are considerably lighter than the metals they replace. The fact is, practically the entire airframe of the 787 is made of composites. In terms of volume, 80 percent of the airplane is made of composites. That includes the fuselage, most of the wings, and the tail assembly. The list below will assist in better visualizing exactly where composites are used:

Fuselage: frame, shear ties, skin, and stringers
Wings: skin, spars, and stringers
Tail assembly horizontal stabilizer: the main torque box is a single composite piece, previously made up of nineteen separate pieces.

Because the 787 is manufactured by various partner companies all over the world, the use of composites to such an extent is even more a substantial step forward. Boeing had to ensure that the various partners involved in the manufacture of composite components clearly understood both the techniques to be used and had the facilities and equipment required for such material processing. The result was that the partners often had to construct new buildings that had, among other things, "clean rooms". They also had to purchase expensive and highly sophisticated equipment required for this type of manufacturing. The clean rooms, which have purified air and a controlled environment, are necessary when working with composites.

These requirements brought about a gigantic job of monitoring by Boeing's engineers and technicians. Translating that application for partner companies involved both a major effort and a certain level of risk. This was particularly true when one considers that single-piece fuselage barrels with 20-foot diameters and wing skins 80 feet long were being contemplated, and were far larger than any composite assemblies ever attempted before. Composites were chosen over steel and aluminum for the following reasons:

1. They are much lighter than metals. For the same strength, composites are 10 to 30 percent lighter than aluminum. This makes possible a lighter

airframe and, as a result, lower fuel burn, lower operating costs, and reduced landing fees, which are based on the weight of the airplane. For example, the 787 is 30,000 to 40,000 pounds lighter than the A330-200, an airplane of comparable size.

2. Composites are stronger than metals, as well as more resistant to puncture and fatigue. In fact, several airliner accidents over the years have been attributed to a failure of the cabin walls, resulting in explosive decompression. The specific strength of composites is almost twice that of aluminum.

3. Composites can be tailored to be more flexible than metals. They are also more conducive to larger and more integrated designs.

4. Composites require far less maintenance, being more resistant to fatigue and corrosion. Line maintenance intervals are programmed to be 1,000 hours, as compared with the 500 hours for the 767 and the 700 hours for the A330. Heavy structural inspections are scheduled every 12 years for the 787, compared with every six years for the 767 and A330. Thus, composites add value to the airplane, giving customer airlines more for their money. This particular cost savings is one that becomes more readily apparent over the life of the airplane.

5. Repairs to composites are often much cheaper and quicker than for aluminum. Many minor repairs to the skin can be completed at the gate within an hour.

6. Composites are extremely resistant to fire.

Additional significant benefits of composites include:

1. Larger assemblies reduce manufacturing and assembly time by 30 to 40 percent.

2. There is a sizeable reduction in the amount of manufacturing waste as compared with aluminum.

3. Composites create a stronger fuselage wall, which allows the passenger-cabin equivalent altitude to be lowered to 6,000 feet, while allowing for larger windows.

4. Using composites enables the wings to be thinner and lighter, thus producing the same lift with less drag.

The use of composites enables design engineers to design a wing that is more aerodynamically efficient and has a higher aspect ratio (10-1) for long-range cruise. The 787 wing is also extremely flexible (*see* p 115).

A problem associated with composites is that they are subject to photooxidation caused by sunlight. Photooxidation is the degradation of a polymer surface when oxygen or ozone is present. The sun's rays facilitate this process. In degradation, a chemical change occurs that can make the composite brittle, with a reduction in its tensile, impact, and elongation strength. To counter degradation, a primer coat of special paint is applied to all surfaces. Since the majority of time a jet transport flies it is in bright sunlight, the photooxidation process continues for a great deal of the time. The solution is the creation of an intermediate barrel coating applied under the exterior paint as a primer.

The composites used in the 787 are carbon fiber reinforced plastic (CFRP) composites made from resins and fibers. The fibers can be made of carbon, fiberglass, or aramid. The resin matrices are thermoset (epoxy) and have slower processing times than thermoplastic material. The fibers are woven into fabric, or they are unidirectional and called *tape*. Both fabric and tape are delivered in rolls, and the width of each roll is specified depending upon its final application. By adding more layers, the strength of the composite can be increased to meet a specific need. The rolls are received already impregnated but not yet cured, which constitutes the final process. All the composites for the 787 are supplied by Toray Industries of Japan, the world's largest producer of carbon fiber. Since 2004, Boeing has placed orders with Toray for composites totaling more than $6 billion.

To make barrel sections for the fuselage, mats of the required thickness and strength are wound on enormous mandrels (40-foot molds) that are the same diameter as the fuselage. The barrel sections are then placed into autoclaves (ovens), where the material is baked at high temperatures and pressures until it reaches the stage of being a finished composite. Composites can then be cut with special cutting tools or high-pressure water jets to create openings for windows, doors, and hatches.

To validate the manufacturing processes for the fuselage barrel sections, Boeing completed the first full-scale one-piece fuselage section at the Developmental Center in Seattle in January 2005. The section was 22 feet long and 19 feet in diameter, and included stringers. Windows and doors were cut into the sidewalls. In all, nine developmental barrel sections were produced.

The highly specialized tooling required in the manufacture of the composite sections of the airplane created a challenge that required innovative design. Janicki Industries, a company located in Seedro-Wooley, Washington, developed tooling for the 787 that has proven successful.

The Fuselage

The fuselage alone is manufactured by four subcontracted companies: Spirit AeroSystems, Kawasaki Heavy Industries, Alenia Aeronautica, and Vought.

There are five separate components to a fuselage barrel section, all made of composites. They are:

• Frames that run the circumference of the fuselage
• Stringers that run the length of the barrel
• Shear ties that attach the frame to the skin
• Skin
• Floor beams

Together, these are the main components that form a complete barrel section.

An additional component to barrel sections is identified as tear straps. These are straps built into the walls. If a puncture occurs in the fuselage while it is pressurized, they prevent the hole or tear from spreading. The concept is similar to staves that encircle a barrel. It is a basic concept that Boeing introduced in its original 707 jet transport. Steel straps were located at roughly 30-inch intervals. In the 787, the tear straps consist of a thickening in the cabin walls achieved by adding composite plies. The thickness and location of each tear strap is a function of the specific local loading and the adjacent skin gage, developed by lab analysis and validated by testing.

The nose section (also known as section 41) is probably the most interesting and complex portion of the fuselage, from a manufacturing point of view. It has a different and more complex shape, since it includes the cockpit. Furthermore, section 41 is delivered to Boeing with windshields, virtually all the cockpit instrumentation, much of the total system hardware, and the nose wheel well and nose landing gear assembly installed. One can visualize how complicated this section is and how it is delivered with a great deal more equipment installed than on any previous aircraft design.

Fuselage Subcontractors
Spirit AeroSystems

The nose section is built by a newer company, Spirit AeroSystems, located at the edge of McConnell Air Force Base, on the east side of Wichita, Kansas. The plant itself has an interesting history; the company name is new, but the facility has been around a long time. This facility was owned by the Stearman Airplane Company, that was purchased by United Aircraft and Transport Corporation (UATC) in August 1929. When UATC was broken up in 1934, the plant became a subsidiary of Boeing, in August 1934. Boeing produced some of its Kaydet trainers there. During World War II, the plant expanded and built the Boeing B-29 Superfortress. Later, the plant also built B-47 Stratojet bombers in large quantities, as well as the B-52 Stratofortress, and support work for both the B-52 and the KC-135 Stratotanker. It also did fabrication work for the Commercial Airplane Division, chiefly on the 737 fuselage.

The facility encompasses an area two miles by one mile. The facility remained Boeing's Wichita plant until June 2005, when it was sold to a new business venture called Onyx, which then became Spirit AeroSystems. Spirit continues to manufacture various portions of Boeing airplanes, including the 737, 747, 767, and 777 models. It also supplies Airbus with some major airframe components.

In November 2003, while the Wichita facility was still a Boeing plant, it was awarded the work for the nose section and immediately began working on the design of the section, as well as the technology and systems required to build this large airframe section.

In August 2007, the author toured the Spirit 787 plant together with Jennifer Cram, a Boeing 787 communication representative. We were escorted by Bob Smith, a Spirit corporate communication specialist, and the technical explanations were handled by John Pilla and Forrest Urban.

The tour began with an explanation of the general layout of the building, enhanced by an excellent model of it. The building is a new, 127,000-square-foot addition to the plant. While the extensive use of composites in the 787 is an important step forward, Spirit—and before it Boeing at this location—had worked with composites dating back to the late 1970s.

The interior of the composite fuselage frame.

The inside of a fuselage barrel section showing a stringer.

Another view of a composite stringer.

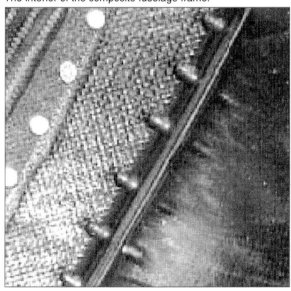
A view of a composite shear tie.

An early barrel section built for testing.

The major components of a 787 composite wing.

The nose section construction begins in an enormous clean room, where all personnel wear protective clothing. Here the composite material is wound around the mandrel, which is a very large tool (40 feet long and 19 feet in diameter) made of steel. The composite material is a tape of varying widths preimpregnated with resin. The tape is wound around the mandrel by an Ingersoll fiber placement machine. At this point in the process, metal strips are attached that attract and direct storm lightning, so that it cannot damage the composite surface. A final coating of gray adhesive is then applied and the entire assembly is encased in an enormous plastic bag. The assembly is then placed inside an autoclave, where it is baked for a specific amount of time at a specific temperature. The autoclave is 70 feet long and 30 feet in diameter and is heated by natural gas. When the mandrel is removed from the autoclave, the plastic bag is removed from the assembly.

Next, the assembly is placed between two parts of a large fixture that resembles a lathe and grips the assembly tightly, turning it as needed. The assembly is next placed in a trim and drill tool manufactured by MTorres of Spain, which cuts out the windows, doors, hatches, and the cockpit windows. In performing this function, the tool scores the mandrel. Before the mandrel can be re-used for another nose section, all the scoring has to be filled in with metal.

The assembly is now ready to have the mandrel removed. This is a step that Spirit and Boeing consider to be proprietary and therefore cannot be divulged. Once the mandrel has been removed, the cutouts are sanded, edged, and sealed.

The fuselage is then inspected ultrasonically, inside and outside, by robots. Then, frames, stringers, and shear ties are automatically installed in the section and tacked in place by a Brotje (Germany) automation installer.

The fuselage section is then revolved upside down, so the nose wheel assembly wheel well can be installed. With the assembly rotated right side up again, the floor is installed, consisting of graphite epoxy beams upon which are laid fiberglass sandwich floor panels. This arrangement makes for a light yet strong floor that does not flex.

The final nose section assembly involves installing the following items (together with their suppliers):

- 15-inch flat-panel instrument displays, flight control electronics, and pilot control information systems (Rockwell Collins)
- electronic flight bags (Astronautics Corp.)
- environmental control system ducting (Hamilton Sundstrand)
- flight deck seats (Ipeco)
- hydraulics (Parker Hannifin)
- nose wheel landing gear structure (Messier-Dowty)
- passenger doors (Latecoere)
- water and waste system components (Monogram Systems)
- window reveals (C&D Zodiac)
- windows (PPG)
- wiring bundles (Labinal)

This list clearly shows how Boeing's Tier 1 partners have the responsibility to deliver all the major assemblies complete in all respects.

With the fuselage assembly completed, it is taken to the paint shop for an initial coat, which acts as a sealer, and Spirit moves the fuselage to a nearby building, where it is signed over to Boeing. From this point, the fuselage is moved to a ramp at McConnell Air Force Base for pickup by one of Boeing's 747-400 Dreamlifters and transported to the Everett plant to be integrated into the final assembly sequence.

Kawasaki Heavy Industries

Kawasaki Heavy Industries (KHI) is located in the Nagoya, Japan, metropolitan area. One of its assignments is the manufacture of part of the forward fuselage section of the 787 (identified as section 43). The manufacturing sequence for this barrel section involves steps similar to those employed by Spirit Aerosystems for the nose section. Section 43 is located just forward of the wing in a completed fuselage assembly.

Alenia Aeronautica

While some 787 partners manufacture composites to fulfill their portion of the total 787 airframe, this Italian partner has the distinction of having won the contract for the single largest portions of the fuselage. Alenia Aeronautica has been manufacturing aircraft parts for decades, and was chosen to create the center fuselage barrels (identified as section 44, which is 33 feet long, and section 46, which is 28 feet long).

To fabricate these two long barrel sections, Alenia built a vast plant in the small town of Grottaglie, near the city of Taranto, on the "instep" coast of Italy. In this former agricultural community, Alenia constructed the plant in 18 months.

The factory boasts a 6.2 million cubic foot clean room—by far the largest in Europe—and employs about 500 people. Dust is kept out of this area by reversible-pressure doors. The temperature is maintained at a constant 66 degrees Fahrenheit and the humidity at 60 percent. Here, the process of creating composite structures is carried out.

The heart of the process is a massive machine 118 feet high and with 32 spools of carbon fiber. The spools unwind the carbon fiber in a set pattern that envelopes a 30-foot mandrel. The mandrel is placed within an enormous autoclave, where the material is cooked at high temperature for a specific period.

Vought

Another supplier of barrel sections is Vought Aircraft Industries, well known in aviation history. The company supplies Boeing with the aft fuselage sections, which are manufactured at North Charleston, South Carolina, in a plant built specifically for the 787 program. Vought originally gained experience with composites when it developed the B-2 bomber intermediate wing section and has further extensive experience with composites in other programs.

Vought is responsible for the aft fuselage (section 47) and part of section 48. Section 47 is 23 feet long and the last passenger section, while section 48 is the first cargo hold section and 15 feet long. These are fabricated in a new Vought facility, a 342,000-square-foot building that houses a 70,000-square-foot clean room with a 40-foot interior clear height, as well as a 14,200-square-foot training facility. Among the major equipment used is a 30-foot-diameter by 75-foot-long autoclave, the world's largest by volume. Vought also has automatic fiber-placement machines (supplied by Cincinnati Machine), a PAR Systems trim–and-drill machine, Brotjie automated riveters, and a nondestructive inspection machine from MTorres of Spain.

Vought also installs an aft pressure bulkhead between sections 47 and 48. This important item measures approximately 14 feet by 15 feet, is made using a vacuum-assisted resin transfer mold process, and is the first composite aft pressure bulkhead ever used by Boeing. It is manufactured by the EADS company's Military Aircraft Division in Augsburg, Germany. The Vought plant eventually changed ownership (see Chapter 14).

Global Aeronautica

Global Aeronautica is another part of the manufacturing complex, a fifty-fifty joint venture between Vought and Alenia North America, a division of Alenia Aeronautica of Italy. Its function is to integrate some of the various major portions of the 787 fuselage before shipment to the Everett, Washington, site for final assembly (see chapter 9). The Global Aeronautica plant eventually changed ownership (see chapter 14).

The Wings

The 787 wings are manufactured by Mitsubishi Heavy Industries (MHI), the center wing box is manufactured by Fuji Heavy Industries (FHI), and the landing gear well is manufactured by Kawasaki Heavy Industries (KHI), all located in the Nagoya, Japan, metropolitan area. The wings, center wing box, and landing gear well together make up the 787 wing assembly.

The main portion of the wing, called the wing box, for which MHI is responsible, is fabricated in a brand-new plant that has a floor space of more than 500,000 square feet. The building is 656 feet long, 558 feet wide, and has a ceiling height of 98 feet. More than 500 workers are employed in the plant. One of the world's largest autoclaves is located at MHI for the curing of the all-composite wings.

In addition, MHI built a second plant to manufacture the composite skin stringers used to reinforce the wing. This second facility is a converted portion of an MHI plant located at its Shimonoseki Shipyard and Machinery Works in Yamaguchi, Japan.

The 787's wings are made up of a main wing "box" structure, to which are attached leading and trailing edges and wing tips. In the case of the wing, the material used is CFRP; it is the first time it has ever been used for a wing this size. The composite tape is stretched over a mandrel, resulting in the wing box. This box constitutes the main part of the wing and stretches from the fuselage to the wing tips. Then, leading and trailing edges, as well as wing tips, are added to the box, thus providing aerodynamic shape to the wing.

The wings are connected to each other by a center wing section that lies within the fuselage and extends out from either side. The wing box itself measures approximately 18 feet wide at its widest point, four feet deep at its thickest point, and is 50 feet long.

The complete wing is made up of stringers, spars, and the skin covering them. The upper and lower surface panels and the spars are all made of the same composite material, but the wing ribs are machined from a single piece of monolithic aluminum plate.

Two skin sections make up a wing box: an upper and a lower section. Each section requires a large mandrel. To cure each wing, MHI uses a very large autoclave that is 131 feet long, 26 feet wide, and weighs 70 tons.

Kawasaki Heavy Industries builds the wing's fixed trailing edge, which is then moved to MHI for assembly to the wing.

Boeing Aerostructures Australia builds the wing's movable trailing edge, as well as the inboard flaps.

Boeing Winnipeg makes the wing-to-body fairings from panels manufactured in Hafei, China, and also makes the main landing gear doors and the engine fairings that fit behind the pylons.

The center wing box, a critical component in terms of structural integrity, is built by Fuji Heavy Industries at a new one-million-square-foot plant also located in Nagoya. The plant has an autoclave measuring 23 feet wide by 23 feet long.

Flow International

Flow International is a company located in Kent, Washington, close to Boeing's Everett, Washington, plant. Flow began to manufacture water jets to cut logs, thus its location near the lumber industry of Washington state. From that beginning, it developed high-speed steam jets that project a pencil-lead-thick stream of water laced with garnet particles at the extremely high pressure of 60,000 psi. This computer-controlled stream can cut through a 12 inch block of titanium. This technology has replaced mechanical milling machines in trimming the edges of composite panels. When milling machines were tried, edges could be rough and sometimes result in delamination.

These trimming machines cost from $3 to $6 million, but are worth the price because of improved final results. For the 787 wing, Flow International built a trimming machine that is 20 feet long.

Tail Structure

The tail assembly is manufactured in various locations. The rudder comes from Chengdu, China, and the leading edge of the vertical fin comes from Shenyang, China. The 30-foot tall vertical fin is made in Boeing's Frederickson, Washington, plant and is the only portion of the airframe built in the Puget Sound area.

Alenia builds the 64-foot wide horizontal stabilizer assembly in Foggia, Italy. The tail assembly comprises five distinct pieces, these being the left and right stabilizers, two elevators, and a center section. The assembly measures 32 feet from front to back. The stabilizer consists of a single co-cured piece of composite called the main torque box.

CHAPTER 7
Details, Details

As the saying goes, "The devil is in the details," or, as some people have been known to put it, "The details are what can kill you!"

Certainly, there is no better example of a very sophisticated and complicated machine where a major effort was exerted in taking care of the details than the 787. Once the main design elements were complete, then it was the details that had to be developed, and carefully at that.

A great deal has been written concerning the efficiency of the 787, the vast and unprecedented use of composites, and its lower fuel use. Yet, in addition to all these rather dramatic advances, Boeing engineers also designed and implemented other interesting innovations that make the 787 a new and different design, even though the external appearance is similar to other Boeing designs. For this reason, it is worthwhile to examine some of the details and innovations.

Design Features

The 787 has several rather unique design features that clearly demonstrate the care that went into the design of the *Dreamliner*.

Fuselage Details

The fuselage barrel sections have smooth butt joints that in turn reduce in-flight drag. An interesting item in the 787 fuselage is the introduction of a structural member known as a keel, which is located at the bottom of the fuselage. Its purpose is to strengthen the fuselage structure, minimize bending moments, and, together with the upper fuselage, carry the body bending loads through the main wheel well.

The keel measures 340 inches in length and stretches from the rear of section 43 forward fuselage to just behind the front of the section 46 center-rear fuselage. The keel runs just below the center wing box. It has a cross section of 2.4 inches by 4.8 inches and is located deep within the fuselage, so that only a small portion protrudes below the fuselage. This protruding section is covered by a fairing only a few inches deep. The fairing uses area ruling to minimize any drag rise at transonic speeds. The keel is manufactured from a solid block of aluminum by Kawasaki Heavy Industries (KHI) of Japan. After fabrication, KHI ships the keel to Fuji Heavy Industries (FJI), which then assembles the keel to the wing center section together with the pressure deck and the aft wheel well bulkhead.

The pressure deck is located just above the main landing gear wheel well and should not be confused with the "pressure bulkhead", which is located at the aft end of the fuselage just in front of the tail. It is a structural member required to maintain pressure in the fuselage and is necessary because the landing gear wheel well constitutes a penetration in the fuselage pressure vessel.

Air Scoops

On one side of the fuselage, adjacent to the wing-body fairings, are two large air scoops, both on the same side. The larger air scoop brings in air for the environmental control system duct. This larger air scoop was needed in order to replace the typical bleed air system, which the 787 does not have. The other, slightly smaller air scoop brings in outside air to cool equipment.

The Cockpit and its Systems

When the general design of the flight deck was first contemplated, the guiding principle was that of improving situational awareness on the part of the flight crew. This approach can be best justified when one considers that in many aviation accidents, where pilot error is found to be the cause, the lack of situational awareness was a contributing factor. The result of this principle can be appreciated in the care that went into the design of the 787's flight deck.

The Flight Deck

The Dreamliner flight deck may, at first glance, look pretty much the same as those found in other Boeing airplanes. The reality is that it is considerably different. Granted, the general layout is similar, with an instrument panel just below the windshield, side-by-side pilot seats with typical control columns and yokes, rudder pedals on the floor, and a throttle pedestal between the seats.

The possible use of conventional control columns with yokes caused a great deal of discussion. Military fighter aircraft and Airbus commercial jets use side arm controllers to activate the ailerons and elevators. Some pilots like this system, while others do not. It appears that what finally tipped the scales in favor of the time-honored yokes previously used on all Boeing transports was that many airlines operate different Boeing airplanes and cross-train their flight crews, so it was finally decided to retain the control column (yoke) system.

Boeing, however, implemented some interesting changes in the control systems. The two yokes are cross-linked to avoid confusion, have large ranges of motion for improved peripheral cuing, and are back-driven to communicate clearly to the pilots what either the auto-flight system or one of the pilots is doing. Additionally, there is a provision for instantly disconnecting the computer-driven auto-flight systems in case the computer malfunctions. This allows the pilots to hand-fly the airplane if it becomes necessary. The control systems are fly-by-wire, which has become common in commercial aircraft. The control system will also automatically change throttle settings and roll and yaw settings in case one engine fails.

Careful scrutiny of the cockpit quickly reveals that, instead of instruments, the panel is made up of four large 12-inch-by-9.1-inch flat-panel liquid crystal displays (LCDs) that measure 15.1 inches diagonally and provide a total 546 square inches of display space, twice the display space that is provided in the Boeing 777. There are two LCDs for each pilot, and they can present all the information available to the flight crew. A fifth LCD is located on the center pedestal that can access various data according to the needs of the crews.

The 787 flight deck comes with the latest technological features, partially listed below together with their respective manufacturers:

- Communication and navigation radios (Honeywell)
- Computer server for handling maintenance and data-loading functions (Rockwell Collins)
- Configuration integrated surveillance system (CISS) with MultiScan weather radar (Rockwell Collins)
- Dual electronic flight bags (Astronautics Corp.)
- Dual enhanced ground-proximity warning systems
- Dual global positioning system (GPS) landing systems
- Dual head-up displays (Rockwell Collins)
- Electronic checklists
- Flight data/voice recorders (Rockwell Collins)
- Flight management system (Honeywell)
- Full-route vertical situation displays
- Large-format map
- The industry's largest pilot display screens (Rockwell Collins)
- Pilot control yokes and central pedestal (Rockwell Collins)
- Traffic alert and collision-avoidance system

The weather radar, which scans up to a distance of 320 nautical miles, is of particular interest. The equipment has tilt-angle capability and automatically varies its scans from long to short range. Systems such as weather radar, enhanced ground proximity warning, and traffic collision avoidance are automatically furnished as dual in all 787s—the various customers do not have a choice. Boeing did, however, agonize over this automatic duality because it increased the total unit price. Nevertheless, it was decided that this was the approach to take for the sake of safety.

Rockwell Collins furnishes the majority of the systems found in the cockpit. These include the display and crew alert systems, pilot controls, communication and surveillance systems, a common data network, and an open-architecture computing system. As noted in chapter five, the use of a common core system and open architecture not only greatly simplify the entire electronic system, but also allow for the eventual updating of the aircraft's systems far more easily.

Another novel system is a flight deck entry video surveillance system furnished by Goodrich. The system uses a set of concealed high-resolution infrared cameras and a security camera interface unit that sends digital video images to the electronic flight bags. The cameras are able to see in total darkness. This enables the flight crew to monitor the entryway visually while on the ground or at night.

A general view of the forward part of the 787 flight deck.

The flight deck windows were designed to increase situational awareness simply by enabling pilots to see through a greater expanse of window surface. The total flight deck window area, which includes the front windshield and the side windows, is approximately 50 percent larger than on the 777 transport. The result, proved in a simulator, is not only better "out-the-window" viewing, but also an improved escape route for the pilots in an emergency.

An additional feature not previously found on commercial jets is the introduction of windshield nozzles that enable flight crews to clean the windshields externally while on the ground without having to request a truck with a hoist and crew. The innovation was requested by All Nippon Airlines, the 787 launch customer.

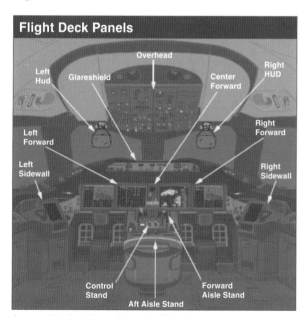

A more detailed view of the 787 flight deck pilot panels.

Flight Deck Panels

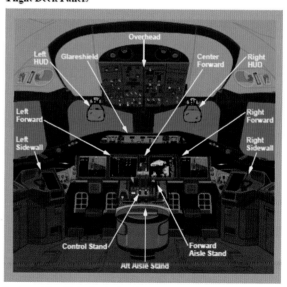

A view of the flight deck clearly showing the throttle control stand and the four LCD displays, two for each pilot.

Pitch & Stabilizer Trim Systems Control Wheel & Column

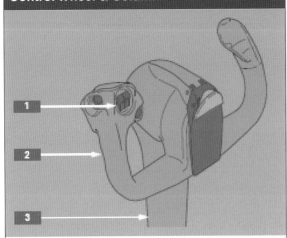

1. Pitch Trim Switches
Spring-loaded to neutral.
Push (both switches)-
• on the ground, directly move stabilizer
• in the air in normal mode, changes the trim reference airspeed
• in the air in secondary and direct modes, directly moves the stabilizer

2. Control Wheel
Rotate - deflects the ailerons, flaperons, and spoilers in the desired direction.

3. Control Column
Push/pull - commands the airplane to pitch in the desired direction:
• in the normal mode, deflects the elevator and horizontal stabilizer
• in the secondary and direct modes, deflects the elevator
Does not move with pitch trim operation.

The control wheel and column, including the pitch and stabilizer trim systems.

Control Wheel Microphone/ Interphone Switch

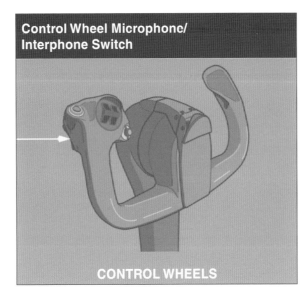

CONTROL WHEELS
The control wheel with the microphone/interphone switch.

Rudder/Brake Pedals

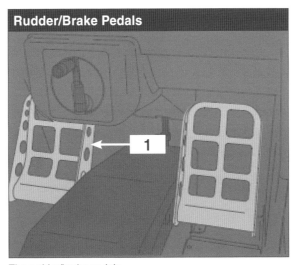

The rudder/brake pedals.

Nose wheel Steering Tillers

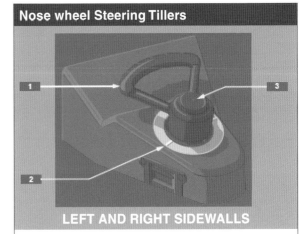

LEFT AND RIGHT SIDEWALLS

1. Nose wheel Steering Tiller
Rotate -
• turns the nose wheels up to 70 degrees in either direction
• overrides rudder pedal steering
2. Tiller Position Indicator
Shows tiller displacement from the straight - ahead, neutral position. There are three tick marks on the tiller assembly. The center mark identifies the neutral position of the tiller, while the other two ticks identify the maximun left and right displacements.

Nose wheel steering tillers, one for each pilot.

Control Stand

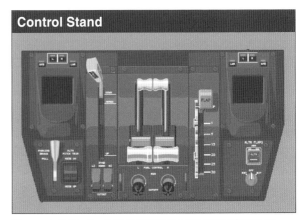

The control stand, which includes the two power levers or throttles.

TO/GA & Autothrottle Disconnect Switches

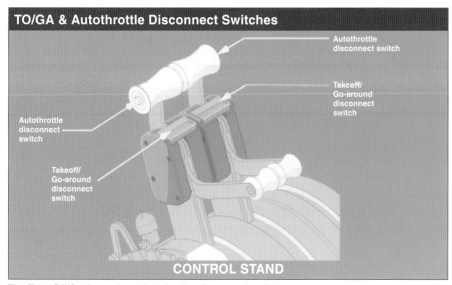

The Take Off/Go Around and Autothrottle disconnect switches.

Flap Controls

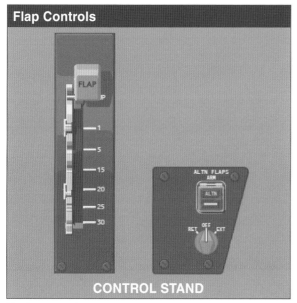

The flap controls located on the control stand.

Speedbrake Lever

The speed brake lever located on the control stand.

Landing Gear Panel

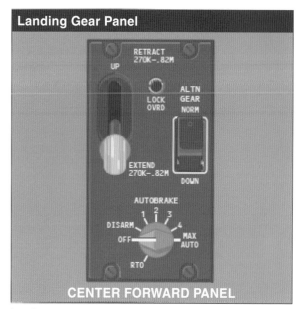

Landing gear control located on the center forward panel.

Aft Aisle Stand

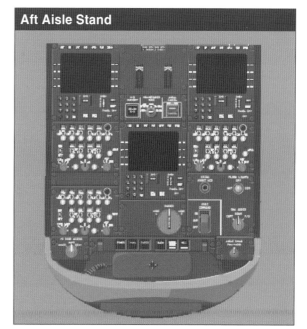

The aft aisle stand.

AFT Aisle Stand

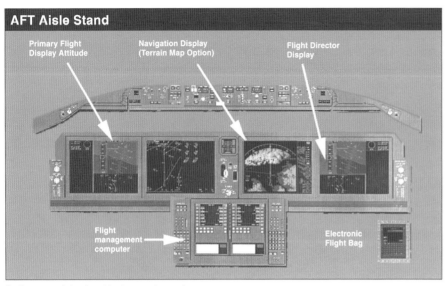

Primary Flight Display Attitude

Navigation Display (Terrain Map Option)

Flight Director Display

Flight management computer

Electronic Flight Bag

A close up of the front instrument panel.

PFD Steering Indications

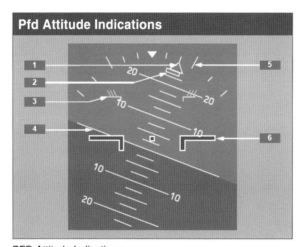

PFD Steering Indications.

Primary Flight Display (PFD)

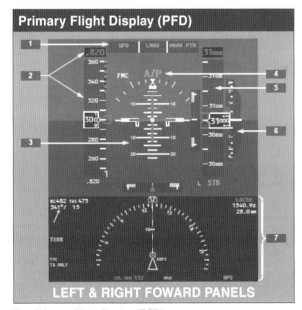

LEFT & RIGHT FOWARD PANELS

The Primary Flight Display (PFD).

Pfd Attitude Indications

PFD Attitude Indications.

Full Symbology Mode

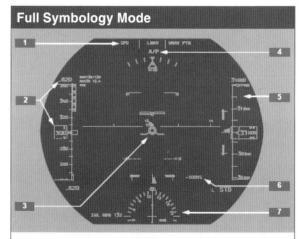

1. **Flight Mode Annunciations**
2. **Airspeed/Mach Indications**
3. **Altitude, Steering, and Miscellaneous Indications**
4. **Autopilot, Flight Director System Status**
5. **Altitude Indications**
6. **Vertical Speed Indication**
Displays ARDS vertical speed.
7. **Compass Rose**
Displays current IRS heading, track, and other related information

Full Symbiology Mode.

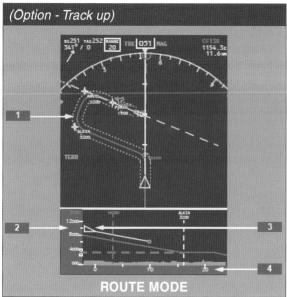

(Option - Track up)

ROUTE MODE

Full Symbiology Mode.

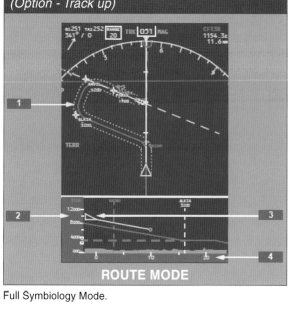

ND Plan Mode

Groundspeed, True Airspeed and Wind Indications

True North Up Arrow

Active Waypoint Information

Center Waypoint

Alternate Airport

Airplane Symbol

Range Circle

Navigation Route Mode.

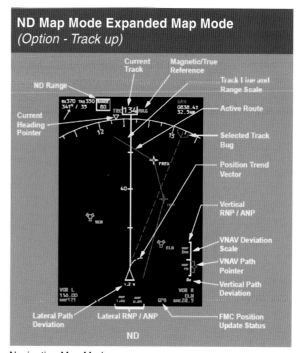

ND Map Mode Expanded Map Mode
(Option - Track up)

ND Range

Current Heading Pointer

Current Track

Magnetic/True Reference

Track Line and Range Scale

Active Route

Selected Track Bug

Position Trend Vector

Vertical RNP / ANP

VNAV Deviation Scale

VNAV Path Pointer

Vertical Path Deviation

Lateral Path Deviation

Lateral RNP / ANP

FMC Position Update Status

ND

Navigation Map Mode.

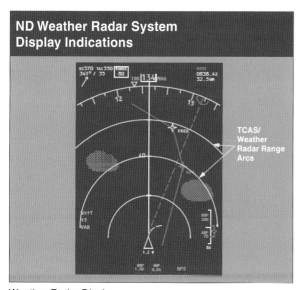

ND Weather Radar System Display Indications

TCAS/ Weather Radar Range Arcs

Weather Radar Display

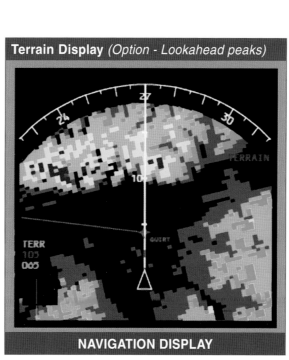

Terrain Display (Option - Lookahead peaks)

TERRAIN

NAVIGATION DISPLAY

Terrain Display.

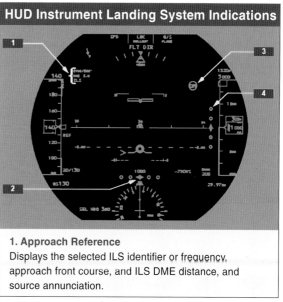

HUD Instrument Landing System Indications

1. Approach Reference

Displays the selected ILS identifier or frequency, approach front course, and ILS DME distance, and source annunciation.

ILS Display.

69

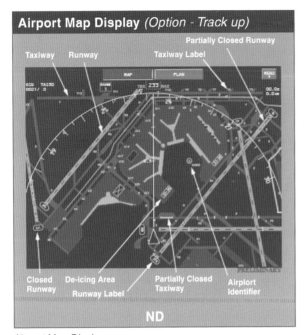

Airport Map Display *(Option - Track up)*

Airport Map Display

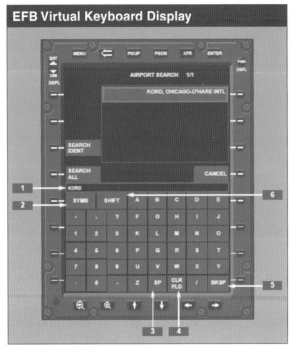

EFB Virtual Keyboard Display

Virtual Keyboard Display

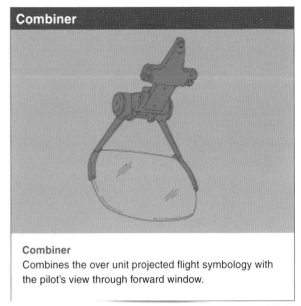

Combiner

Combiner
Combines the over unit projected flight symbology with the pilot's view through forward window.

The combiner enables the pilot to see both the projected flight symbiology and the outside terrain simultaneously.

The Wing De-Icing System

The de-icing of airplane wings is critical to safe flight. In the Dreamliner, because there is no hot-engine bleed air that can be pumped directly onto the wings, an electrical system had to be developed. The company selected to develop this system, GKN Aerospace, of Luton, United Kingdom, realized that it could not simply place electrical heating wires within the wings because of the stringent limits of the composite material. Instead, GKN designed a heating mat embedded in the wing's composite structure. The mats are created by spraying metallic elements into the wing's structure. The system allows for localized heating and more effective power management through the use of zones. This novel approach also prevents the weakening of the composite material that could be caused by the application of excessive heat.

Crew Spaces

The 787 forward fuselage was designed with extra space for a crew rest area. This was dictated by the long range of the 787, which in many cases will require augmented flight crews, thus allowing individual crew members to take turns having rest periods. The rest area is above and behind the cockpit, but is designed in such a way that an airline can customize the space. Because of its location, it does not affect any revenue space within the fuselage.

Passenger Luggage and Cargo Space

The Dreamliner has an important advantage over other similarly-sized airplanes: it has more revenue cargo space. Compared with the Airbus A330, the 787-8 has a 20 to 45 percent advantage in cargo-carrying capacity. The fuselage has two cargo bays located in the lower lobe: one forward of the wing and one aft. The forward cargo bay can accommodate either five 88-inch-by-125-inch pallets, five 96-inch-by-125-inch pallets, or a combination of the two

Carries an additional pallet of revenue cargo

- ■ Revenue Cargo
- □ Passenger Baggage
- ■ Bulk Cargo

types. The aft, or bulk, cargo bay can handle four of the smaller pallets or three of the larger, with two LD-3s. Additionally, instead of just pallets, a combination of pallets and LD-3 containers can also be loaded in these cargo bays. This is just one more example of how Boeing added value for the airlines when designing the Dreamliner.

Cargo Capacity by Model

Model	Pallets	LD-3s	Total Cargo (cubic feet)
787-8	9	28	4,400
787-9	11	36	5,400

Forward Cargo Bay — **Aft Cargo Bay** — **Bulk Cargo Bay** 398 cu ft (11.3 cu m)

5 pallets (88 x 125)

4 pallets (88 x 125)

5 pallets (96 x 125)

3 pallets (96 x 125) + 2 LD-3s

16 LD-3s
Forward cargo bay
Mixed cargo capacities
(96x125 or 88x125 pallets

4 pallets + 2 LD-3s
3 pallets + 6 LD-3s
2 pallets + 8 LD-3s
1 pallets + 12 LD-3s

12 LD-3s
Aft cargo bay
Mixed cargo capacities
(96x125 or 88x125 pallets

3 pallets + 2 LD-3s
2 pallets + 4 LD-3s
1 pallets + 8 LD-3s

A detailed breakdown of the 787's cargo capacities.

Wing Movable Control Surfaces

The wing movable control surfaces constitute an area where Boeing made innovative advances. As in virtually all modern jet airplanes, the 787 wings boast a number of movable control surfaces. These surfaces are critical not only to the in-flight maneuvering of the airplane, but also to slow it down during descent, approach, and landing. They also result in slower takeoff speeds and thus shorter takeoff distances—an important consideration. In the case of the 787, however, these control surfaces also manage to accomplish jobs that have never been done before. The control surfaces are found on both the leading and trailing edges of the wings. A quick review of the control surfaces reveals an item that no commercial jet has ever employed before: the wing trailing edge variable camber (TEVC) system (detailed below).

The primary flight control actuation system uses thirty actuators, both electric and hydraulic, that are manufactured by Moog, an Aurora, New York, company that furnishes actuators for all the Boeing commercial transports.

At right is a detailed list of all the control surfaces found on the 787, what they do, and how and where they are used in flight.

Leading Edge Control Surfaces

Inboard and outboard three-position slats. These slats increase the camber, or curvature, of the wing during low-speed flight, increasing lift and enabling the 787 to operate at much lower speeds on takeoff and landing. The slats work as a function of the

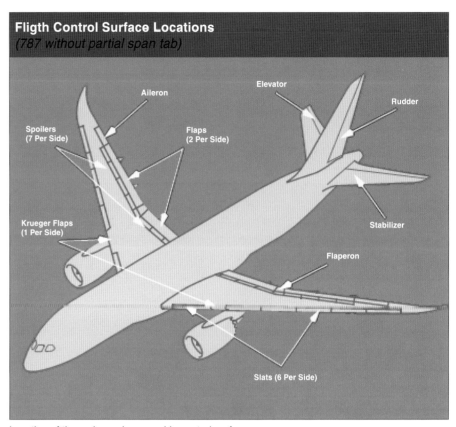

Fligth Control Surface Locations
(787 without partial span tab)

Aileron · Elevator · Rudder · Spoilers (7 Per Side) · Flaps (2 Per Side) · Krueger Flaps (1 Per Side) · Stabilizer · Flaperon · Slats (6 Per Side)

Location of the various wing movable control surfaces.

trailing edge flaps. The three positions are fully retracted, halfway extended, and fully extended. If partially extended and the airplane is slowed down sufficiently, they will fully extend. Below 250 knots they partially extend, and at around 220 knots they will fully extend.

Trailing Edge Control Surfaces

- The sealing Krueger flaps are located adjacent to the engine pylons and seal off air that swirls around those pylons.

- Inboard and outboard single-slotted flaps. There are four segments each to the inboard and outboard flaps. These operate as normal flaps to permit slower speeds on takeoff and landing. There are six positions to which the flaps can be extended. They can also be raised in 0.5 degree increments, as described below.

- Single outboard ailerons. These are standard ailerons that are used at low speeds, load alleviation during high-speed flight, and are deflected downward during takeoff and landing to increase lift. They are locked out above medium speeds, but these surfaces are somewhat smaller than one might expect for an aircraft this size.

- Single outboard flaperons. These surfaces do double duty. During high-speed cruising, they control the roll of the airplane. At low speeds, they act as inboard flaps.
- Trailing edge variable camber system (see right).
- Spoilers, or speed brakes, are vertical surfaces that are hinged and swivel up in flight. They can be raised from one degree to 90 degrees. They have the dual function of slowing the aircraft down when required and are also used to roll the aircraft. There are seven of these on each wing.

The result of all these various movable control surfaces is not only a greater level of maneuverability, but also the ability to operate into mid-size airports, where airplanes the size and weight of the 787 would normally be excluded because of takeoff and landing runway length requirements.

The reduced complexity of the wing trailing edge mechanism is another improvement. This mechanism has been simplified and reduced in size, allowing for much smaller aerodynamic coverings, called canoes, which can be seen trailing back from the wings. These canoes cover the flap tracks, which allow the flaps to extend. In the 787 these are called flap-support fairings. There are also fairings over the aileron actuators called blister fairings, as well as over the flaperon actuators, which are called flaperon support fairings. In the case of the 787, however, they are all smaller than are usually found owing to the 5,000-psi hydraulic pressures used, which result in smaller mechanisms to move the control surfaces. Previously, the standard hydraulic pressure used was 3,000 psi.

Wing Trailing Edge Variable Camber System

The TEVC system and its application in the 787 series are believed to be the first time this system has ever been introduced in a production aircraft. The TEVC system automatically deploys trailing edge flaps in 0.5-degree increments while in the cruise mode, resulting in materially-reduced cruise drag. The system is expected to save between 750 and 1,000 pounds of fuel per typical flight. The system is driven by an electrical power drive unit. It is controlled by both the flight management system and the digital flight control system. The system is limited to a maximum arc of three degrees.

Load Alleviation

One of the more fascinating yet invisible details that was incorporated into the 787 design was a sophisticated system known as *load alleviation*. Using sensors in the nose of the airplane and elsewhere which can predict air turbulence by a few seconds, the system automatically moves control surfaces to reduce the load on the wings. With this system, Boeing engineers were able to reduce the total wing structure, since it will bear reduced loads.

Fly-by-Wire Control System

The 787 uses a fly-by-wire control system. Fly-by-wire is a well-proven system, whereby the control surfaces are not operated by cables connected directly to the cockpit control column and pedals. Rather, the physical input from the pilots is translated into electrical signals, which in turn go through wires to actuators that move the control surfaces electrically. Furthermore, the autopilot is also integrated into this control system through a central computer. The basic system has been successfully used in many commercial and military airplanes with absolutely no problems. Boeing's first commercial transport using fly-by-wire was the 777.

Yet, when Airbus developed its single-aisle A320, which used the fly-by-wire system, it elected to design the computer software in such a way that it was difficult for pilots to override the autopilot. This in turn led to some incidents and considerable controversy among flight crews, the majority of whom believed it was critically important that the final decisions should be left in the hands of the pilots themselves and not up to the autopilot. To make matters somewhat more complicated, the Airbus autopilots were programmed never to allow the airplane or its engines and systems to exceed normal operating limits, but flight crews firmly believe that in emergencies, an airplane and its passengers can be saved if these operating limits are in fact exceeded.

This basic controversy had to be resolved one way or another by Boeing's engineers. The verdict was that final decisions during a flight had to be made by the flight crew. While this particular controversy may last for many years, in the meantime, Boeing has opted for what it believes to be the safest approach to the problem.

Landing Gear

Messier-Dowty, headquartered in France, is the company that furnishes both the main and nose landing gear assemblies to Boeing, all of which are built at its plant in Gloucester, United Kingdom.

Taxiway Requirements

The 787 has a nose-wheel maximum steering angle built into it that is greater than that found on a Boeing 767 or MD-11. The angle is 65 degrees, compared with 61 degrees used previously. This translates into a minimum pavement width of only 138 feet for the 787-8, as compared with 166 feet for the 767-400. While this difference may not appear significant to the reader, in the real world of flight operations, it could be important in terms of allowing the 787 to operate into a greater number of mid-size airports.

The 787 and the Environment

The design of the 787 will contribute positively to the environment. It is worthwhile to look at these positive contributions.

Quieter Takeoffs

An advantage of the 787 that will be noticed by a great many people is that the level of its takeoff noise is considerably less than many other airplanes of similar size. Using FAA standards, Boeing determined that the footprint of the 787-8's 85 dBA noise level would fit the requirements of all the airports that this airplane was designed to fly into. Moreover, this footprint is considerably less than such airplanes as the A330-200/300, A340-300, and the Boeing 767-300.

Reduced Fuel Use

The 787's reduction in fuel use, as compared with older airplanes of the same size, means lower emissions, as well as less waste of precious fossil fuels.

Reduced Engine Emissions

The operation of jet engines results in carbon dioxide (CO_2) emissions. Using less fuel results in

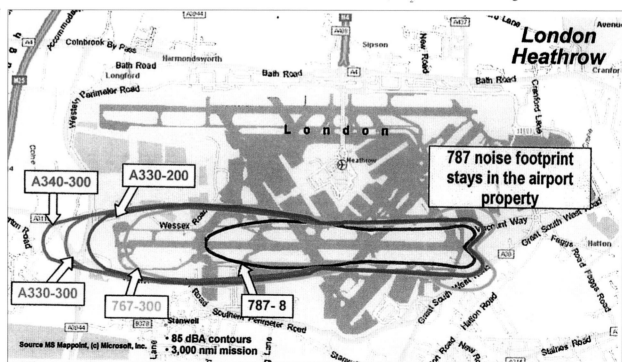

Diagram comparing the take-off noise footprint of the 787 versus other jet transports within airport boundaries (London Heathrow).

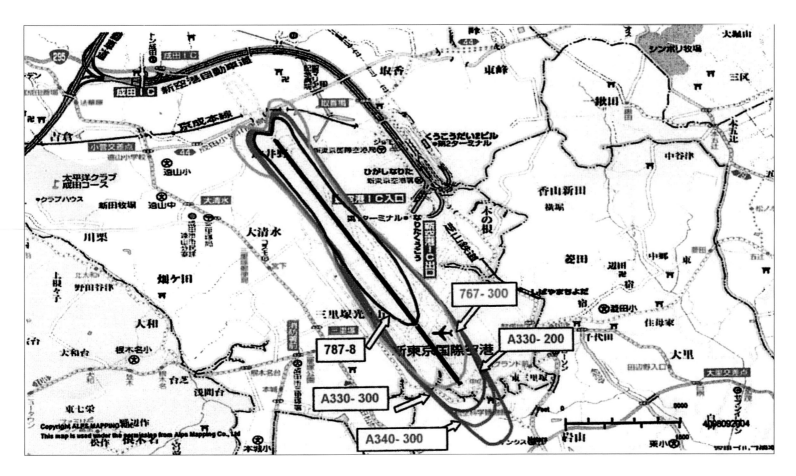

Diagram comparing the take-off noise footprint of the 787 versus other jet transports in the vicinity of a major airport (New York, JFK).

less CO_2 emissions. Nitrogen oxide (NO_x) is also exhausted from jet engines. The 787's engines put out 30 percent less NO_x than the Boeing 767 and will actually better the standard for these emissions currently being drafted.

Point-to-Point Travel
The fact that the 787 is designed to achieve more point-to-point travel will result in far fewer takeoffs and landings, and therefore lower fuel usage and emissions.

Reduced Manufacturing Waste
The unprecedented level of use of composites greatly reduces manufacturing waste. In previous airplanes, where metals such as aluminum were the major material used, as much as 90 percent of the raw material wound up as waste.

End-of-Life Recycling
Boeing is already working with other companies, studying ways to scrap and possibly recycle materials when 787s begin to be retired 30 to 40 years in the future.

Putting all these various factors together clearly shows that having a large number of 787s replacing older airplanes will materially lessen the effect of flying these jet transports on the environment.

Conclusion
This multitude of details is certainly important in understanding what went into the design of the 787. In the next chapter, the reader will find more details about topics that will directly affect the crew and passengers.

CHAPTER 8

Keeping Passengers Happy

At the time Boeing committed to the 7E7, it also decided that two of the three models offered would be long-range, with flights of up to 12 to 14 hours. Although this was the market that Boeing's salespeople identified as having great potential, the downside of such long flights is that they result in tired passengers. Therefore, Boeing targeted the general comfort of passengers as a primary goal. It would not be enough simply to replicate what had been done before. The passenger's environment had to be substantially improved in significant areas.

When Boeing designs and sells a passenger jet transport, it has to satisfy two different and entirely separate customers whose goals and wishes are often different. One customer is the airline that will operate the airplane, and the other is the flying public who will ride in said airplane.

The airline is looking for profits, maintainability, and safety. The passengers are usually looking for comfort, safety, and affordability. So when Boeing was thinking about the passenger needs of the 787,

it developed a whole range of issues that it felt needed to be resolved.

Boeing calls its approach to the interior design of the Dreamliner a *differentiation strategy*. This is a unique philosophy, whereby Boeing took into account the needs of the pilots and cabin crew, the passengers, and the mechanics who service the airplane. This approach is also an attempt to make the 787 truly different from competing transports, thus making it more attractive to both airlines and passengers. This differentiation strategy is led by Blake Emery, a longtime Boeing employee with a background in both communication and psychology who has led this effort since August 2000. *Differentiation philosophy* is defined as an effort to make a product visually different so that it will appeal to a wider audience. To that end, it crosses many cultures and applies to both the interior and exterior of an airplane.

The internationally-known design firm Teague, an industrial design studio, had input in this entire

process. Teague's input included the nose, wing tips, wing-to-body fairings, and the detail on vertical and horizontal stabilizers. However, any design input that could affect the aerodynamics of the airplane had to be approved by Boeing's design department. An example of the difference between aerodynamics and design is the wing-tip dihedral, which is a design feature, and the wing-tip rake, which is an aerodynamic feature. *Wing-tip rake* is defined as the tip of the wing having a higher degree of sweepback than the rest of the wing. *Wing-tip dihedral* is defined as the tip of the wing having a higher degree of dihedral, or upsweep, than the rest of the wing. The main entrance to the cabin was another important design consideration. Customers have reacted positively to the various design features, and no further changes are contemplated for the -9 model.

An unprecedented research effort was undertaken to clearly identify the specific areas passengers consider to be important during a commercial flight.

Boeing conducted traveler surveys and collaborated with various distinguished universities to find the best solutions. This effort started with the Sonic Cruiser program, so that the actual design could take into account the results obtained.

Included in this list of improvements were the following:

1. Cabin environment, including internal air pressure, air quality, and ambient sound
2. Cabin luggage storage
3. Interior architecture and lighting
4. Ride quality
5. Seating comfort
6. Window size and location

All these areas had to be examined in detail, and related issues considered and resolved. Let us take a careful and discriminating look at all these areas and the solutions that Boeing developed.

Cabin Environment

Included in the cabin environment are air quality and the level of humidity, cabin pressure, and general ambient noise levels. Each of these four items required separate examination. A two-year study of cabin environment conducted in conjunction with the Technical Institute of Denmark (DTU) revealed a surprise. Increasing the humidity alone did not materially help to solve the problem often voiced by air passengers that the air in airplane cabins is too dry. Instead, the research determined that air purification, which reduced gaseous contaminants, together with moderate increases in humidity, did much to improve the general breathing comfort of passengers. Cabin air is a mixture of outside and recirculated air. The outside air passes through an ozone removal step. The recirculated air is first passed through a HEPA (high-efficiency particulate air) filter, which removes bacteria, viruses, and fungi. The particle-free air then goes through a gaseous filtration system to remove odors, irritants, and gaseous contaminants. The resulting air that passengers breathe, combined with higher levels of humidity, is expected to result in far fewer cases of headache, dizziness, eye irritation, and membrane dryness.

Ambient Sound

Ambient sound in flight has a definite effect on the level of fatigue experienced by passengers, especially on long flights. A clear indication of that recognition is demonstrated by the type of headsets that are currently given to passengers in first and business class only by some major airlines on such long flights. These are noise-canceling headsets that completely cover the ears. Since these headsets are quite expensive and sophisticated pieces of equipment, the airlines would not be using them unless they recognized the serious fatigue factor brought on by noise on long flights.

The great majority of ambient sound is generated from two sources: engine noise and the aerodynamic noise caused by the outside air scrubbing against the airframe, particularly against the fuselage. Further, since the 787 is designed to operate at a cruise speed of 0.85 Mach—somewhat faster than many current airplanes—the ambient noise would be greater.

Boeing did some things to reduce the sources of noise. The fuselage and wing surfaces are now perfectly smooth, with no rivets or other protuberances, which in turn means less aerodynamic noise. The engine noise is partially muted by the use of serrated chevrons, which form part of the engine package. The interior of the cabin is very well insulated, and the average noise level inside the cabin is lower than that found on other transports of comparable size.

Cabin Altitude

The cabin altitude was another area that required research. Cabin altitude refers to the equivalent altitude achieved within an airplane cabin by use of pressurization. Here again, academia was called in to assist in achieving the best solution. Working together with Oklahoma State University, Boeing ran a large number of tests on 500 subjects at various cabin altitudes.

The tests were based on U.S. Army Research Institute of Environmental Medicine methodology, which used 68 possible altitude symptoms. The results of this survey clearly indicated that lowering the cabin altitude to 6,000 feet from the commonly used 8,000-foot cabin altitude resulted in measurable improvements to passenger comfort, while lowering it still further made little difference.

That the 787 fuselage is made entirely of composites was the key to lowering cabin altitude without the potential for increased metal fatigue, which may occur in other airplanes. This fatigue is the result of the cabin walls flexing during flight as the internal cabin pressure maintained is much higher than the outside air pressure.

The luggage racks feature a new design that makes it easier for passengers to stow their luggage.

Interior Architecture and Lighting

The interior architecture of the 787 was specifically designed to avoid the typical "long tube" sensation that a passenger gets when boarding most jet transports. To begin with, the larger total size of the *Dreamliner*'s fuselage results in a feeling of more spaciousness. The designers went further. The entryway is larger, and beyond that point, a sweeping, backlighted overhead archway directs the passenger's eyes upward. This particular feature exists only at door number two, the main entry.

The ceiling is decorated with sweeping vistas of blue sky. At carefully chosen locations along the length of the cabin, additional archways add to the feeling of space. The overhead lighting is provided by light emitting diodes (LEDs) that can be changed in color and brightness throughout the flight, supplied by the Diehl Corp. This particular feature permits the cabin attendants to control both aspects of the internal lighting. Thus, as an example, on a long-haul flight, the lighting might be gradually lowered and changed to blue tones as night falls, then changed again to bright orange hues in the morning.

With the ability of a composite fuselage to withstand a greater pressure differential without fear of any fatigue over the life of the airplane, Boeing was able to significantly improve the cabin environment for passengers.

Luggage Bins

In response to the ever-increasing amount of carry-on luggage that passengers bring aboard, Boeing is installing the largest luggage bins in the industry. The bins are large enough to accommodate 11-inch by 16-inch by 25-inch-long bags, plus there will be enough total bin space to enable each passenger to have one such suitcase at his seat. The bins swing down for easier loading and then swing back up so as to allow an unobstructed view of the cabin.

A related problem was the difficulty some passengers have with luggage bin latches, with broken nails resulting, as well as a slowing down of loading and unloading of the airplane. The solution was to design latches that would work regardless of whether they are poked or pushed from the top or the bottom.

Lavatories

With increasing numbers of older and handicapped people traveling, Boeing knew it was essential that accessibile lavatories had to be designed with these passengers in mind. To ensure such design, Boeing went to the National Center for Accessible Transportation at Oregon State University. The results are impressive.

The *Dreamliner* will have two wheelchair-accessible lavatories, each with significant

Ride Quality and Gust Attenuation

Boeing was familiar with the reaction of many passengers to even mild turbulence. Anyone who has flown commercially and encountered even mild turbulence must have noticed how the faces of passengers change expression. Some people even start clenching their hands. It is not uncommon on some flights for passengers to experience this type of sensation for extended periods. Boeing engineers also discovered that only certain types of turbulence cause motion sickness. Constant and frequent mild turbulence merely makes passengers uncomfortable or nervous, but continued swooping motions within a certain frequency band will induce motion sickness in a percentage of passengers. In addition, the mere sight, sound, and smell associated with motion sickness can cause it in others.

To mitigate this type of motion and make the flight more comfortable, Boeing installed a sophisticated gust suppression system on the 787. The system uses sensors installed in the nose of the airplane, as well as throughout the fuselage. These sensors measure changes in angular velocity and pressure distribution. Gyroscopic sensors detect changes in yaw, roll, or pitch caused by wind gusts. In like manner, accelerometers detect vertical and horizontal forces. As soon as the various sensors detect the beginning of even minor turbulence, they immediately send the information to the central computer system that controls flight. This system then sends electronic signals that in turn actuate the rudder, elevators, spoilers, ailerons, and flaperons. These control surfaces then move in such a way as to counteract the turbulence.

The main entry to the 787. An effort was made to create a more appealing entrance for passengers.

accessibility advancements. Each facility is 56-inches long and has a repositioned entryway door to provide more usable space.

A 56- by 57-inch lavatory includes a movable center wall that allows two separate lavatories to become one large, wheelchair-accessible facility. These lavatories also include an additional toilet flush button on the sink cabinet and a fold-down assist bar to aid independent transfers.

Another innovation, triggered by launch customer All Nippon Airlines, is the introduction of a combination toilet and bidet. Bidets are standard in European bathrooms, and evidently ANA must have felt that their inclusion in the 787 would be something passengers would appreciate.

Another interesting feature is the use of dampers on toilet seats so that they will not bang if they are dropped. This particular feature was first introduced on Boeing's 777.

Galleys

The galleys are all manufactured by Jamco of Tokyo, Japan, and its subsidiary Jamco America, located in Everett, Washington. These galleys include steam ovens, microwave ovens, air chillers, and bar counters.

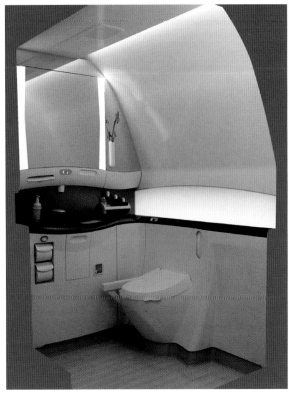

A typical 787 lavatory.

Essentially, the system predicts how the aircraft will react to gusts and acts to neutralize their effect, resulting in a far smoother ride. For example, the system is expected to reduce a gust-induced, 20-foot free fall to only six feet. While eight percent of passengers experience motion sickness during turbulence, only one percent are expected to experience it with the new gust suppression technology.

Cabin Space and Seating Comfort

The first design item that Boeing effected was to make the cabin wider. The 787 cabin is 15 inches wider than comparable twin-aisle wide-body transports. Furthermore, the widest part of the cabin occurs at an average shoulder height. This is more important than having the greatest width at hip level.

If an airline chooses an eight-abreast configuration for economy class, then the widest economy seats in the industry can be used, at 18.5 inches wide.

Likewise, an eight-abreast seating arrangement in economy class results in the two aisles being 21.5 inches wide, or 2.5 inches wider than is typically found. In business class, the aisles are 25.5 inches wide.

Boeing worked closely with various airline seat manufacturers and chose a total of seven companies to offer first, business, and economy seats to the airlines that purchased 787s.

The majority of the airline customers elected to go with nine-abreast seating in economy class, thus effectively removing the advantage of the extra space. With nine-abreast seating in economy class, the aisles are somewhat narrower, at a width of 18 inches. At the beginning of the program Boeing chose the seat manufacturers listed below:
• Avio (Italy)
• B/E Aerospace (North Carolina, U.S.)
• Contour (United Kingdom)
• Koito (Japan)
• Recaro (Germany)
• Sicma (France)
• Weber (Texas, United States)

Cabin Windows

While some passengers truly dislike looking out their windows during flight, others find it both comforting and interesting. Still, even for those seated next to a window, and tall passengers especially, seeing out is often difficult because the windows are generally too low for them. For anyone not seated next to a window, seeing out is close to impossible. Here again, the basic design of the 787 offered a way to solve the problem. Because the 787 fuselage is made of composites, it is stronger than metal fuselages and flexes far less. Having larger windows in a metal fuselage would require heavier window frames to prevent flexing, with a corresponding weight penalty. In addition, the flexing of window frames can lead to windows popping out—an extremely dangerous condition. In fact, the writer knows of two high-rise buildings that had their windows pop out during high winds because the buildings swayed and the window frames flexed. Consider that high-rise buildings do not even have the problem of the much higher interior pressures that jet airplanes must contend with!

The shape of the 787's fuselage allows for windows that are not only larger, but are also placed higher on the sidewalls relative to the floor. This positioning became possible because of the vertical size of the upper fuselage lobe. Thus, an average adult seated upright can easily see not just down and sideways, but also upward. The increased general size of the windows also enables passengers seated one or two seats away from the window seat to have some outside visibility, as well. Furthermore, the larger windows also allow more direct sunlight to enter the cabin.

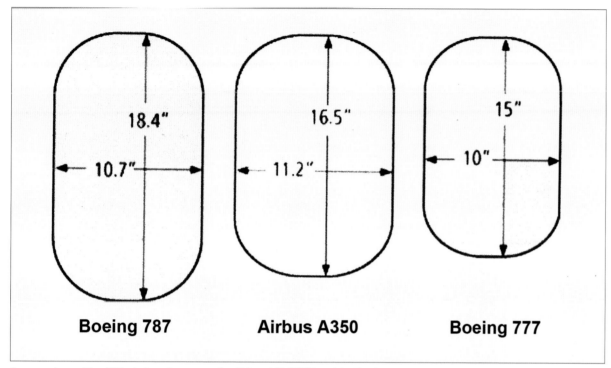

A comparison of the 787 window size versus the Airbus A350XWB and the Boeing 777.

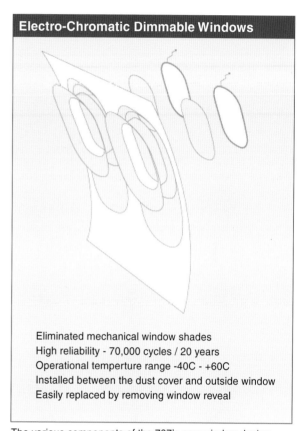

Eliminated mechanical window shades
High reliability - 70,000 cycles / 20 years
Operational temperture range -40C - +60C
Installed between the dust cover and outside window
Easily replaced by removing window reveal

The various components of the 787's new window design.

The windows measure 19 inches high by 11 inches wide, a size that Boeing claims is 65 percent bigger than the competition. The windows feature a highly innovative design known as *electrochromatic technology*, a term used when referring to a window that is electronically dimmable. It allows each passenger seated next to a window to dim his or her window individually, using a solid-state controller. In addition, a cabin attendant can dim all the windows simultaneously when a movie is being shown. Even then, while the window allows far less light in, the passenger can still view the outside quite easily.

The windows were developed by PPG Aerosystems of Pittsburgh, Pennsylvania, but only after considerable prodding by Boeing. PPG's reluctance was based on the fact that these new windows are far more expensive compared with the type used previously. PPG believed that no airplane manufacturer wanted to bear the much higher cost. Boeing, however, in its quest for a more user-friendly passenger cabin, felt that the additional expense was worth it. What is more, using this type of window does away with the mechanical pull-down shades, thus materially reducing maintenance costs over the life of the airplane. PPG teamed with Gentex, a company located in Zeeland, Michigan, to manufacture the windows. Figure 8-7 clearly show the cross section of this advanced window design.

Airbus was initially opposed to the use of these windows, but eventually decided to offer them as an option on its new A350XWB transport, which is in direct competition with the 787.

Conclusion

Now that the reader has an idea of what goes into making a 787, it is appropriate to examine how the 787 is assembled; another highly innovative way of doing things developed by Boeing.

Passenger Cabin Window

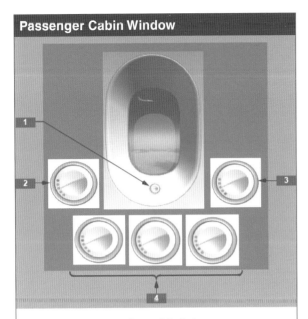

A close-up of the passenger window controls.

1. Window Dimming Control Switch

Individual window dimming is controlled by using this switch. Push the upper part to lighten the window. Push the lower part to darken the window. Blue LEDs indicate the level of dimming.

The idividual control feature can be partially overidden at the cabin Attendant Panel. Only the two darker settings are available while in the cabin attendant override mode.

When the switch is not in use, the LED turns off. Selecting the control again illuminates the LED at the last position.

2. Clear

This indicates a clear window (no dimming) has been selected.

3. Dark

This indicates a dark window (full dimming) has been selected.

4. Intermediate Levels

One of these three indications is displayed when an intermediate level (partial dimming) has been selected.

The new window size allows the passengers to look out far more comfortably.

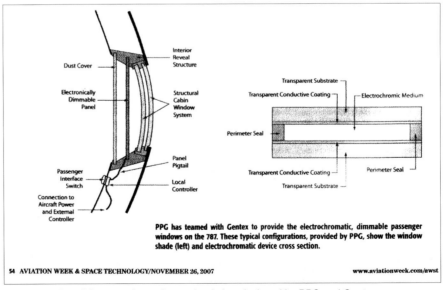

PPG has teamed with Gentex to provide the electrochromatic, dimmable passenger windows on the 787. These typical configurations, provided by PPG, show the window shade (left) and electrochromatic device cross section.

A cross section of the new electrochromatic window designed by PPG and Gentex.

CHAPTER 9
Putting It All Together

While much has been written about the advanced design concepts of the 787, the way in which this airplane is manufactured is equally innovative and might even be called revolutionary. The assembly of a huge, wide-body commercial jet would normally be viewed as a complex, interesting, and possibly even exciting process. That is the way it used to be, but in the case of the 787, things are different. Much of the work is accomplished far away from the final assembly site. As has already been shown, the 787 assemblies are built in many places, but not in Everett, Washington. Large sections of the airplane, as well as other components, all arrive at the Everett plant ready for final assembly. This final phase is really a short step in the entire process of bringing the airplane to the point where it will fly. Many events, steps, facilities, and developments, all leading to the final assembly, are of interest and importance to that goal.

For Boeing to accomplish the rather amazing feat of bringing together all the major parts of the airplane ready to be assembled at just the right time, an entirely new way of controlling the design, manufacture, and delivery was developed and put in place. Not only were portions of the 787 built at locations thousands of miles from Everett, but the people at these distant locations spoke various languages, came from different societies, and some used different measuring systems. It becomes clear that Boeing's new way of building an airplane required a tremendous amount of planning and improvising. The items that Boeing introduced to the manufacture of the 787 family of airplanes include:

1. Outsourcing major portions of the airplane to manufacturers throughout the world
2. Using several software management systems that would guarantee the just-in-time scheduling of delivering of the assemblies
3. Using a fleet of converted Boeing 747-400s to bring main airframe assemblies to Everett
4. Using new tools and fixtures innovatively in the final assembly process within the largest building in the world

The Global Collaborative Environment (GCE)

At the time Boeing was putting together its business plan for the 787 program, it was decided that much of the work previously conducted at the Everett plant would be accomplished by other companies, identified from that time on as partners. Approximately 50 partners, known as Tier 1 companies, would contract directly with Boeing. There would also be a category of Tier 2 companies supplying the Tier 1 partners.

Contracts signed by the Tier 1 partners are all long-term and stipulate that the partners are responsible not merely for the fabricating of various major assemblies, but further, they must also do the design work. This design work must be carried out within a strict set of guidelines called a commonality matrix. Combined with specifications for more than 100 computer applications, the commonality matrix spells out how the partners are to execute their contracts, delineating everything from design and development standards to manufacturing requirements.

Getting major companies from various countries with greatly differing cultures to meet contractual obligations was a major challenge. Boeing had to disperse hundreds of managers, engineers, and technicians throughout the world, until it became clear that all the partners truly understood how the entire business plan functioned. At the core of this plan was the use of extremely advanced digital computer software that tied everyone together, showed the various companies what had to be done and how to do it, and acted as the glue that held the entire Global Collaborative Environment (GCE) together.

One usually thinks of Boeing products as being those of an American company, but in these days of ever-expanding globalization, that view has changed. Thus, early in the 787 planning process the decision was made to bring in as equal partners large, worldwide manufacturing companies having the capability of both designing and producing major portions of the 787 airframe. A large percentage of the 787 airframe is manufactured by companies other than Boeing and the various components are brought to Everett, Washington, for final assembly. In fact, the visual picture of an airplane manufacturing plant with workers crawling all over the airframe becomes a thing of the past as the 787 reaches the production stage.

On previous airplanes, Boeing had outsourced approximately 50 percent of the work to be done on each airplane. That meant that Boeing manufactured half of the airplane, while the other half was manufactured by other companies. In the case of the 787, Boeing planned from the start to have a 70-30 split, with 70 percent being outsourced and 30 percent made in-house.

By outsourcing so much of the 787, Boeing hoped to reduce costs and thus the price of the airplane. One reason for the lower costs realized overseas, particularly in Asia, was the lower labor costs across the board. Keeping in mind that Tier 1 partners were required to design as well as manufacture their portions of the airplane, this meant that Boeing could reduce the number of in house engineers required for this project. Still another factor that would reduce the cost of the airplane was that major assemblies of the airframe were to arrive in Everett already "stuffed." This meant such major units as the fuselage barrel sections would already have installed floors, windows, electrical wiring, and so forth, so that all Boeing would need to do would be to connect them or, as they say, "snap them together." This approach to the assembly of the 787 was designed to greatly simplify the assembly process and to provide huge cost savings for that assembly.

For Boeing to maintain the ambitious schedule it set up in May 2004 for bringing the 787 into production, careful monitoring and scheduling of the various partners was necessary. The pieces all had to come together at the precise times. To that end, Boeing sent its engineers abroad at critical times to work with the partners, while the partners

also sent their engineers and lead technicians to Everett for coordination and training during the initial design phase.

Of the major assemblies of the 787, the largest come from Japan, Italy, and the United States (Kansas, South Carolina, and Washington state), with the jet engines being supplied either by General Electric in Ohio or Rolls-Royce in Derby, United Kingdom (see page 86 for a list of the major suppliers, together with the portion of the 787 they furnish). Altogether, there are seven companies that furnish major sections of the 787 structure, plus two engine manufacturers.

In April 2004, Boeing set a deadline for delivering the first 787 in four years and one month (by May 2008). This was by far the most ambitious schedule in Boeing's history. What made it even more remarkable was that the 787 was chock full of new and complex technology. In July 2006, the company revealed that it had added $333 million to the research and development program, and followed this amount with a further $50-$100 million later that same year. In 2007, another $100-200 million was added for the same purpose. (These are all approximate amounts, as Boeing does not reveal financial data of this kind.) While some of the additional funding also went to other programs, such as the new 747-8, the majority was for the 787 program. Boeing was taking no chance that its original investment might be compromised by any sort of delay or misstep on the part of the partners. In turn, the partners, who had a lot of money invested in the 787 program by 2007, could clearly see that the soaring sales totals for the 787 meant many years of profitable work.

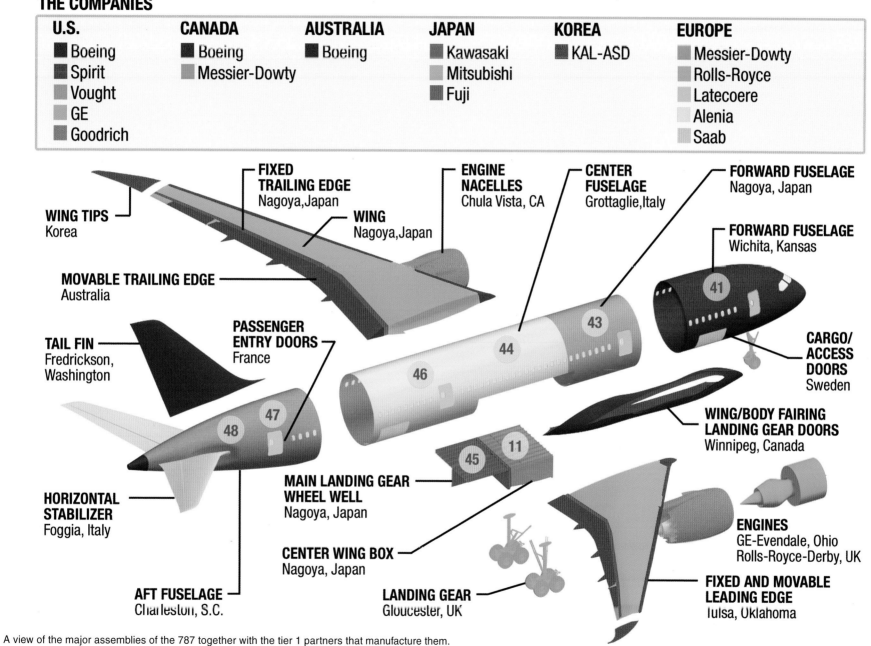

THE COMPANIES

U.S.	CANADA	AUSTRALIA	JAPAN	KOREA	EUROPE
Boeing	Boeing	Boeing	Kawasaki	KAL-ASD	Messier-Dowty
Spirit	Messier-Dowty		Mitsubishi		Rolls-Royce
Vought			Fuji		Latecoere
GE					Alenia
Goodrich					Saab

WING TIPS
Korea

FIXED TRAILING EDGE
Nagoya, Japan

WING
Nagoya, Japan

ENGINE NACELLES
Chula Vista, CA

CENTER FUSELAGE
Grottaglie, Italy

FORWARD FUSELAGE
Nagoya, Japan

FORWARD FUSELAGE
Wichita, Kansas

MOVABLE TRAILING EDGE
Australia

TAIL FIN
Fredrickson, Washington

PASSENGER ENTRY DOORS
France

CARGO/ ACCESS DOORS
Sweden

WING/BODY FAIRING LANDING GEAR DOORS
Winnipeg, Canada

HORIZONTAL STABILIZER
Foggia, Italy

MAIN LANDING GEAR WHEEL WELL
Nagoya, Japan

ENGINES
GE-Evendale, Ohio
Rolls-Royce-Derby, UK

CENTER WING BOX
Nagoya, Japan

FIXED AND MOVABLE LEADING EDGE
Tulsa, Oklahoma

AFT FUSELAGE
Charleston, S.C.

LANDING GEAR
Gloucester, UK

A view of the major assemblies of the 787 together with the tier 1 partners that manufacture them.

Section	Description	Company	Country
11	Center wing box	FHI	Japan
41	Nose section	Spirit	United States
43	Forward fuselage	KHI	Japan
44	Center fuselage	Alenia	Italy
46	Center fuselage	Alenia	Italy
47	Aft fuselage	Vought	United States
48	Aft fuselage	Vought	United States
	Center wing box and landing gear wheel well	KHI	Japan
	Horizontal stabilizer	Alenia	Italy
	Main wing box	MHI	Japan
	Vertical fin	Boeing	United States

On March 19, 2007, the company declared that the first 787 would be rolled out July 8, 2007. Although last-minute glitches did appear, on the appointed day, the first 787-8 was rolled out for the world to see. This happened at the Everett plant, where approximately 15,000 employees, customer representatives, and partner executives witnessed the unveiling. The event garnered worldwide attention and set the stage for the Dreamliner's first flight.

Managing the Logistics of the 787

A key element in the critical scheduling of production and delivery of thousands of parts was the use of a software system that enabled Boeing to maintain control of the process. This software was created by Exostar of San Francisco, which was founded in March 2000 by a consortium of Boeing, Lockheed Martin, BAE Systems, and Raytheon. These companies all saw a need for developing a better way to manage manufacturing programs that were increasingly more complex and dispersed throughout the world.

For Exostar to create the necessary software for the 787 program, it first had to clearly understand the requirements of the process. To this end, it spent a year working with Boeing as a consultant. Next, it contacted the company E2open, of Redwood City, California, which identified commercial, off-the-shelf software that would be used as part of the new management program. Called SCP, for *supply chain platform*, the program accomplishes what Boeing needed to bring the 787 to flight status on time.

However, Exostar was only one of the software systems employed. As may be recalled from Chapter 2, Boeing elected to employ three innovative software systems designed by Dassault Systèmes, identified as CATIA, ENOVIA, and DELMIA. CATIA enables the airplane design to be accomplished with much greater sophistication than might otherwise be possible, while simultaneously saving engineering work hours. ENOVIA comes into play by coordinating the component designs carried out by many separate companies. This coordination is critical when employing a global collaborative approach, such as Boeing did with the 787. DELMIA is also critical, because it enables users to plan, create, monitor, and control production and maintenance processes digitally. By using DELMIA, Boeing is able to tackle three critical areas of the production (assembly) function. The primary job of DELMIA relates to process engineering and establishes a *build procedures network*. This term means that DELMIA establishes all the guidelines necessary to set up the flow of parts and assemblies that will result in an efficient production line. Such coordination includes scheduling deliveries from approximately 50 partners, plus two engine manufacturers; it is truly critical. Boeing did not want major assemblies to be sitting around the plant floor, taking up space and adding to an overstock of parts which would be inefficient and costly.

The secondary job of DELMIA is to evaluate product and tool design within the manufacturing context. Included in this step is assembly simulation, which in turn permits the early training of technicians, plus the ability to forecast production problems. Finally, DELMIA issues detailed work instructions, which are an invaluable tool in doing assembling within a tight time frame while adhering to extremely high quality standards.

The various software systems employed by Boeing enabled a level of manufacturing sophistication possible to achieve its goals. By using these software systems, Boeing was able to create a real-time logistics system that keeps all suppliers coordinated. It further enables Boeing to monitor the critical on-time flow of parts and assemblies.

The *Dreamlifter*

Early in the planning process for the Dreamliner, the question of delivering large assemblies came up. It was determined that, by far, the most efficient method of manufacturing the airplane was to have the main assemblies arrive in Everett just in time to be slipped into the manufacturing sequence for a particular airplane. That approach immediately ruled out shipment by sea, and further, it indicated to Boeing's logistics planners that the cost of shipping huge structural assemblies could be accomplished at a 20 to 40 percent cost reduction over traditional shipping methods. Shipment by air, however, was questionable, owing to the size and weight of the assemblies.

The answer Boeing found was the modification of four used Boeing 747-400 airplanes it had bought back from China Air Airlines. The modification consisted of installing a new upper lobe that runs the length of the fuselage, plus strengthening the main floor. The fuselage is three feet, four inches longer than the normal fuselage, while the wing remains the same. Additionally, the extreme rear of the fuselage was configured as a swing tail operating on two huge hinges. The height of the vertical stabilizer has been increased by seven feet

A drawing that illustrates how major 787 assemblies fit in the Dreamlifter, as well as the way the Cargo Loader enables this to work.

to 70 feet, eight inches. Because the assemblies the *Dreamlifter* carries are large but not extremely heavy, the zero-fuel weight of the airplane is greater than the original airplane, while the maximum gross takeoff weight is reduced by 72,000 pounds to 803,000 pounds. The modified fuselage has a 65,000-cubic-foot capacity, which is three times that of a standard 747-400 freighter. The resulting airplane is truly an awesome machine.

The conversion was carried out by Evergreen Aviation Technologies Corp. (EGAT) of Taipei, Taiwan, as a joint venture between Evergreen International Aviation of McMinnville, Oregon, and General Electric. The large swing tail allows such items as the 787's wings and the fuselage

barrel section to be easily and quickly slid in and out of the airplane.

An additional piece of equipment was needed, however, to load and unload these Dreamliner parts. This turned out to be a specialty transport vehicle called the cargo loader. Designed and built by TLD, a specialty manufacturer in Sherbrooke, Quebec, Canada, the loader is identified as a DBL-110. Six of these 220,000-pound monsters were ordered by Boeing. Each is 118 feet, one inch long by 27 feet, 6 inches wide. The loader can be raised from five feet, 10 inches off the ground to a height of 33 feet, one inch, which enables it to mate with the Dreamlifter floor. The loaders are designed to handle major composite fuselage sections and entire

composite wings. They can carry loads of up to 150,000 pounds and move at 10 miles per hour.

The six loaders are distributed: two at the Everett plant and one each at Global Aeronautica, the Vought-Alenia partnership in North Charleston, South Carolina; Spirit Aerosystems in Wichita, Kansas; Alenia Aeronautica in Grottaglie, Italy; and the Centra International Airport in Nagoya, Japan, which serves three partners: Fuji, Kawasaki,

and Mitsubishi. The loader somewhat resembles a miniature aircraft carrier and has been jokingly referred to as "the darn big loader".

Two Dreamlifters were originally placed in service in 2007. A third Dreamlifter began airlifting assemblies in 2008. A fourth airplane of this small, yet truly unique fleet was flown to Taiwan in March 2008 to begin the major work to transform it into a Dreamlifter. The fourth Dreamlifter entered service in February 2010.

Integrating the Major Pieces

The airframe of the 787 is manufactured in various locations, as previously described. In addition to these manufacturing locations, there is one other site where assemblies are further combined. This is generally referred to as *integrating the airframe*. It is a rather fascinating process.

At the Fuji plant, where section 11 is assembled, the center wing box from Fuji and section 45, the main landing gear wheel well made by Kawasaki, are assembled. Both this assembly and the forward fuselage section 43 made by Kawasaki are then individually barged to the Nagoya Central Airport. This is a new facility built on an artificial island off the coast of Japan. From there, these two large items are airlifted by a Dreamlifter to North Charleston, South Carolina.

Global Aeronautica

Located adjacent to the Vought facility is a similar plant co-owned by Vought and Alenia, identified as Global Aeronautica. This is a 334,000-square-foot building used to integrate several major components. These include sections 44 and 46 made by Alenia (Italy), plus the items listed above. This facility was later sold to Boeing.

The combined assembly, consisting of all the components listed above, measures 84 feet in length and constitutes the major part of the 787 fuselage. To better visualize how all the major assemblies are moved, consider the following steps:

• The wings are flown directly from Nagoya, Japan, to Everett, Washington.
• The center wing box (section 11) and forward fuselage section 43 are flown from Nagoya, Japan, to North Charleston, South Carolina, for further mating.
• The horizontal stabilizer and center fuselage sections 44 and 46 are flown from Italy to North Charleston, South Carolina.
• The large, assembled, integrated center fuselage is flown from North Charleston to Everett.
• In Wichita, Kansas, Spirit attaches the nose landing gear made by Messier-Dowty in the United Kingdom and the forward cargo door made by Saab of Sweden to the nose section, which is then flown to Everett.
• Spirit's Tulsa, Oklahoma, plant builds the wing leading edges. The fixed leading edges are shipped to Mitsubishi for assembly to the wing, while the movable leading edges are shipped directly to Everett.
• The rear fuselage (sections 47 and 48), built by Vought in North Charleston in two sections, is first fitted with the aft passenger entry door, which comes from the French company Latecoere, and is then flown to Everett by the Dreamlifter.

From this list, the reader can visualize that the Dreamlifter fleet is kept busy and operates as a constant shuttle. In Wichita, Kansas, for example, where the nose section is delivered to Boeing by Spirit, the Dreamlifter lands at McCoy Air Force Base and is off again within two hours at the most. No time is wasted!

The Production Integration Center

Early in the 787 planning process, Boeing personnel had concluded that it would require a highly sophisticated production control system to maintain control over the supply system it was creating for its new airplane. The result became known officially as the Production Integration Center, or PIC. The impetus for the PIC came when Boeing vice-president Bob Noble, a longtime supply chain specialist, decided that having a center to collect and distribute information relating to production was absolutely necessary. A forerunner to the PIC had been developed and implemented at Boeing's Commercial Aviation Services Division in 2005. For the 787 program, Boeing moved more slowly, as it began to receive components for the Dreamliner. Boeing went back to Dassault Systèmes of France, which furnished other critically important production scheduling software. Together, the two companies fashioned a system that provides information about and control of the entire supply chain; a highly significant achievement, considering the complexity of the supply chain and the fact that it is spread out virtually throughout the world.

In designing the PIC, Boeing looked at such other organizations as NASA, the Burlington Northern Santa Fe Railroad, and the Federal Homeland Security Department. The result of all this research and planning is a large room situated on the fourth floor of the final assembly building, high above the 787 assembly line. The facility has more than 5,100 square feet of space and features 27 workstations. It also boasts a 40-foot-long situational awareness video screen that can be sectioned off to receive a large variety of information, from cable news to reports from supplier facilities throughout the world. It entered service in December 2008 and operates 24 hours a day.

Not only can the PIC bring up information on any of the 787's multitude of parts being shipped, it also tracks the movements of the Dreamlifter fleet hourly. The PIC staff represents supplier management, engineering, and production support. This staff communicates with 1,600 PIC-trained personnel working for the various suppliers. Thus, the PIC maintains a constant track of parts from all suppliers, not just the main "partners." This ability constitutes a giant step forward from the way that previous airplane programs were managed.

As an information collecting and distributing focus, the PIC really goes considerably further. It keeps constant track of such environmental events as hurricanes and earthquakes that can affect both manufacturing and the delivery of manufactured items. It also monitors news channels for any events that can affect a distant supplier. They might be a large-scale power failure, a political event or riot, or even an outright military operation. By collecting and then having available this information, the PIC can act to keep the supply chain moving smoothly and on schedule.

The Final Assembly Building

The final assembly of the 787s takes place at Boeing's Everett plant, 30 miles north of Seattle, Washington. Here, on a 1,025-acre site, sits a building that Guinness World Records recognizes as being the biggest in the world by volume. The original building was constructed in 1966 to build 747s, increased by 45 percent in 1980 to accept the 767 production line, and further expanded by an additional 50 percent in 1993 for 777 airplane production. While the building is anything but new, it is still a manufacturing facility second to none and worth examining.

The building is 3,500 feet long, 1,614 feet wide, and 114 feet high. There are six gigantic hangar doors: four measuring 300 feet wide by 81 feet high and two additional doors that are 350 feet wide by

81 feet high. The area of the plant is 4.3 million square feet, the volume 472 million cubic feet, and it covers 98.3 acres. Under the plant are 2.33 miles of pedestrian tunnels, while overhead rumble 26 cranes. The largest of the cranes can lift up to 34 tons. On May 1, 2007, the facility reached 40 years of production. During the summer of 2007, it delivered its 3,000[th] wide-body jetliner, a notable accomplishment by any standard.

When construction of the plant started in 1966, the entire area was a sea of mud, which is not surprising, considering the frequent Seattle area rainfall. This site in Snohomish County had been chosen by Boeing after long and careful consideration, even though other sites had been contenders, including some in states other than Washington. The plant sits adjacent to Paine Field, a county airport, and has good access to rail and shipping facilities. The original plant was completed in only 16 months, with Boeing pushing for quick completion so it could begin fabricating and delivering its brand new 747 wide-body jetliner. This now is the site of the final assembly of the 787 Dreamliner.

The building encloses and accommodates four discrete assembly lines for the 747, 767, 777, and now the 787. The production lines stretch down the short side of the building (see diagram, figure 9-4). There are six subdivisions to the building, each with its own identifying number. To make room for the 787 assembly line, part of the 777 assembly line was moved from the 40-36 building to the 40-34 building.

The Assembly System

The assembly of a wide-body jetliner is normally viewed as a complex affair requiring many weeks. In the case of the 787, the entire process is so fast and simple as to make veteran aerospace workers' eyes pop. This assembly has been characterized as "click-click," or snapped together, an astonishing improvement in the process. The reasons for this huge advance in manufacturing are twofold. First, the major airframe sections arrive at the Everett plant in a state of completion far more advanced than any previous airplane. For example, fuselage sections are pre-wired, with electrical and hydraulic systems in place and wall insulation blankets installed. Interior sidewalls are not included at this point.

Second, the result of this level of completion before reaching the Everett plant enables Boeing to connect the major portions of the airframe quickly and easily. Still, the manhandling of these large and heavy sections resulted in a separate problem. Boeing production managers did not want to employ overhead cranes as had been done in the past, because the scheduling and coordinating of crane movements is too inefficient. Instead, Boeing developed tools and fixtures to make the joining of the various sections fast and rather simple. Tools and fixtures are items used to move, hold, and connect major portions of the airplane. It is worth examining some of these tools and fixtures because of their unique designs.

Mobile Gantry Crane

Called the "boat loader" because it resembles a crane used to lift pleasure boats in and out of the water, the mobile gantry crane offloads major assemblies from the cargo loader once they arrive at building 40-36. The cargo loader is the self-powered piece of equipment that loads and unloads the Dreamlifter.

Wing and Wing Tip Cradles and Stands

These cradles and stands are used to hold the wings and wing tips when they are in a laydown position.

Section 41 Cradles

Section 41 cradles support the main sections of the fuselage and are used to move them into position.

MOATT

MOATT stands for the "Mother of All Tools Tower". Its function is to hold the vertical fin in place while it is aligned and joined to the fuselage.

Circumferential Join Tool

This tool holds portions of the fuselage in place while they are being joined.

Jacking and Alignment System

This system moves the airplane so that necessary joining work can be performed. The stands are motorized so that the airplane can be moved from position 1 to position 2.

Large-scale Mapping and Alignment Truss Installation

These laser installations, located in the ceiling beams, keep the airplane properly aligned.

Turning Jig

This jig rotates the fuselage.

Heavy Moving Equipment

These are remotely-controlled units that can move large portions of the aircraft anywhere within the plant.

Turning Jig

Heavy Moving Equipment

787 Final Assembly Overview

40-36 Building

40-26 Building

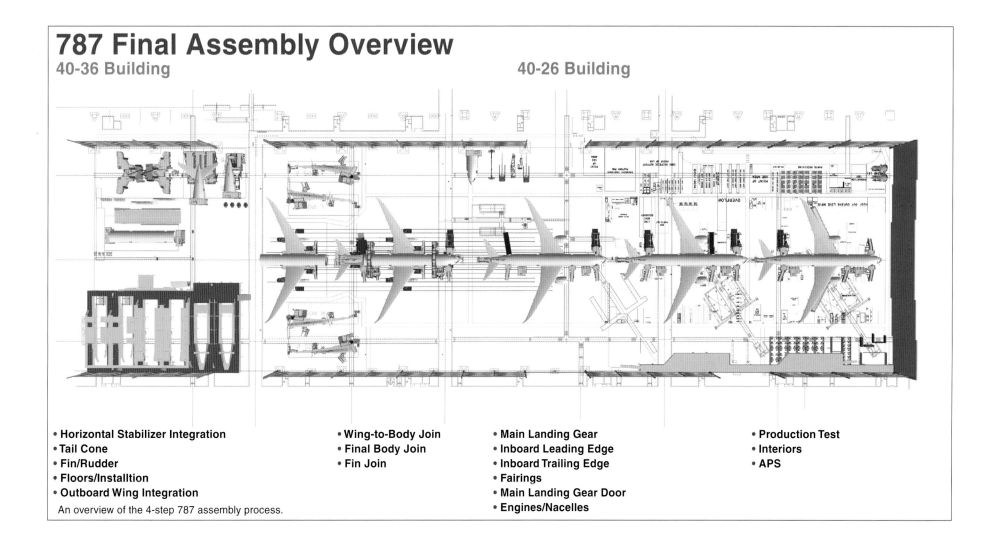

- Horizontal Stabilizer Integration
- Tail Cone
- Fin/Rudder
- Floors/Installtion
- Outboard Wing Integration

An overview of the 4-step 787 assembly process.

- Wing-to-Body Join
- Final Body Join
- Fin Join

- Main Landing Gear
- Inboard Leading Edge
- Inboard Trailing Edge
- Fairings
- Main Landing Gear Door
- Engines/Nacelles

- Production Test
- Interiors
- APS

The Assembly Process

The assembly process that Boeing developed for the 787 is far simpler than for preceding airplanes, such as the 767/777. The simplicity of the process is a result of major portions of the 787 arriving at the Everett plant ready to be connected and already stuffed with such items as all electrical wiring and floors. Thus, the entire 787 assembly line has one station in the 40-36 building, identified as "pre-integration", and four stations in the 40-26 building where the majority of the assembly is carried out. As shown in the accompanying illustrations, the assembly process follows a logical sequence.

Major components arrive by air, carried by the fleet of Dreamlifters. Step 1 begins a Dreamlifter arrives at Paine Field and is unloaded using one of the two cargo loaders assigned there. The cargo loader slowly carries the just-delivered component(s) to the 40-36 building, where the mobile gantry crane unloads it, then moves it to the appropriate position. At this location, the horizontal stabilizer and the vertical fin are fully assembled.

Step 2 takes place in position 1 in the 40-26 building. Here the wings are joined to the center section of the fuselage, identified as section 44. Then the remaining fuselage sections are attached, as well as the previously assembled tail assembly. These sections are joined with a bolt-and-nut system, rather than with traditional rivets.

Step 3 occurs in position 2 in the 40-26 building. Here the engines and landing gear are installed, as well as the interior. Structure and system testing begins and electrical power is fed to the airplane.

Steps 4 and 5 take place at positions 3 and 4, again in the same building. All installations are completed, including production testing.

The primer coat of paint is previously applied to each major subassembly by the Tier 1 companies that manufactured it. This is the coat that is designed to neutralize the effects of photooxidation.

The assembled airplane is now ready to be towed to the paint shop for the final exterior coat. After that, the airplane is ready for pre-flight and delivery activities, including engine runs (see Chapter 15).

The 787 assembly line operates three shifts each day, with full shifts five days a week and much lighter shifts on weekends.

Interior Assembly

An advanced assembly system was also developed for the interior components of the cabin, including passenger seats, galleys, overhead bins, and cabin linings. Back in 2001, an "interiors team" was organized with the goal of assembling the cabin interiors with such speed and efficiency as to fit the concept of a 787 being put together at Everett in just four days. Beyond that, the team had the vision to design interior architecture that would allow both the factory and airline to build, reconfigure, refresh, and service the interior easily with speed and precision. To meet this extremely ambitious goal, the team determined it would have to change the culture in which the work was carried out. Part of the inspiration for its work came from viewing how professional auto racing pit crews are able to refuel a race car and change four tires in less than 10 seconds—a truly amazing achievement.

The team felt that what was needed were components that fit intuitively and were capable of being installed easily, quickly, and safely with few or no tools. To accomplish a task which many felt was not achievable, the team brought together personnel from both manufacturing and engineering. Ideas on how items should be designed and how they should be assembled into the cabin were thus worked out in tandem.

The result has been parts that are simpler, lighter, and ergonomically easier to install. To prove the validity of the basic concept, the team first installed the various components into replicas of the 787 fuselage. Then, in March 2008, 25 interior items, including lavatories, floor coverings, dimmable windows, and crew rests underwent simulated installation in the number 3 airplane. The results were extremely successful.

The Dreamliner Gallery

When an airline orders a quantity of airplanes, such as the 787, one of the tasks it has to complete is to determine exactly what goes into the interior of the airplane. With previous airplanes, this involved a long, drawn-out process, as airline personnel traveled everywhere to view such products as seats, galleys, coffee makers, bathroom units, and fabrics manufactured by competing firms. But with the 787 program, an exciting and downright revolutionary system was introduced.

As the 787 Dreamliner project evolved, the matter of interiors eventually came to the fore. At that time, Boeing received a suggestion from an industry source for creating a one-stop location to handle the entire matter of the interior furnishings. The Boeing individual chosen to lead the creation of this facility was Patricia Rhodes, a mechanical engineer and veteran Boeing employee who in 1998 was a program manager of the 747-400X program. Rhodes moved ahead with the project proactively. The result, inaugurated in January 2007, is called

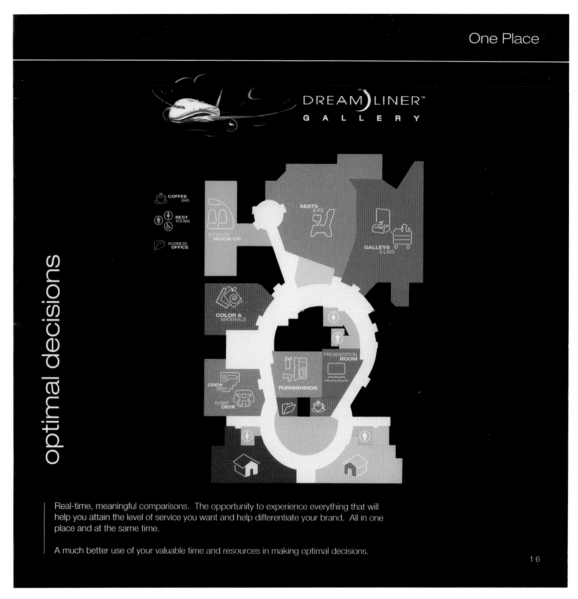

The layout of the Dreamliner Gallery.

the Dreamliner Gallery, a separate 54,000-square-foot facility in a one-story building located about one mile north of the Everett facility. The building is owned by the well-known industrial design firm Teague. The design of the building was created by various groups, including consultants from MY Design, Inc., and Boeing and Teague personnel. The Gallery is a one-stop shop for 787 customer airlines that results in savings for both customers and Boeing.

With manufacturers of such items as seats, galleys, and lavatories sprinkled all over the globe, airline representatives previously had to travel extensively to compare products. In many cases, Boeing personnel traveled with them. Now, airline representatives simply fly to Seattle and make all the choices relating to the 787 interior in one location. In addition to the obvious savings in cost and time, Boeing has further simplified interior choices in another way. Only a limited number of manufacturers for each type of product are offered, and all these are previously certified. Rhodes compares the concept of the Gallery to going to an automobile showroom and picking out the accessories from a catalog. To that end, she has led a team of cross-functional employees who gather all 787 catalog offerings. Gallery customers can make choices in the following categories:

- Attendant seats
- Attendants' rest compartment
- Bar units
- Bun warmers
- Business class seats
- Chillers and freezers
- Closets and bins

The seat section of the Dreamliner Gallery. Note that seating for all classes is shown here.

- Coffeemakers
- Convection ovens
- Economy class seats
- Espresso makers
- Exterior décor
- First-class seats
- Flight crew rest compartment
- Flight deck elements
- Folding trolleys and carts
- Galley waste disposal units
- Galleys
- In-flight entertainment
- Interior decor
- Lavatories
- Lighting
- Meal and beverage carts
- Premium seats
- Steam ovens
- Trash compacters
- Water boilers

By quickly reviewing the above list, the reader can easily see how time consuming it must have been for airline personnel to travel to many different locations to examine various products. Plus, it was difficult to compare and select from the various choices. Boeing had already reduced the offerings available in an effort to simplify the entire process. This next major step was long overdue. Consider, for example, that one Boeing supplier offers 105 coffee maker models. Now, with fewer choices available, plus having everything available to view in one location, an airline can make quicker and better-informed choices. An example is one airline that previously spent four months traveling extensively just to choose seats for its 777s. For the

787, that same airline brought a team of purchasing specialists together with a few frequent-flyer passengers and made the necessary choices in one afternoon.

Entering the Gallery, one comes into a beautiful and relaxing reception area that doubles as a place where various interior LED lighting choices are displayed. Part of the reception area floor is covered with carpet representing what is available for the 787. This carpet is recyclable and ecofriendly.

The Gallery facility is subdivided into several separate sections, each dedicated to a single item type. There is a seat and in-flight entertainment section, a kitchen or galley section, a cabin mockup section, a section for furnishings, one for crew rest and cockpit systems, and another for colors and materials. In the galley section, customers can test the various choices by cooking with real food. All the various rooms are carpeted in some of the carpeting choices available for the Dreamliners, thus allowing customers to test various equipment on carpeting and floors that would be found on their airplanes.

Boeing designed a visual reality system called eConfig. This is a three-dimensional configuration tool that greatly enhances the already considerable advantages of the Gallery, since it leads the client on a virtual tour of the cabin interior with all the items previously chosen. To accomplish this, there are computers in each section that enable customers to upload their selections and view the result on a large screen in a presentation room. Thus, a customer can see them on a viewing screen and make changes if desired.

Customers' reactions to the Gallery have been enthusiastic. They clearly see the savings in time, cost, and travel stress that the Gallery affords. The only negative comments relate to premium seating, where some clients seek more choices. Boeing does encourage customers to select premium seats from outside their catalog of options. For Boeing, the advantage, in addition to keeping customers happy, is that it simplifies the process of identifying, ordering, receiving, and installing all available equipment.

Boeing Expands the 787 Assembly Process

On November 30, 2009, Boeing began construction of a second 787 final assembly plant located at North Charleston, South Carolina. This new facility is adjacent to the other two 787 plants at that site, these being the former Vought and Alenia assembly integrating plants. The new plant has six buildings, including a 610,000-square-foot final assembly hall that measures 1,037 feet by 460 feet and is completely open, with no implanted structures or columns. This allows for great flexibility in how the assembly lines are structured.

One section innovation is the use of *barges*, small, mobile shipside support stations that hold six workers. Unlike the much larger stations used at Everett, these can be easily relocated. Another improvement that has been implemented here is the use of a U-shaped assembly line. It has been shown to be far more efficient than a long, straight assembly line.

The South Carolina plant will assemble the -8 model, while the original Everett plant will assemble both the -8 and the newer -9 models. This plant benefitted from previous experiences, such as the improved Boeing plant in Renton, Washington, which assembles 737s, and the Everett, Washington, plant assembling the initial 787s.

Conclusion

The innovations now found in the 787 have changed the way that crews are trained, as will be explained in the next chapter.

CHAPTER 10

Training and More Training

Early in the 787 planning process, the subject of training came up. Three distinct types of training were considered. The first was the training that would be required of engineers, technicians, and manufacturing employees worldwide under a production system Boeing contemplated, namely the Global Collaborative Environment. The second type of training involved pilots and cabin crews. The third type dealt with airline maintenance crews who perform regular scheduled maintenance, plus on-call short-term line maintenance.

Boeing's Approach to Flight Training

Boeing's approach to training has changed radically over the years. When the "Dynamic Duo" of the 757/767 were being introduced in 1982, the training essentially involved stand-up lectures. In 1991, with the arrival of the 777, electronic presentations were employed, but with the 787 program, a brand new approach was instituted. Now the entire training system is predicated on the use of digital training equipment.

With the 787 program, Boeing believed it was time to make fundamental changes in its previous training programs for two reasons. First, the 787 represented a quantum jump in the technology employed in its design and manufacture, especially when one considers an all-composite airframe and the 787's highly integrated electronic system. The second reason was that a general advance in the training systems had become available. It was Boeing's feeling that the all-new digital technology used in the 787 required a digital training solution. In addition, Boeing was considering changes in its philosophy of training. One change included implementing a program that utilized computer-based training (CBT). This, together with simulation and working with virtual reality systems, forms the backbone of Boeing's flight training program.

Another new approach Boeing took involved having pilots qualify in the 787 simulator only, with no real 787 flying hours. This applies only to pilots with Boeing 777 flight experience and is possible because of the many similarities in the flight characteristics of the 777 and 787.

Boeing Training & Flight Services (Formerly Alteon Training)

A big factor in the training process was a wholly-owned subsidiary of Boeing, originally called Alteon Training. The history of Alteon dates back to 1997, when Boeing needed a new strategy for training customers' personnel. At that time, Boeing created a joint venture company with highly respected FlightSafety International. The cooperative venture began with 11 training facilities worldwide, but soon grew to 20 sites. Boeing bought out FlightSafety in 2002, and created a wholly-owned subsidiary called Alteon Training. The name of this entity was changed again, in 2009, to Boeing Training & Flight Services, as part of Boeing Commercial Airplanes.

Training Flight Crews

787 training is based on using the advanced technologies in the 787. The result is an electronic performance support system; an all-digital, Internet-based teaching system that encompasses both flight and maintenance training. Furthermore, the system is based on "just-in-time" training, a marked break from previous training systems. Airline flight and cabin crews now travel to the training site of the airline's choice shortly before the beginning of 787 deliveries.

Flight crews previously trained to work on the 777 can complete 787 conversion courses in 50 percent of the time it would have taken previously. Procedures for the 777 and 787 have a lot in common: similar extended two-engine operations, cruise speeds, flight maneuvers, takeoff and landing techniques, autoland or autocoupled controlled landing, non-precision approaches, and in general, the same flight deck operational and design philosophies. Many of the air carriers ordering 787s are already operating 777s. The result is that 777 crews can move to the 787 with as little as five days of training.

Another aspect of this program is its flexibility. Each airline is given a certain quantity of training points. The total number of points depends on the number of airplanes being purchased, the type of operations of the particular air carrier, and any regulatory requirements that may apply. The airline's employees then undergo whatever amount of training is necessary to bring them to the desired level of proficiency. For example, a 777 pilot requires far less training than one who has been flying a non-Boeing aircraft, or even a Boeing 757.

The training equipment itself is fascinating. Each pilot receives a personal tablet already programmed with the necessary software and information. Back in June 2005, Alteon revealed that it had chosen Thales, a French-based electronics and communication company, to supply these tablets.

Boeing's tablet is merely the first device to be used to train flight crews.

A trainee is introduced to a flight training device (FTD), which is also supplied by Thales of France. The FTD is essentially a mockup of the 787 cockpit and duplicates the flight management and flight control systems of a 787. It is an ideal way for students to become totally familiar with the location of all the 787's cockpit levers, knobs, controls, and other mechanical elements. Touch-screen displays, however, substitute for the switches found in a real

An airline crew in the 787 simulator.

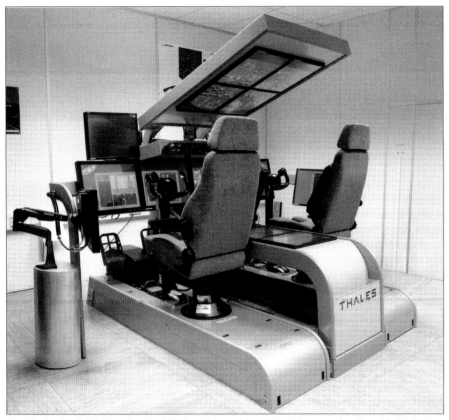

The Thales Flight Training Device (FTD), which enables pilots to become familiar with the 787 cockpit layout and instrumentation.

An exterior view of the Thales full-flight simulator.

cockpit. This part of the training is also far less expensive when done in an FTD, rather than using a simulator. While it is true that the 787 flies in a manner similar to the 777, the cockpits are by no means identical. Thus, the FTD enables the student to reach the necessary cockpit familiarization fairly quickly and simply.

Finally, the trainee has access to a full flight simulator (also a Thales product) with six degrees of freedom, or motion. Note that the simulator could not be certified for training until the flight test program was completed, since data from the test flights was used to continually update the simulator software.

For the 787 program, Boeing Training & Flight Services set up five training facilities in Seattle, London (Gatwick), Shanghai, Singapore, and Tokyo. By creating these training sites throughout the world, Boeing has succeeded in greatly reducing the travel costs required for airline personnel to reach a training site.

Flight Training

The flight training system includes the following individual courses:

• Airplane Flight Training
• Flight Attendant Transition Training: 2 days
• Full Transition: 20 days
• Instructor Pilot Training
• Route and Line Training
• Shortened Transition and Rating (STAR): 13 days
• 777-rated Pilots Transitioning to 787: 5 days
• 787 Emergency Exits/Doors Training: 1 day

The author, Claude G. Luisada, standing in front of the 787 simulator in Seattle, Washington.

Let's Go Fly the 787

So you want to fly a Dreamliner? We can't fly a real one, but we can do the next best thing and fly the 787 simulator. In August 2010, the author had the opportunity to fly the simulator, and in many ways it was a real eye-opening experience! Follow me as we go fly.

Accompanied by Scott Lefeber of the 787 Communications organization, I went to the Boeing Commercial Airplanes office complex at Longacres, a part of Tukwilla, a community south of Seattle. Here, in one of the large buildings, is the Training & Flight Services Department, where we are met by Capt. Robert Botnick, the 787 chief standards pilot. After introductions, he takes us to the simulator room, which is a large, high-ceilinged area with big doors to the outside that permit easy delivery of the bulky simulators located there. The 787 simulator is a large, rather nondescript enclosure mounted on hydraulic legs. It is completely surrounded by open space so that it can move freely, since it is a six-motion simulator. To enter it, one walks across a short gangway, which is then retracted after personnel are inside and the entryway

is sealed. Entering this simulator almost makes one feel like entering an ancient castle by way of a drawbridge over a moat! Interesting, to say the least!

The simulator is a perfect replica of the 787 flight deck, with all the consoles, yokes, rudder pedals, and two pilot seats. Behind the pilots' seats is the instructor's seat, with two consoles flanking it. Behind that are more seats for observers. These additional seats are not found on the real 787. The flight deck is dark, except for the illumination that enters through the cockpit windows.

I had not really expected to fly the simulator. As a result, I am somewhat flustered and unsure of myself. Captain Botnick indicated that I should take the left-hand seat, and once I am seated, he helps me manipulate the seat controls to move the seat forward and upward to a comfortable position. He tells everyone in the simulator to put on their seat belts and adds that during some maneuvers the simulator can throw people around. I comply immediately. As I look outside, I realize that the view is of Sea-Tac Airport, located between Seattle and Tacoma, Washington, and it shows that the airplane is sitting not far from runway 16 Left.

Captain Botnick gets the two fan jets started, and their sound is extremely realistic. So is the view, for that matter, which Botnick tells me is the first simulator to show a complete 180-degree view. He tells me to go ahead and taxi to the runway. I grasp the tiller on my left with my left hand, put my right hand on the two throttles located in the center console, and add some power. After a little hesitation, I can see that the view outside shows us moving forward, so I reduce power in order to taxi slowly and manipulate the tiller as I head for the

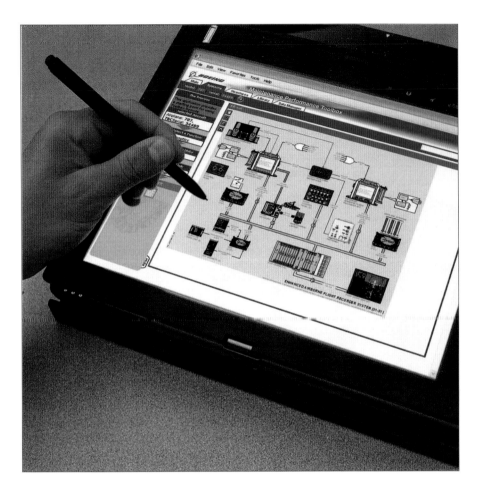

The tablet issued to every airline crew member starting 787 transition training.

them for me. Both typical noises and vibrations are heard and felt as he carries out these two operations. As we climb out, Botnick cautions me to maintain a substantial angle, and as we reach pattern altitude and I start to level off, he tells me that at that airspeed the 787 is flown at a 3-4 degree nose-up angle.

I fly around for a few minutes, but Botnick evidently realizes I am thoroughly intimidated by both the airplane and the "glass cockpit." Many years before I had been a student pilot and still occasionally fly right seat in a Cessna 182. However, having no familiarity with glass cockpits and being hampered by poor vision, it is harder for me to read the gauges and makes it difficult to do a particularly effective job.

Botnick now takes over and explains that we will do an autoland back at SeaTac. He sets up the autopilot, and the 787 obediently circles and lines up for the approach to runway 16 left. As we get close to the runway, I am startled by a recorded voice that reads off the altitude above the ground starting at 200 feet above ground level. In a nose-up attitude, the plane smoothly approaches the runway, and as it touches down I feel a definite thump in the seat of my pants.

My flight is over, and I wish I had been able to carry out my pilot duties in a far more competent manner, but I guess that at age 79, my time for that is long past. Still, I am truly awed by the realism of the 787 simulator! In fact, as we leave the facility, Scott Lefeber reveals that at one point he was feeling a bit queasy! I have been told that this is not uncommon, especially on the part of observers who are sitting behind the pilots in an almost pitch black area.

threshold of runway 16 Left. Botnick quietly reminds me that the turning point of the 787 is 18 feet behind me, and I try mightily to compensate for that.

I discover that the 787 has a ground steering tiller for both pilots, the first airplane to feature this particular arrangement. Reaching the threshold of the runway, I somewhat gingerly turn left onto the runway and stop the airplane for a few seconds. This may be just a simulator, but I'm feeling nervous!

Then, placing my feet on the rudders and my left hand on the tiller, I advance the throttles to what I'm guessing is takeoff power. My seat gives me a gentle shove as the view outside shows us beginning to accelerate, and the sound level rises accordingly. Botnick reminds me that at 80 knots indicated air speed (IAS) I can switch hands to the yoke. As he calls "VR" for rotating velocity, I pull back on the yoke firmly and we are airborne! I am so far behind the airplane that I forget to call for "Gear Up" and "Flaps Up," but Botnick calls out when he does

It has been a most rewarding experience, and I only wish I could repeat it, but better prepared mentally. Not only was I not really ready, but there was no pre-briefing, so I was constantly playing catch-up!

Having flown the 787 full-motion simulator, it became much easier to understand how line pilots with Boeing 777 certification can move to the 787 with relatively few hours in the simulator and no real flight time in the Dreamliner.

Training on Emergency Exits and Doors

Boeing has built a small section duplicating the left side of the 787 cabin that includes the main exit door, the adjacent bulkhead, and three rows of seats. Nearby is a control panel operated by a simulator instructor. The cabin trainers are included at all Boeing Flight Training campuses.

The exit doors of the 787 are another new feature. Because there are basic differences from the doors found on Boeing's previous transports, both cabin attendants and pilots are trained to use these doors with a special door training device.

The exit doors on the 787 incorporate what is officially referred to as the *individual emergency pneumatic door opener*. The main door, as well as all the others, can be operated in one of two ways. It can be used as a regular door, or it can be opened in such manner that the attached emergency slide will automatically deploy and inflate. In the case of emergency crash landings, a pneumatic actuator will open the 200-pound door once it is unlocked.

Airlines normally send only one or two instructor cabin attendants for training. These airline employees, plus all the pilots, are required to take exit door training.

Training Airline Mechanics

In a manner similar to the flight training approach, maintenance training is carried out using personal tablets, interactive computer-based training, three-dimensional images, and desktop simulation. These digital tools replace a large number of printed volumes. There are two distinct disciplines under the general category of maintenance: one is avionics, the other is airframe, or power plants.

Customer airlines purchasing the 787 send maintenance instructors and senior mechanics to one of Boeing's training facilities. In April 2010, Boeing completed the training of the first ten 787 mechanics from 787 launch customer All Nippon Airlines (ANA), plus two inspectors from the Japan Civil Aviation Bureau. The course lasted more than 30 days, including 20 days of theoretical training, two days of engine runs and taxi tests, five days of practical training, component identification exams on production airplanes, and five days of troubleshooting exams in the full-flight simulator. These ten mechanics were the first of 150 from ANA to train in Everett, Washington, over a period of seven months.

The student mechanics do much of their training using Boeing's Maintenance Performance Toolbox, a notebook-size computer that shows them how to remove and install components. The system as a

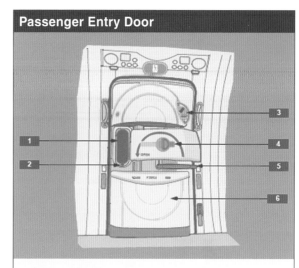

Passenger Entry Door

1. **Viewing Window**
Allows observation outside the airplane.
2. **Closed, Latched and Locked Indicator**
Indicates the current state of the door. The indication displays either an open symbol; or a closed, latched and looked symbol.
3. **Door Mode Select Panel**
See the detailed Door Mode Select Panel description in the next graphic.
4. **Gust Lock Release Handle**
Grab and pull inward to release the gust lock and move the door inward.
5. **Door Operating Handle**
To open the door - rotate in the direction of the arrow.
To close the door - rotate in the opposite direction of the arrow.
6. **Slide/Raft**
The bustle contains the slide/raft.

The Passenger Entry Door Simulator.

whole is less about learning specifics than about learning the electronic tools that enable the mechanics to locate the data they need quickly. The training system is so streamlined that Boeing expects line maintenance personnel to be trained in half the time it took to train the 777 mechanics.

Training Plant Employees

Far more than in any previous aviation production system, the manufacturing of the 787 required production workers from all over the world to have a great deal of training. This was necessitated by the Global Collaboration Environment employed for this project, which spread manufacturing not only to many suppliers, but more importantly, to many countries.

The training of plant employees at both Boeing and at the sites of Tier 1 partners was more of a cooperative developmental effort, rather than a well-orchestrated effort. The reason for this becomes readily apparent if one considers that large composite structures had never been manufactured before, and thus, manufacturing them was a learning process for everyone involved. The Tier 1 partners sent their lead technicians and engineers to Seattle, where they worked together with Boeing personnel at the Development Center.

Working together, this group developed the manufacturing processes and technology needed for making large composite barrel sections and long sections of the wings. After the Tier 1 employees returned to their home locations, Boeing sent personnel to assist these companies in setting up their manufacturing facilities.

Conclusion

Boeing made dramatic changes to its basic training program when it developed the training approach for the 787. The net results should be that personnel will become proficient far more quickly and at far lower cost than previously. Obviously, the Boeing Training Department spent considerable effort and thought in developing this training program and utilizing up-to-date tools available to them.

CHAPTER 11
A Bump in the Road

An Ambitious Schedule

The 787 has the distinction of being the single commercial jet transport with the most sales orders placed before its first flight. By October 2008, the order book had swelled to a majestic total of 751. This number meant the Boeing assembly line was already totally committed through at least 2013.

A hallmark of the 787 program has been its extremely tight design, development, testing, and manufacturing schedule. When Boeing launched the 787 program in April 2004 on the basis of the All Nippon Airways order for fifty aircraft, it set in motion the fastest design-to-delivery program in its history. Somewhat to the surprise of many, it kept to this extremely ambitious schedule up until the first airplane rollout in July 2007. At that time, however, potential delays had already begun to appear, and Boeing executives had to be asking themselves whether this was just "a bump in the road" or, "Were the wheels starting to come off of the cart?"

The Production Schedule

It was Boeing's intent to outsource major manufacturing assignments, thereby enabling them to receive large sections of the airplane ready to be assembled. In fact, the entire assembly of a single 787 at the Everett plant was originally scheduled to last just three days. This was predicated on having the major assemblies not only arrive from various Tier 1 partners on time, but also having them stuffed.

Unfortunately, when the initial major assemblies began to arrive in Everett in January, February, and March 2007 for the assembly of the first 787, a different picture began to emerge. What happened next was not only interesting and fascinating, but it reveals what happens in big business and large industries, and in the relationships between different cultures.

By May 2007, Boeing was beginning to see the effects of various problems on the total 787 production schedule. It was apparent that Boeing had an inkling about potential delays, as indicated by the extra funding it made available in the 2006-2007 period that paid for additional engineering and technical support to be sent to Tier 1 partners.

A problem that arose was the amount of time required to certify the millions of lines of software code in the computers that control and operate the airplane. A second, and much greater problem was that the major assemblies had not been stuffed. *Stuffing* refers to the various items the Tier 1 partners were supposed to have placed within the fuselage barrels, such as insulation, side walls, floors, electrical and hydraulic lines, and windows, to name a few. As a result, merely assembling the first airframe in time for the July 7, 2007, rollout became a frantic effort to avoid delaying that first showing of the 787 to the outside world. Still, no real sense of emergency was revealed at that time. That may have been because Boeing truly believed that only the first assemblies from each partner were lacking the necessary stuffing to complete the job.

Boeing did manage to finish the basic assembly of all the major sections of the first airplane in time

The 787 production line in early 2008. Note the many additional workstations necessitated by the delivery of major sections that were not "stuffed."

for that inaugural rollout, but the condition of those arriving assemblies was beginning to send out some negative vibrations throughout the Boeing hierarchy.

There were many effects of missing "stuffing" on the first new airplanes being assembled. Additional personnel, many of whom were contract workers, had been hired or transferred on short notice. These workers were congregated in temporary workstations arranged on either side of the production line. Computer terminals and drawings were visible everywhere. Workers were clambering inside the 787 fuselages, installing all the "stuffing" that the Tier 1 companies had not completed. Keep in mind that it was not in the original plan to have these supplementary workers trained on the installation of the items comprising the missing stuffing. In fact, the same physical items themselves had to be brought in on short notice. No wonder there were delays!

Another nasty problem was apparent, the timely procurement of fasteners. A summary of the reasons for this stumbling block in the assembly of the 787 is revealing:

- After 9/11/2001, some fastener companies shut their doors, going out of business because of a rather severe downturn in orders for their products.
- This downturn was followed a few years later by a strong and unexpected upswing in aircraft orders, both commercial and military, which stretched the capabilities of the now-downsized fastener industry to the maximum.
- The fasteners required for the 787 were of a new design, dictated in part by the fasteners having to

be connected to composite, rather than metallic, components.
- Certification requirements had to be met for this new design of fasteners. This step was delayed because of the lack of the small quantity of fasteners required for testing.
- Fastener companies had not developed second-source backups, partially because of the new technology.
- The redesign of the specialty fasteners used in the composite structure occurred because of concerns over the lightning protection system. Both Boeing and Mitsubishi had concerns that gaps between fastener and composite surfaces might cause arcing. As a result, the redesigned fasteners form a tighter seal with the composite surface.

To assemble the number 1 airplane in time for the planned and advertised rollout July 8, 2007, Boeing was forced to use non-aerospace fasteners. Later, all these had to be drilled out and replaced with the proper, but late-arriving, fasteners. It is ironic in the extreme that this lack of fasteners was affecting an airplane that, because of its composite airframe, requires only a fraction of the number of fasteners required by other jet transports of comparable size.

Still another problem was the difficulty in obtaining small assemblies or components on time. Precisely why this was happening is not clear, although the steep downturn in aviation manufacturing beginning in late 2001, combined with the unexpected recovery beginning in 2005, may have caught many small suppliers shorthanded. Perhaps they were simply not ready to respond to the needs of the aviation industry.

"The Best Laid Plans of Mice and Men"

Finally, by the summer of 2008, work on the 787 test airplanes was moving along at a reasonably brisk rate, and Boeing was looking at an October or November date for the much-anticipated first flight. Unfortunately, more obstacles lay in wait for the program.

As the well-known saying goes, however, "The best laid plans of mice and men . . ." That phrase pretty well describes what transpired in the months before and after that initial rollout. (To read about and follow the flow of these events, beginning in the spring of 2007 and continuing until the 787's first flight in December 2009, Appendix I presents them in chronological order.)

The Saga Continues

With ground testing of the first 787 continuing through the summer months, one might have expected that the corner had been turned in the program. Yet this was not the case, as events clearly indicate.

September 6, 2008, a strike by the machinists and aerospace workers' union stopped all work. This work stoppage lasted for almost two months, until October 27, 2008. A small amount of work continued on the 787 line during this almost two-month period, but the program ground to a halt. The timing of this strike was truly unfortunate, when one considers the following:

- Work on the ZA001 airplane, the first of six flight test aircraft, was almost 100 percent complete.

- The first flight was on schedule for either late October or early November.
- The ground testing was well under way, with test results nominal.
- A drastic drop in stock markets and the toll on financial entities was already having a negative effect on all activities for U.S. companies, including Boeing.

There was more fallout from the strike. All Nippon Airlines, the 787 launch customer, indicated it would stick with its order for a total of 50 787s, but would accept its first delivery in August 2009, as well as a reduction in deliveries from the original seven per month to six per month.

An ironic twist to the delivery delay and general slowdown was the revelation that ANA was ordering nine 767-300ER airplanes to help tide it over. This meant that the 767 production line, which only a few months earlier Boeing thought would have to be closed down for the immediate future, now had an extension on its life.

In early November 2008, Boeing revealed that a revised delivery schedule was being developed because of the strike and fastener problem. The fastener problem was said to affect only three percent of the total fasteners on a 787, and as of that date, the problem had been identified on the first four flight test aircraft, as well as on the two static and fatigue test airplanes. There was also some indication that an additional 15 airplanes might be affected.

The problem was not with the fasteners themselves, but with their installation; some fasteners were not being inserted far enough, while others had pins that were either too long or too short. Boeing believed the root cause of the problem was that the installation instructions were not clear and they were attempting to isolate all the contributing causes of the situation.

The delay of the 787 introduction may have inadvertently caused another event to occur at Boeing. Because the 787-10 model had been envisioned to carry 310 passengers, this put it in the same category as the 777-200ER. In mid-2008, with the delays in the -8 and -9 models, Boeing revealed that it was considering dropping the 787-10 and creating a new family of passenger airplanes that might fit in between the 787 and the new 747-8. Only time would reveal events in that area.

In any case, at the end of June 2008, when the first test airplane was powered up, the fastener problem can be considered to be the end of the "bump in the road" part of the story and the beginning of the test phase. This phase lasted from June 2008 to December 2009 (approximately 17 months), but by the end of this phase, the 787 program emerged considerably stronger, more organized, and better equipped to face the challenge of ramping up production.

The Economic Crisis and the 787

Beginning in the spring or summer of 2008, signs began to appear that a world economic crisis was coming. This trend worsened quickly in the fall and winter of 2008 and into 2009, and unavoidably it affected Boeing and the 787 program. To begin with, air carriers worldwide were seeing shrinking passenger loads and resulting red ink in their corporate financial statements. This, in turn, brought about a reduction in scheduled flights and a general belt tightening throughout the industry. A further result was the cancellation of some aircraft orders by a few airlines and a deferral of deliveries by others. A few new orders were received in late 2008 and into the early months of 2009. Then, in May, there was a cancellation of 25 additional aircraft by a single customer. The result of all this was that by June 2009, the order book for the 787 showed a total of 861 orders—down six percent from a year earlier. Thus, while the world economic crisis of 2008-2009 had made itself felt on the program, it did so in a relatively minor way. The total number of orders for the 787 was still extremely large.

The Quiet Period

During the latter half of 2008, surprisingly little was heard about the 787 program. Boeing was trying to fix all the items that needed correcting, including the replacement of fasteners on the test airplanes. This cumbersome process took considerable time to complete. The fastener issue, together with the other "travel work" that needed to be completed, required many months. Not until late January 2009 did regular production resume. At that time, the fifth 787 (ZA005) began going through the final body-join process. ZA005 was also the first 787 that would be powered by GE engines. At this point, only the first aircraft had its fasteners completely replaced, while on the other three airplanes requiring the rework they were still in process.

As of the end of January, Boeing had the sixth (and last) flight test airplane under construction at its various partner sites, while assemblies for a further 30 787s were in various stages of production.

Engine Improvements

The two-year delay in the 787 program enabled Rolls-Royce to upgrade the Trent 1000 engine it was providing for the 787. The company called this modified engine an *upgraded standard* model. The major change implemented was a six-stage, low-pressure (LP) turbine with high lift, high-aspect-ratio blades. With these changes, the Trent 1000 achieved specific fuel consumption (SFC) that was 0.5 percent better than called for in the specifications. The engine was thus able to give 16.5 percent better SFC than the GE CF-6 engine that powers the Boeing 767.

During this two-year delay in the program, Rolls-Royce worked hard, further developing the Trent 1000, with a resulting 9,300 cycles and 5,200 hours of test operation and more than 7,000 starts.

Another Nasty Surprise

On June 23, 2009, in a move that was no doubt painful, Boeing revealed that a structural weakness had been discovered in the wing-body joint. Specifically, stress tests showed that where the top of the wings joined the fuselage there was greater strain than had been predicted by the computer models. As a result, the first flight of the 787 was now delayed indefinitely until the problem could be resolved. It was hoped that the delay would be short-lived, since the fix involved reinforcing small areas of the top of the wing with stiffeners. In fact, it was planned that 18 stiffeners of only one or two square inches in size would be needed. The fix, which was being initially installed on the static test aircraft, would then have to be validated with new wing bending tests.

This delay came as the 787 number 1 aircraft was finishing the last of three gauntlet system tests and was being prepared for taxi tests. In the meantime, this sixth delay in the 787 program had some uncomfortable results for Boeing. Wall Street investors did not take the news well, and rumors were swirling that some Boeing heads might roll.

The problem of the wing-body joint was thought to have occurred at Kawasaki Heavy Industries, where the wings were designed and manufactured. Thus, the entire subject of major outsourcing came to the fore once more. Specifically, the problem arose when the stress analysis data from the wing bend exercise did not match the predictions of the computer models. As a result of this unfortunate development, Boeing pulled design authority from its partners and went to its in-house design team. This change was in place as the final configuration of the 787-9 model was being worked on.

While of no real comfort to Boeing, it is a fact that the Airbus 380 had a similar wing problem that also delayed that program. Interestingly, some of the 787 customers accepted the news of the delay calmly. The severe downturn in air carrier traffic that continued into mid-2009 caused many customers to request delays in airplane deliveries.

Ironically, a week before the revelation of the wing-body joint problem, in an interview, Boeing CEO James McNerney talked about the previous delays and admitted that the 787 program had so many new aspects that it outran the ability of Boeing to manage it effectively. Throughout the remainder of 2009, many people held their breath, wondering whether that long-awaited first flight was ever going to happen. Finally, on December 14th, it was announced that the next day, ZA001 would begin the flight test program, weather permitting. And so, at last, the long bumpy journey that stretched from July 2007 to December 2009 was coming to an end. Boeing was looking forward to much better days. (For more detail covering the period October 30, 2006, to December 14, 2009, please see Appendix I.)

CHAPTER 12
Testing and More Testing

Many people wait anxiously for the first flight of a brand new aircraft. For some, it is simply the excitement of seeing that first flight. For many others who have been directly involved in the design, development, testing, and production of the airplane, that first flight is an affirmation of what they contributed to and have accomplished. For those who have financed the new airplane or who have placed orders for it, this is a nerve-wracking time, wondering whether their gamble will pay off. And of course, the competition also waits to see the results.

Much work must be satisfactorily complete before that first flight. Airplane manufacturers carry out a great deal of testing long before the first flight. Much of it is required for certification of the airplane by U.S. and other government agencies. Additionally, a manufacturer conducts testing to be absolutely satisfied as to the structural and operating integrity of a new airplane. This was particularly true in the case of the 787, because this was the first large passenger transport built mostly of composite materials. As well, other technological

advances, such as more fuel efficient engines, meant that even more testing than usual was needed. This testing takes various forms and is a particularly interesting part of the entire process that brings a new airplane into airline service. Consider, however, that there are so many different tests performed, both on the ground and in flight, that it would require more than one book of this size to list and describe them all. Moreover, because the Dreamliner boasts so much new technology, the FAA required more testing than would be required of a more conventional design.

This testing was divided into two broad categories: ground testing and flight testing. These were each subdivided into many other categories. Listed below are just a few of the testing areas.

Ground Testing
- Brakes
- Computer software program lines of code
- Engine
- Electronic systems and components
- Environmental systems
- Individual electrical circuits
- Landing gear operation
- Operation of moveable wing surfaces
- Structural integrity of total airframe
- Structural strength and integrity of airframe components
- Structural tests of landing gear

Flight Testing
- Aborted takeoff distances
- Aircraft response during excessive maneuvers
- Fuel efficiency at various weights and altitudes
- General maneuverability of aircraft
- Landing distance at various weights
- Low- and high-speed response to controls
- Maximum range at various weights
- Stability at all speed ranges
- Stall speeds at various weights
- Takeoff distance at various weights
- Total flight envelope

In the case of the 787 program, the period of testing may be said to have started June 11, 2008, when power was first applied to the number 1 airplane. From that time on, various tests conducted in various ways continued nonstop.

Testing the Airframe

Separate tests are made for the fuselage barrel sections, wings, empennage (tail assembly), and the landing gear. Individual composite sections are thoroughly tested. One possible failure mode of multi-layer composites can occur if these layers separate, also known as delaminating. Therefore, composites are checked carefully for that possibility.

The strengths of various parts of an airframe are tested to a potential ultimate load—the 150 percent load—and in some cases to destruction. A full-scale wing box was sent to Farnborough, United Kingdom, for testing. The piece measured 17 feet from front to rear and 4 feet in height, was 50 feet long, and weighed 55,000 pounds. This weight includes test-only hardware and instrumentation. The piece is basically the wing box starting at the fuselage centerline and extending out to about halfway to the wing tip. The wing is then tested to the failure point, which should be 150 percent of the maximum load or more.

Boeing tested a barrel section of the fuselage, in this case section 46, in a special test rig built at its Everett location. It consisted of a rather majestic steel frame that holds the barrel section in place. Twenty-five hydraulic jacks strategically located exerted tremendous loads on the barrel section. To quantify precisely how the test piece reacts to the stresses imposed by the jacks, 4,000 strain gauges and 25 displacement indicators were located throughout the exterior of the barrel.

This barrel section was tested to 150 percent of the limit load. The limit load is defined as the maximum load that an aircraft would be expected to experience during its lifetime. In addition, the barrel section was tested to 200 percent of the limit load, or twice what it might ever encounter, at which point the barrel wall failed in some spots and tears became visible.

Boeing also tested two full-scale 787 airframes built for just that purpose that are part of the validation and certification process. Other items that are tested include engine nacelle fittings and main landing gear fittings.

One of the static test airframes had to be tested for durability in various ways. The initial test, known as *high blow*, was merely the first of three such tests required before the first flight. This test involves sealing the fuselage, then building up the internal air pressure to 14.9 pounds per square inch,

A wing box, shown here after being tested to ultimate load.

In 2008, a barrel section of the 787 was tested to 150% of normal limit load, then beyond to 2 ½ Gs in this test rig. At that point, far beyond the load any airplane might ever experience, the barrel finally showed signs of failure.

Testing for fire propagation was another area that was examined. The test results revealed that while aluminum is able to resist flame without burn-through for only 20 seconds, composites showed no burn-through after 20 minutes.

The effect of lightning strikes on the airframe—a fairly common occurrence in normal airline operations—is another area Boeing thoroughly tested. In fact, the potential problem of the effect of lightning strikes on an all-composite airframe had been researched years earlier. The Beechcraft Company, when it designed and built its futuristic "Starship" business jet, was aware of the potential problem of lightning strikes. Boeing's solution, similar to Beechcraft's, was to embed a phosphor bronze fine-wire mesh in the first layer of the composite skin, plus a ground-plane system to shield various electronics present. The fuselage was then tested to a 200,000-ampere simulated lightning strike. During the certification evaluation, the aircraft was struck by lightning with no negative results.

Component Testing

One area all airplane manufacturers and the federal government focus on is the physical testing of such major airframe components as the wings and fuselage.

With the barrel section having successfully passed these two rigorous tests, it was then subjected to increasing loads until it collapsed. This load turned out to be more than two and a half times the force of gravity. In spite of this stress level, the section did not collapse as much as expected, and

or one and a half times the maximum level likely ever to be reached during flight operations. This test was successfully completed September 27, 2008.

Boeing also completed an ultimate load test on an entire airframe. It was carried out in a special test rig, and the surrounding area of the building was cleared of all employees. This was done in the unlikely case that a failure of any part of the airframe launched small pieces of composite material at high speeds in all directions. The total airframe was subjected to 150% of ultimate load. At that point, the wings had flexed so much that the wing tips were at 90 degrees to the wing roots! The test was a complete success and certainly demonstrated both the strength and flexibility of the composite airframe.

From this description of how composites are tested in the 787 airframe, it becomes clear how critically important this material really is to the success of the entire project.

the barrel was then extensively tested and the test results were carefully analyzed. The entire structural integrity of the barrel section was clearly proven to be far beyond the required limits. During a seven-month period, beginning in late 2007 and stretching to June 2008, Alenia Aeronautica tested a 787 horizontal stabilizer to destruction. Working at its Naples, Italy, plant, the company first tested the stabilizer to 150 percent stress load, then further tested it to destruction. The latter test was for the sole benefit of Boeing and Alenia, while the initial test was carried out to comply with FAA requirements.

The Icing Lab

Boeing has one of only seven icing labs worldwide built specifically to test the effect of ice on aerodynamic surfaces. Built in 1991 as part of the model 777 test phase, it is located just south of Seattle and is the third largest icing facility in the world. It is officially known as the Boeing Research Aerodynamic Icing Tunnel, or BRAIT. The tunnel measures 4 feet wide, 6 feet high, and 20 feet long. Icing conditions are created artificially within the tunnel by lowering the internal temperature to between 32 and -22 degrees Fahrenheit, blowing air through at speeds of up to 288 miles per hour, then spraying a cloud of water upwind against the aerodynamic surfaces being tested. The result is that ice begins to form on the surfaces almost immediately.

Sections of the wing were then tested in the tunnel to determine how much ice forms on them. This is a critical concern, because in acute icing conditions two dangerous events can occur simultaneously. Ice forming on the wing can change the aerodynamic shape of the wing, thus reducing or even destroying the necessary lift. At the same time, ice accumulation can add considerable weight to the airplane. The weight factor can become critical if the airplane has just taken off at its maximum gross takeoff weight. Using this tunnel reduces flight testing by as much as sixty to seventy hours and thus also its cost. As Gene Cain, a Boeing technical fellow and the tunnel's designer, puts it, "We help ensure the safety of an airplane in natural icing conditions. And we provide this capability in a cost-effective manner."

Other Boeing Test Labs

Boeing has developed and uses other test labs in an effort to work all the bugs out of any airplane design, as well as minimize the time wasted and additional cost if unexpected problems in a new design should suddenly surface. Further, these labs test and validate that the new design meets certification requirements and Boeing standards. Boeing has 250 labs in the state of Washington, as well as additional labs located in other places. Listed below are several of these test labs, together with a brief description of the function of each.

Aerodynamic Wind Tunnels

Boeing has three aerodynamic wind tunnels: one is the BRAIT described above; a second is a transonic wind tunnel for testing speeds up to Mach 1.1; and the third is a 9 by 9 foot low-speed propulsion aero-wind tunnel that tests engine nacelle inlet performance and thrust reversers.

Noise Labs

Seattle area commercial labs test for cabin, flyover, and ramp noise levels.

Propulsion Lab

The propulsion lab is located at Boeing Field and generally tests various parameters relating to jet engines.

Structural Dynamics Lab

This lab evaluates the dynamic behavior of structures. To accomplish this, the lab performs component vibration, wind tunnel flutter model, and ground vibration tests, and provides real-time data processing support of in-flight flutter tests.

Integrated Airplane Systems Labs

This Seattle lab tests avionic, electrical, flight control, hydraulic, mechanical, payload, and propulsion systems on the ground, both individually and in combination. The lab also has six flight simulators, allowing pilots to test simulated flight characteristics.

Structural Labs

These labs validate the design strength, damage tolerance predictions, and the minimum expected service life of an airplane. The tests also help determine how much growth remains in an airplane structure. That information is then used in future models of the same basic design.

Metrology Labs

The sole function of these laboratories is to calibrate, repair, and maintain Boeing's measurement and test equipment.

Flame propagation test.

The 787 wing was tested in this rig past ultimate load. Note the wing tips bent almost 90 degrees upward!

Preliminaries to Flight Testing

Eventually the flight testing stage is reached, and company test pilots begin what was planned to be a six-month-long period of such flying. Of the first nine aircraft to roll off the assembly line, six will take part in the flight test program. These are the number 1 airplane, plus the number 4 through number 8 planes. Number 2 is a static test aircraft and number 3 is a fatigue test aircraft.

Taxi Tests

Flight testing begins with taxi tests at various speeds of up to just below the predicted liftoff speed. During these taxi tests, such items as landing gear shimmy and vibration, longitudinal control of the aircraft using both nose wheel steering and the rudder, and the response of the airplane in cross winds are all checked and verified. The braking and engine reversal systems are also checked.

In addition, the engine reverse thrusters and the wheel brakes are tested under both normal and emergency conditions. An emergency condition would occur during an aborted takeoff when the aircraft has to be stopped before it runs out of runway. This is generally considered to be the most rigorous test of the braking system.

The Flight Tests

Eventually, the big day finally arrives. In the case of the 787, the "Big Day" was December 15, 2009. Let's see the *Dreamliner* fly!

CHAPTER 13

Flight Testing

People who are not familiar with the certification and testing process required for a new passenger jet transport may be under the false assumption that flight testing makes up most of the testing program. In fact, the reverse is true. All other testing, plus certification documentation, account for close to 90 percent of the entire process. Nevertheless, flight testing is the phase where unexpected results may show up, and it is certainly the most exciting and visible phase to the average outsider. Thus, while it represents a relatively small portion, it is nevertheless critical to the total process. The flight testing stage was eventually reached, and company test pilots began what was planned to be a nine-month period of test flying.

The Test Operation Center

In the months before the beginning of the testing period, Boeing came to the conclusion that a new approach was required to the entire company flight test program. Heretofore, testing was accomplished by groups assigned to any new aircraft models that required such testing and certification. But back in early 2007, Boeing suddenly became aware that a period of testing loomed that would include no less than five separate and distinct models: the 777F, 767-300BCF, 767-200SF, 787-8, and the 747-8.

One of the solutions Boeing derived was to systematize the flight operations, test and validation (FOT&V) organization. The result was the creation of a new test operation center (TOC) within the flight test center located at Boeing Field in Seattle, Washington, which monitors all flight test activities. The TOC operates 24/7, with flight testing during the day, ground tests during the second shift, and maintenance at night. Employees from major suppliers and the FAA are also housed at the same location so as to improve communications relating to problems, as well as to expedite the validation process.

The staffing of the flight test center numbers more than 600 pilots and mechanics. If this seems like a large number, remember that in addition to the previously mentioned aircraft models, the test center will also be testing no fewer than four additional models for Boeing's Integrated Defense Systems. For the 787 test program, 34 pilots were assigned to the program to support at varying levels, with a captain for each airplane. For example, Capt. Mike Carriker would always be assigned to ZA001, and so on.

To understand the flight test process better, one has to consider Boeing's approach. The company uses four key milestones to mark progress, these being:
1. Initial airworthiness
2. Type inspection authorization (TIA)
3. Certification testing
4. Function and reliability (F&R) testing. Reliability includes determination of extended twinjet operations (ETOPS).

Preliminaries
to the First Flight

Several steps are taken before the first flight of any new design, and in May 2009, Boeing was ready to begin the countdown to that flight.

Gear Swing Tests

In August 2008, gear swing tests were completed on ZA001. This required putting the aircraft on jacks, then extending and retracting each individual gear (the nose gear, left main gear, and right main gear), then repeating the same operation with all three together, which would duplicate flight operation. This sounds like a fairly simple test, but in reality it is not. That's because the 787 systems are so sophisticated that this gear operation requires the integration of avionics, common core system, electrical power system, hydraulic system, and the major airplane structure itself.

The Gauntlet
Test and Other Tests

Initially, a *factory gauntlet test* was performed for the 787, in which the airplane was connected to test equipment that simulated flight. This took place April 20, 2009, and was successfully completed in less than 12 hours.

On May 21st, tests that require operating the entire electrical system of the airplane were performed, which in the case of the 787 involved just about all the various systems in the airplane. The problem with running such tests is that the airplane's computers have to be fooled into thinking that the aircraft is in the air and flying while it is on the ground with the engines off. This necessitated some rather brilliant work on the part of the software engineers but was eventually successful. As part of these tests, the Rolls-Royce Trent 1000 engines on the ZA001 were started for the first time using the auxiliary power unit and operated at various power settings.

This test was followed by the *intermediate gauntlet test*, also carried out in May 2009. This test further evaluated all the airplane systems as though in flight and was carried out outdoors on the ramp; it took a week to complete. By late June, *Aviation Week and Space Technology* magazine was reporting that the first flight of ZA001 was likely to be only a week away. But, as explained in chapter 12, on June 23rd, Boeing revealed that a structural weakness had been found in the connection of the wings to the fuselage which brought the initiation of flight testing to a sudden halt. This further delay was a bitter pill for the corporation after all the previous delays. In the meantime, flight test pilots and engineers continued to familiarize themselves with the intricacies of the 787's sophisticated systems by "flying" the *integrated test vehicle*, also known as the Iron Bird simulator.

The Test Fleet

Boeing committed the first eight airplanes off the assembly line to certification and flight testing. Aircraft number 2 was designated to be used for a static test, with aircraft number 3 for a fatigue test. The remaining six airplanes are all for flight test, as shown below together with their individual power plants. Keep in mind that customers for the 787 have the choice of ordering the airplane with either Rolls-Royce Trent 1000 or General Electric GEnx power plants. For this reason, aircraft with both engines were tested.

1. ZA001 – Rolls-Royce Trent 1000
2. ZA002 – Rolls-Royce Trent 1000
3. ZA003 – Rolls-Royce Trent 1000
4. ZA004 – Rolls-Royce Trent 1000
5. ZA005 – GEnx
6. ZA006 – GEnx

Here are a few references that might help refine this section:

Q1: *When were the first flights of the flight test 787 Dreamliners?*

A:

Airplane	First Flight Date
ZA001	December 15, 2009
ZA002	December 22, 2009
ZA004	February 24, 2010
ZA003	March 14, 2010
ZA005	June 16, 2010
ZA006	October 4, 2010

Q2: *What specific flight tests does each airplane perform?*

A: The following chart notes some of the tests each flight test airplane will conduct:

Tests

- **ZA001** Flutter, Systems – Landing Gear/Brakes/Hydraulics, Aerodynamics – Low-Speed Performance, Stability and Control, Flight Controls
- **ZA002** Stability and Control, Systems – Electrics, Autopilot, Avionics – miscellaneous, Propulsion
- **ZA003** Systems, Noise, Flight Deck, Avionics,

Electromagnetic Effects/High Intensity Radiated Field (EME/HIRF), Cabin – miscellaneous, Extended Twinjet Operations/Functional and Reliability (ETOPS/F&R)

- **ZA004** Aerodynamics – High-Speed Performance, Propulsion Performance, Flight Loads Survey, Community Noise, ETOPS/F&R
- **ZA005** Flutter, Aerodynamic Performance, Propulsion, Systems, Stability and Control, Flight Controls, Avionics, Community Noise, ETOPS/F&R
- **ZA006** Misc. tests with minimal analog requirements, EME/HIRF, ETOPS/F&R

The flight test program was designed to complete 2,430 flight test hours and 3,100 ground test hours on the Rolls-Royce Trent 1000 and 670 flight-test hours and 600 ground-test hours on the GEnx engine.

On December 12th, high-speed taxi tests were completed, with ZA001 reaching a speed of 130 knots and the nose gear being lifted off the runway. At this point, all the preliminaries to a first flight were accomplished. The only other item to be considered was the weather.

The First Flight

December 15, 2009, the big day finally arrived; Boeing was ready to carry out the first flight of the 787. Once again, there was anxiety, because the weather at Paine Field in Everett, Washington, was marginal. The first flights of a new model are always flown in "VFR" (visual flight rule) weather conditions, which means a minimum 1,000-foot ceiling and three mile visibility. Early that morning,

however, Paine Field had ceilings of around 1,500 feet, which, while legally VFR, were not quite what Boeing wanted for a first flight. As the morning progressed the ceiling slowly lifted, and by 10 a.m.—the original scheduled takeoff time—it was decided to begin preparations for the flight. Shortly thereafter, the two-person crew climbed aboard: 787 Chief Test Pilot Mike Carriker and Engineering Test Pilot Randy Neville. Within a few minutes, the twin Rolls-Royce Trent 1000 engines were started. Then the 787 began a long, slow taxi around toward runway 34 Left. Lining the runway were emergency and fire trucks placed there as a precaution. Watching all this was a large crowd estimated to be as large as 13,000 people, made up mostly of Boeing employees with some customer representatives and media, all somewhat uncomfortable in the cold, drizzly weather. In addition, 81,000 Boeing computers logged on to watch the historic flight.

Finally, ZA001 arrived at Runway 34 Left and slowly moved into position for takeoff. There was a short delay as the two-person crew went through its *pre-takeoff checklist*. Then the engine noise grew and the big 787 began rolling at 10:27 a.m. With a takeoff weight of only 390,000 pounds—far below its design maximum gross takeoff weight of 502,000 pounds—the 787 quickly accelerated, rotated at 140 knots, lifted off, and climbed slowly, followed by two T-33 chase aircraft. The 787 remained beneath the low ceiling and soon disappeared in the murky weather. Those television networks that followed the takeoff showed the large crowd cheering enthusiastically.

The plane headed out over Puget Sound, where the weather was marginally better. Three hours and

six minutes after takeoff, ZA001 landed at Boeing Field, 40 miles south of Paine Field and the location where many of the test flights would originate. During the flight, the crew climbed to an altitude of 13,000 feet and reached a speed of 180 knots, which was below the planned parameters because of the limiting weather conditions. The crew found the handling qualities of the airplane to be excellent, and everyone was impressed, despite the curtailed flight envelope caused by the bad weather.

Upon their return, the pilots commented favorably on the flight characteristics of the 787. They also mentioned that while they were flying around the general area, they received direct radio calls or heard radio calls on the frequency from crews in other aircraft congratulating them. Both Carriker and Neville said that this radio traffic was most welcome and showed the high level of interest in the 787 program on the part of the aviation community.

The Flight Test Program Continues

So finally the great day had arrived, and the first flight of the 787 was now history. It was regrettable that it occurred approximately twenty-one months later than originally planned, but then, long delays in the development of a new airplane are not at all rare. Remember that the 787 was not just a new design, but in fact one that involved greatly advanced materials, aircraft systems, and manufacturing procedures.

Now Boeing had to move ahead with an ambitious flight test program. Boeing decided to implement a different testing schedule than used

ZA001 shown during touchdown.

on other new models. Each aircraft in the test program would be available for flight beginning at 7 a.m. for eight hours. After that period, each aircraft would have up to 16 hours for maintenance and configuration changes, then be ready for the next day's 7 a.m. flight. This schedule would be maintained 24/7.

The progress of the test program as it reached various milestones and the events involving the six test airplanes are shown below in chronological order. The listing represents one approach to communicate to the reader the level of activity during the test program.

- **December 22, 2010** ZA002 completes its first flight.

- **January 15, 2010** Initial airworthiness tests are completed. This allows the test program to expand. ZA001 and ZA002 complete 15 flights totaling 60 hours. Test crews reach a speed of Mach 0.65 and a 30,000-foot altitude.
- **January 29, 2010** ZA001 is subjected to 1.5 G load and checked for buffeting.

Boeing 787-8 (aircraft ZA001) on its inaugural flight. Note the landing gear left extended.

- **February 24, 2010** ZA004 joins the test fleet and will be used to test aerodynamics, high-speed performance, propulsion performance, flight loads, community noise levels, and etops.
- **March 12, 2010** ZA002 is flown to Victorville, California. The testing consists of low-level flights over the runway, duplicating typical approaches and landings. These tests, called ground effect tests, show that the controls of the airplane are effective at low altitudes. All tests were successfully completed.
- **March 14, 2010** ZA003, the fourth and final Rolls-Royce-powered test aircraft, joined the test fleet with a three-hour initial flight. ZA003 has portions of the passenger interior installed, as well as cabin and crew support systems. ZA003 will be used to test the interiors, plus other operational parameters.
- **March 20, 2010** The ultimate load test of the 787 wing was successfully completed on the test rig. In the test, the wings were flexed upward to the point that the wing tips were forcibly raised 25 feet. The test took two hours, during which thousands of data points were recorded. In addition, the fuselage was successfully pressurized to 150 percent of its normal operating condition.
- **April 20, 2010** The FAA grants Boeing expanded *type inspection authorization* (TIA), clearing the way for the remainder of the 787 flight test program. This is a critical milestone in the testing and certification of a new airplane. As of this date, the four test airplanes have accumulated a total of 505 flight hours.
- **April 22, 2010** ZA003 is flown to Eglin AFB, Florida, for both high- and low-temperature testing. The tests are conducted in a special hangar, with temperatures ranging from a high of 115 degrees Fahrenheit to a low of minus 45 degrees Fahrenheit.
- **May 12, 2010** The first GE-powered 787, test aircraft ZA005, begins engine run-up tests. The test fleet completes 231 flights, amassing 700 flight hours.
- **May 26, 2010** The test program reaches 283 flights, totaling 863 flight hours. The test program is lagging slightly behind the original schedule, but is now running so smoothly that it is expected to be finished on or before the original completion date set at the time the first test aircraft flew.
- **June 16, 2010** ZA005, the first GE-powered 787 test airplane, completes an initial three-hour, forty eight minute flight successfully. The test program reaches 311 flights, totaling 1,000 hours of flight. Flutter testing took 108 flight hours over 27 days. Also completed was margin testing of the flight control system and structural tests on the static test airframe. Another completed test was minimum control ground velocity.
- **July 25, 2010** Flight testing of the Rolls-Royce-powered 787s is 50 percent complete.
- **July 30, 2010** The flight test program reaches 430 total flights and 1,366 flight hours.
- **August 15, 2010** The flight test program reaches 472 total flights and 1,482 flight hours.

A portion of the total testing is used to validate the idea that the 787 is similar enough in handling to the 777 that a pilot can make the transition from one to the other in as little as five days. This validation requires three distinct steps or phases, of which two have been successfully completed. Six non-Boeing pilots who flew the 787 said it flew like the 777.

- **August 16, 2010** Hairline cracks have been discovered in some of the tail horizontal stabilizers supplied by Alenia. Boeing is now checking all of them carefully and does not believe the problem will affect the delivery schedule.
- **August 23, 2010** It was revealed that on August 2nd, a Trent 1000 "Package A" engine experienced an uncontained failure of the intermediate pressure turbine, with parts of the turbine penetrating the casing.

The engine was being tested on a test stand at the Rolls-Royce engine plant in Derby, England, and the test site also received damage. Initial investigations led Rolls-Royce to indicate that it believed the engine was being tested in what they called an inappropriate operating regime.

During the test, an oil fire broke out and the resulting high temperatures caused the turbine shaft to weaken and fail.

Boeing has already put some design changes in place for the production version of the engine, identified as "Package B." This latter model will be installed on ZA004 for testing.

The results of this event, plus other unspecified issues that arose during testing, caused Boeing to postpone first deliveries to February 2011, which was an additional delay of six weeks. Beyond that, Boeing scheduled the addition of two more test aircraft, these being regular production airplanes. One of these will undergo ground testing and the other further flight testing.

In still another part of the total test program, Boeing began the long-term testing of ZA998, the fatigue test airplane without engines. Encased in a giant test rig that uses a multitude of hydraulic jacks, the composite airframe was subjected to thousands of cycles, each of which reproduces the stresses of a real flight. Each cycle simulates a flight, including taxiing, takeoff, ascent, cruising, descent, landing, and taxiing again. This program will last three years and provide Boeing with real data as to how its all-composite airframe will hold up during its service life.

- **September 3, 2010** As part of the flight test program, individual test aircraft are dispatched to various airports all over the United States and even to other countries. ZA001 flew for several days from Edwards Air Force Base, California; ZA002 went to Keflavik, Iceland, for high-altitude and cold-weather tests; ZA003 flew to Yuma, California, for hot-weather operations, and overseas to Farnborough, in the United Kingdom, for the prestigious air show there; ZA004 operated out of Victorville, California, conducting flight load surveys and went to Mesa, Arizona, for low-elevation hot-weather tests; to Colorado Springs, Colorado, for high-elevation tests; and also operated from Glasgow, Montana. ZA005 was tested for flight in icing conditions. This is but a partial list of the various places these aircraft visited.

- **September 8, 2010** Testing at Roswell, New Mexico. I had the opportunity to go to Roswell, New Mexico, where ZA001 spent some days carrying out various tests. The Roswell Airport is the former Walker Air Force Base, at one time a U.S. Air Force Strategic Air Command base, and thus boasts a very long main runway. Furthermore, the area is blessed with excellent weather year-round and little air traffic. For these reasons, Roswell is often used by various organizations for testing airplanes. I flew down to Roswell from Albuquerque in a Civil Air Patrol (CAP) Cessna 172 together with a CAP colleague and former Air Force pilot.

As we neared Roswell, we heard the tower clearing ZA001 to land on the long runway that had just been sprayed by water tank trucks. At that point, the 787 was being tested for braking on wet surfaces. Later that morning, it made numerous touch-and-go landings which further expanded the test envelope.

At midday, the 787 landed and parked on the ramp for several hours. The crew consisted of two pilots and eight to twelve technical test personnel. The entire crew went into a hangar for debriefing on the flight tests just completed, after which they took time out for lunch. On this particular day, the morning flights were under the command of Captain Mike Carriker, but then he was to hand over to another Boeing test pilot.

While the aircraft was on the ramp, the crew opened it up for anyone who wished to go onboard, which we promptly did. This particular 787, as well as the other five test aircraft, do not have a standard airline interior. On the contrary, the airplane is outfitted in a functional manner. The ceiling is a makeshift affair. The interior sidewalls are missing and only one half of the insulation is installed. As one Boeing tech admitted, this makes for a noisy airplane. The cockpit, however, is the same as the production version. In addition to the two pilot seats, there are two additional seats for test personnel.

The cabin itself has only a few passenger seats. On either side of the cabin are interconnected water tanks. These are used to transfer weight and thus move the center of gravity while in flight.

Part of the testing involves determining how the airplane flies with the center of gravity located farther forward or aft. Farther back in the fuselage there are large racks containing electronic test gear, including monitors, recorders, and displays.

A visible advantage of the 787 is its cargo bay. A hatch to this bay was open, and it was readily apparent that this airplane has a really deep belly with considerable cargo space.

Another rather interesting event while in Roswell was our encounter with an FAA flight test pilot while we were on our way to the terminal restaurant. This former Navy pilot was willing to talk about what the FAA does during the tests. He, for example, had been taking turns with Captain Carriker in the left seat. He said that the 787 handles easily and is indeed similar on the controls to the Boeing 777. He also gave us a glimpse into the quantity and variety of tests that Boeing is required to complete successfully in order to receive FAA certification. As an example, when testing for the ability to make successful aborted takeoffs, the takeoffs have to be performed at various speeds and weights. What this boils down to is a very large total number of tests that would require many, many pages just to list. This same gentleman also subtly indicated that the 787 was performing very well and that no problems had arisen to date.

An interesting aspect of the 787 design brought up by this FAA pilot was the way that designing with composites enables the designer to do things that would be impossible using metal. He pointed out that the top fuselage above the front of the airplane is manufactured with extra layers of material to make it stronger and more able to withstand the bending moment experienced in hard landings. In aluminum fabrication, the wall thicknesses are generally the same throughout.

• **September 20, 2010** A second problem was experienced September 10th during the testing of ZA001 in Roswell, New Mexico. While the aircraft was taxiing and some certification brake tests were being conducted, an engine surge was experienced. There was no damage to either the engine or the aircraft.

• **October 4, 2010** The sixth and final 787 test airplane (ZA006) made its initial flight October 3rd. This aircraft is the second powered by GE engines.

• **November 9, 2010** Test aircraft ZA002 suffered a fire in a power control panel while operating out of Laredo, Texas. The fire lasted less than 30 seconds, but primary electrical power was lost as a result. Backup systems automatically kicked in, including the ram air turbine. The airplane, which had 42 test personnel onboard, landed safely in Laredo after the incident. The pilots reported that positive control was maintained at all times. As a result of this incident, the entire test fleet was grounded.

• **November 25, 2010** It was revealed that the power panel on ZA002 that suffered the fire November 9th was the P100 panel, one of five major electrical panels on the 787. Because of this incident, minor design changes to the power distribution panels were developed and the system software was updated. The incident, while most unfortunate, demonstrated the general safety and redundancy of the 787 systems. In fact, the backup systems would have enabled the airplane to continue on to any airport that was suitable for landing from any point on a typical 787 mission profile.

• **November 15, 2010** The various recent incidents, such as the Rolls-Royce engine fire and the electrical panel fire, have prompted Boeing to indicate to its 787 customers that further delays in deliveries may be in the works. While flight testing is temporarily on hold, various ground tests are ongoing, including brake cooling tests, ground and steering handling tests, and other required tests. Boeing has indicated that a delay of two to three months in deliveries to ANA is possible. To date, there are 20 completed production 787-8 airplanes parked at Paine Field in Everett, Washington.

The eventual disposition of the six test aircraft had not been clarified at the time the flight testing was being conducted. The thought was expressed at that time to the author that these aircraft might be reconditioned and sold to airline customers. However, as of late December 2012, the word from Boeing was that the first three test aircraft (ZA001, ZA002, and ZA003) would not be reconditioned and sold because the cost of the refurbishing would outweigh the value of the aircraft. A further use for these three airplanes was still being studied. The other three airplanes (ZA004, ZA005, and ZA006) may be reconditioned and sold to airline customers.

CHAPTER 14

How Did It Happen?

During the life of the 787 program, Boeing has received a great deal of criticism for two unfortunate events that transpired: namely, the nearly three year delay in deliveries and the billions of dollars in overruns in development and start-up costs. While this writer agrees that Boeing did indeed make mistakes, it is worth digging a little deeper to find the causes of the two events in order to reach a better and more informed evaluation.

The Timetable

To begin with, Boeing set itself the fastest development timetable ever attempted for a new commercial jet transport, particularly in light of the advanced materials and production systems it introduced. Often overlooked, however, is the rather startling fact that from the official inception of the program in April 2004 to the end of the design phase, the original timetable *was* met. Furthermore, the designs produced were almost entirely validated in testing, which is a huge testament to Mike Bair, the project manager of the entire 787 team. So, we know the delays did not occur during that 26-month period.

The Global Production System

Outsourcing this project to the extent that Boeing did had two built-in risks. One was whether the various Tier 1 companies could produce their portion of the detailed designs correctly. A second risk entailed the ability to produce assemblies that met the required specifications. Problems arose in both areas. The result was that Boeing had to invest large amounts of capital and time to ensure valid results. Only then could the company be sure of acceptable quality.

It appears that at least some Tier 1 companies were so enthralled with the idea of the project that they neglected to consider both the amount of work involved and the level of capital investment required. In overlooking these two factors, it was preordained that the project would encounter significant delays. At least one company (Vought) eventually admitted that it had totally underestimated the amount of capital investment that would be required.

As reported in 2013 in the media, the main reason for the outsourcing was to lower the unit cost of the 787, and it was mandated from the very top of the Boeing management chain.

The Rollout Schedule and "Target Date Fixation"

If there was one area for which Boeing was truly culpable, it was in its total lack of flexibility in recognizing that the July 8, 2007 (7-8-7), rollout date was simply impossible to meet. The author believes that Boeing compounded the error by not leapfrogging the initial test aircraft (ZA001) and using the second or third airplane as the first airframe to fly. This truly made no sense and only added to the delays and frustrations experienced by everyone connected with the project, including the customer airlines. It also added a certain measure of confusion, with no one quite sure what was happening or why, and added to start-up costs. In retrospect, Boeing's top management would have done itself a huge favor if it had simply bitten the bullet and scrapped the 7-8-7 rollout date. Additionally, Boeing supposedly tied the rollout date and first deliveries to the 2012 China Olympics, a questionable decision at best.

Looking back at those decisions, the author wonders whether Boeing management, especially at the Chicago head office, was not afflicted with a serious case of "target date fixation," a malady that can badly damage any program.

Fastener Delays

The delays encountered in the fastener industry probably could not have been foreseen. Too many factors combined to create those delays. Ironically, the 787 uses considerably fewer fasteners than a similarly-sized aircraft, such as the 767. This particular delay of the 787 truly falls in the "act of God" category and Boeing cannot be faulted.

The Production Debacle

There seems little question that many of the Tier 1 suppliers were simply not prepared for the challenges of the 787 program. Specifically, many of the companies overlooked several necessary considerations. These were:

a. The requirement to complete detail designs according to specifications
b. The further obligation to oversee design work on the part of the Tier 2 subcontractors under them
c. Challenges related to dealing with such new materials as composites

d. The level of investment necessary to build and operate new, dedicated plants

All this conspired to cause delays, required Boeing to spend money to hire additional technical personnel and to dispatch them to Tier 1 companies all over the world, and finally, even to buy out some of the Tier 1 operations entirely.

Although it is difficult even in hindsight to determine what Boeing might have done to prevent delays and financial losses, an interesting point came out of a press interview with Mike Bair. Shortly after he was replaced as program manager, he made several highly illuminating comments to the media which were reported in the *Seattle Times*. He pointed out that the original expectations that Boeing had of its Tier 1 and Tier 2 partners had, in some cases, simply not been met. Companies that were to design as well as manufacture major assemblies had subcontracted the design work to others. This led, unavoidably, to a reduction in Boeing's level of control in monitoring the quality and progress of various portions of the program.

To his credit, what Bair did not mention was that first, the decision to outsource to such a large extent was likely made by top-level Boeing corporate management in Chicago, which probably meant that program managers such as Bair had little or no input in the decision. Second, Bair also did not mention that under his leadership the design of the 787, a challenging effort that encompassed much new technology, was completed not only on time, but in the shortest span of time ever for any brand-new jet transport.

Was the Business Plan at Fault?

The basic business plan Boeing embraced was by no means a totally new approach. Outsourcing had begun at Boeing years earlier. This time, however, it was increased dramatically. A possible weakness in the plan may have been that Boeing management never fully realized the extent of oversight that would be necessary over Tier 1 partners in order to ensure their work would be complete and on time. This related more to actual production than to design function. Beyond that was a further requirement for those Tier 1 partners to institute a greater level of oversight of Tier 2 companies. The writer believes that such an increased level of oversight would have not only spotted production problems earlier, but would also have set off alarms at Boeing that much sooner.

It is difficult to fault the business plan out of hand. Boeing had sound reasons for what it formulated and then implemented. The question is, however, whether it had accepted the promises of the Tier 1 companies too quickly. As protection against the possibility that those promises were not realistic, Boeing might have assigned more personnel to oversee the Tier 1 partners. One also has to wonder whether the specifications incorporated in the contracts failed to stipulate clearly and fully the responsibilities of these same companies.

Moreover, Boeing must have thought it would save money and be able to produce the 787 at a lower cost. Unfortunately, the outsourcing had two negative effects. First, it cost so much additional funding to start the production cycle that the first 787 to show a profit will be much further down the production list than originally planned. Second, the level of outsourcing caused a great deal of insecurity and hard feelings on the part of Boeing's unions.

To its credit, Boeing admitted that the delays were forthcoming and moved to limit them as much as possible. Customers of the 787 appeared to take the delays mostly in stride, as did investors and financial institutions.

A Lack of Communication

Looking back, it is fairly obvious that some Tier 1 companies were unwilling to reveal to Boeing the fact that they were falling behind in the execution of their contracts and duties. This may be particularly true for those companies that farmed out their design responsibilities, rather than carry them out in house. Another problem may have been that some of the companies did not have sufficient design or production capabilities and knowledge, and were suddenly faced with the need to educate themselves and their employees and to ramp up production quickly. Thus, rather than faulting the business plan, the writer sees the problem as being one of a lack of understanding of the realities of introducing and implementing such a plan by the Tier 1 companies.

A "Cultural Clash"

Another possible contributing factor to the 787's delays was that Boeing may have been too willing to accept the promises made by Tier 1 and 2 companies. As well, the business plan that envisioned a global community had the built-in challenge of monitoring many companies from various countries, some of which have considerably different cultures. As an example, the Japanese firms involved, which had landed important contracts, had always operated behind a veil of secrecy and confidentiality that made it much more difficult for Boeing to have advance warning of potential problems.

An example of this diversity of cultures occurred in either late 2005 or early 2006. Boeing had begun a program that brought technical personnel from the major Tier 1 companies to Everett in order to integrate design, tooling, and manufacturing processes between those companies and Boeing.

With Mitsubishi (MHI), the manufacturing of the wings was the object. Boeing recommended immediately building full-scale test tools to check the design validity of the wing spars. MHI's people said they saw no need for any of that. Boeing convinced them of the usefulness of such a move and MHI agreed. Boeing built the initial test tools, which, in turn, revealed flaws in the spar manufacturing. MHI followed up with their own testing system that eventually corrected all the manufacturing problems. Still, notwithstanding this successful result, it was obvious early on that these cultural differences could, and in fact did contribute to production problems and delays.

A New Hand at the Helm

The announcement of Mike Bair's replacement set off several events in October 2007. Bair, as the Vice-President and Project Manager who had ably directed the 787 program from its inception, was given a sideways transfer to a strategic planning position in commercial airplane sales. This move was interpreted in some circles as a slap on the wrist over Bair's management style. Bair was universally viewed by 787 employees as being a fair and approachable executive. He was not just well liked, but also highly respected. His replacement was Vice-President Pat Shanahan, who moved over from Boeing's military programs and had the reputation of being a hard-nosed driver.

In retrospect, one has to wonder whether any other manager at Boeing could have possibly done a better job than Bair of staying on schedule, considering the basic difficulties caused by the extent of outsourcing.

Some Tier 1 Companies Fail the Test

Certain events that took place in 2008 and 2009 bear directly on the question of whether Tier 1 companies that contracted with Boeing really understood the full dimensions of the contracts they were signing. Witness the following:

- In 2008, Boeing buys Vought's 50 percent share of the Global Aeronautica integration plant in North Charleston, South Carolina.
- In July 2009, Boeing buys Vought's assembly plant adjacent to Global Aeronautica in North Charleston, South Carolina.
- In October 2009, Boeing commits to building a large manufacturing facility adjacent to both the former Vought plant and to Global Aeronautica.
- In December 2009, Boeing buys Alenia's 50 percent share in Global Aeronautica, thus becoming its sole owner.

Thus, over a period of a little more than a year, Boeing took over two large Tier 1 facilities in South Carolina, as well as initiating the construction of a second assembly line for the 787. The result of all this was the removal of both Vought and Alenia as major assemblers of the 787. Given these rather expensive moves, was Boeing's top management in the process of rethinking its strategy *vis-à-vis* the entire approach to the Global Collaborative Environment? Further, did these moves reflect the thinking verbalized by former General Manager Mike Bair shortly after his removal from the 787 program, that in the future, Boeing might have to reduce its dependence on foreign manufacturing and return some of the work to the United States? This certainly appears to be the case.

Interestingly enough, in July 2010 Mitsubishi, which had the contract for producing the 787's wings, expressed its ambition to garner yet larger portions of such projects as the 787. The two streams of thinking—namely, Boeing rethinking its outsourcing strategy and MHI's expressed ambition to do more major subcontracting—appear to be at odds, and only the future will reveal which philosophy prevails.

Effects Downstream

Several effects can be deduced from all these delays that Boeing faced:

- A few orders were cancelled.
- Boeing received additional 767 and 777 orders to act as stopgaps while awaiting 787 deliveries.
- It was reported that Boeing reduced the prices on early production deliveries in order to pacify airlines that were negatively affected by the delayed deliveries.
- Boeing had to invest additional funds in order to overcome production difficulties. The actual

figure will probably never be released, but it was certainly in the billions.

- Because of the world economic downturn, some airlines were in fact relieved to be able to postpone deliveries.
- The final outcome of the sales battle between the Boeing 787 and the Airbus 350XWB will not be known for 10 to 15 years, but the initial sales of the 787 of over 1,000 airplanes by the end of 2012 could prove to be an insurmountable lead for Airbus.

Conclusion

In the months to come, there will undoubtedly be a great deal of speculation as to what led up to the long delay on the 787 program and what Boeing might have done to prevent delays or to mitigate their length. Here are a few additional thoughts by the author.

The major causes appear to fall into two categories. One is the delay in the delivery of fasteners, a critical item. It does not appear that Boeing could really have done very much, if anything, to change the outcome of this particular situation. There were too many factors within the fastener industry for it not to have affected Boeing. However, the question does arise as to whether Boeing took the delay seriously and whether it factored it into its total schedule. This brings up three major issues.

Boeing should have had an inkling that the global supply chain was having initial difficulties. At that point, it should have revised its entire schedule, including the first rollout. It appears that the 7-8-07 rollout date, a date arrived at strictly for

marketing reasons, was forced on the project by top-level management. This was a mistake. Having initial supply problems with a totally different and very sophisticated aircraft design using a new supply concept, a further delay should not have caused any embarrassment to Boeing, considering the complexity of what was being attempted.

Beyond that, insisting that the number 1 aircraft be built to be used for a first flight was probably also an error. The second and third airplanes delivered were in far better condition and much closer to being totally stuffed by the Tier 1 partners.

Boeing's overriding concern over the Airbus A380 and A350 may have been a contributing factor. Yet, by early 2007, the A380 was already showing very long production delays, and the A350 program seemed to be having difficulty in determining a final configuration. Combine that information with the ever-increasing order total for the 787, and it would seem that Boeing could have easily declared a six- to nine-month delay in early 2007 without suffering any serious consequences. When it refused to recognize reality, it only compounded its own problems.

In retrospect, it is fair to say that Boeing probably should have been more prepared for some of the problems that arose. It did, however, manage to recover, and worked resolutely at resolving the problems encountered. Luckily for Boeing, the delays and other problems do not seem to have materially damaged the future of the 787 program.

CHAPTER 15

First Deliveries – The 787 in Airline Service

Finally, the day arrived when Boeing was ready to deliver its first brand-spanking new 787 Dreamliner. However, delivering a $200 million wide-body jet transport is a bit more complicated than, say, delivering a new car. Before a delivery, a rather elaborate and rigid procedure takes place. It is worthwhile to take a look at this process, which is a reflection of the care Boeing takes with its products.

The Delivery Process

Listed below are the various steps that Boeing follows before actually turning a new airplane over to a customer:

1. The 787 is towed to the Everett Delivery Center at Paine Field, located adjacent to the factory, where the airplane is assembled.

2. The airplane then enters what is known as Phase 1, which lasts approximately seven days. During this phase there are fuel tests, engine run-ups, airworthiness inspections, avionics tests, preflight servicing, taxi tests, and a standard production test flight identified as B1. This test flight is required on each and every aircraft that Boeing delivers. As part of the aircraft systems testing, these systems, including the power plants, are checked as if the aircraft was in actual flight. These tests, called gauntlet tests, are based on test scenarios for both standard flights and flights with single and multiple engine failures. Any problems that are identified, known in the trade as "squawks," are documented and resolved.

3. On Day 8, Phase 2 begins. The green protective paint which was originally applied is removed. The exterior is sanded, cleaned, taped, and primed. Then, the airplane is painted in the airline customer's own unique paint scheme.

4. Now the 787 enters Phase 3, the Final Delivery Phase, which begins on Day 11. Any squawks still remaining are corrected. Pre-delivery flight checks are conducted. A second Boeing test flight may be flown if it is considered necessary. Then, the FAA airworthiness certificate is issued, without which the airplane cannot be flown in revenue service. At this point, the customer airline's flight crew conducts a walk-through of the airplane and then carries out its own test flight.

5. After the customer indicates it is ready to accept the airplane, a final quality assurance inspection is carried out.

6. Now the customer, in this case its flight crew, hands over a check or a wire transfer covering the total cost of the airplane. At this time, the customer receives all of the remaining documentation, manuals, etc. Then, finally, the customer's flight crew can climb aboard and fly the brand-new 787 to its new home.

The first Dreamliner to be delivered to Japan Air Lines departs Paine Field, Everett, Washington, March 26, 2012.

One interesting aspect of the activities that lead up to delivery concerns the engines, which constitute the biggest single expense on a new airplane. Both Boeing and the customer airline prefer to receive and install the engines at the last possible moment, thus deferring the very large payment due to the engine manufacturer. That is why the engines for a particular Dreamliner are delivered by air just prior to the installation date.

Thus, the reader can see how this delivery process is quite long and very exacting. Normally this process takes 17 to 19 days from beginning to end, but can actually run as long as 30 days, depending on any problems encountered along the way.

Eventually, on Monday, September 26, 2011, Boeing held a ceremony at Paine Field, Everett, Washington, to mark the contractual delivery of the very first 787-8 Dreamliner to a customer. In this ceremony, which included both Boeing Airplane Company and All Nippon Airways executives, the airplane was formally turned over to ANA ready for delivery and its ferry flight to Japan. Among the executives attending were Boeing Chairman, President, and CEO Jim McNerney; Boeing Commercial Airplane President and CEO Jim Albaug; and the 787 program Vice-President and General Manager, Scott Fancher. Representing ANA was its President and CEO Shimchiro Ito. More than 500 Boeing employees, attended as well as thousands of interested individuals.

The contractual transfer of the first airplane to ANA was actually completed the day before on Sunday, September 25th. September 27th, the day after the ceremony, a ANA crew flew the airplane (Boeing number ZA 101) from Everett to Tokyo, arriving there September 28th. The 5,037 mile flight required 9 hours and 47 minutes for an average speed of approximately 517 nautical miles per hour. The flight departed Everett at 7:16 a.m. and arrived in Tokyo at 5:03 p.m. (all times Pacific time).

The First Revenue Flight

October 27, 2011, All Nippon Airways, the original 787 launch customer, was finally able to operate the very first 787 revenue flight, some seven and a half years after it ordered the airplane. This first flight was a relatively short charter flight from Tokyo, Japan, to Hong Kong, China, and took only 4 hours 10 minutes. Passenger reaction was very favorable, although the true test would not take place until the Dreamliner entered service on routes where much longer flights of 12-14 hours could occur. These are the types of services the 787 was specifically designed for.

Early Services

In November 2011, ANA began using its first two Dreamliners on local services within Japan. November 6, a domestic flight carrying 249 passengers from Tokyo Haneda to Okayama, in western Japan, experienced an in-flight problem. Approaching Okayama, the crew attempted to lower the landing gear, but got a warning signal from a monitor indicating the mail gear was not fully deployed. A backup system was then used to lower the gear and the 787 landed safely only a few minutes late. An inspection revealed the failure of a hydraulic valve. This was the first in-flight problem encountered by the Dreamliner while in revenue service.

Engine Improvements and Other Events

Throughout the gestation period of the 787, Boeing had been trying to obtain improved fuel burn from both Rolls-Royce and GE. The original versions of both engines were showing a fuel burn that was 3-5% below the performance specifications. Japan Air Lines (JAL), which had originally expected to receive its first Dreamliner in November 2011, got its first two aircraft in March 2012 powered by an improved version of the GE engines with a better fuel burn. Both engine manufacturers were continuing to make changes to their respective power plants and were achieving improved fuel burn and greater thrust. This type of gradual improvement is expected to extend for a considerable amount of time.

The deliveries to JAL were preceded by the FAA certification of the GE-powered 787. This version of the engine is already an improved version over the original prototype.

In March 2012, it was also announced that the 787 Dreamliner had been awarded the coveted Collier Trophy for 2011, the aerospace industry's most prestigious award.

During March 2012, more news were revealed that may have an impact on the future of the 787. The World Trade Organization (WTO) declared that Boeing had, over a period of four decades, received $5 billion in subsidies, which in turn had damaged its rival, Airbus, and further, was prohibited under international trade rules. However, this amount was far less than the $18 billion that the U.S. alleged that Airbus had received over the same period. The subsidies that Boeing has been charged with receiving were for the most part for programs other than commercial aircraft. Precisely how this entire controversy will be resolved, if at all, is anyone's guess as of the date of this publication.

Also during March, a news release by Steven Udvar-Hazy, CEO of Air lease Corp. and possibly the most influential man in commercial aviation, made for some rather earth-shaking news. First Udvar-Hazy declared that Boeing will do very well in the commercial airplane business over the next 25-30 years. But he tempered this piece of optimistic foresight by saying that he believes that Boeing will need to equip the 787-8 model with more powerful engines, due to the fact that its current weight is greater than originally specified. He also said he sees the 787-9 as a better aircraft than the -8 and the proposed -10 as the best of the three.

Then he exploded a small verbal bomb by saying that he sees the financial break-even point of the 787 occurring with almost twice as many airplanes sold as what Boeing has been indicating. It is likely that the actual break-even point of sales for the 787 will not be known for a number of years. For one thing, it is not unreasonable to predict that in the next three to five years, Boeing may be able to reduce the cost of the 787 through more efficient production management, as well as reducing the cost of outsourced assemblies. Nevertheless, this last piece of news from Udvar-Hazy must have sent uncomfortable vibrations through the upper ranks of Boeing's management.

In the meantime, one of the main premises on which the 787 design and parameters were originally based appears to be coming true. Both ANA and JAL, the first two carriers to put the Dreamliner into service, are initiating services that fall into the category of "long thin routes." ANA will start Tokyo-San Jose, California, service and JAL Tokyo-San Diego service. Both these U.S destinations have airports with runways too short to safely accommodate larger aircraft, such as the Boeing 777. Additionally, neither city is likely to be able to generate passenger loads that would justify the larger aircraft. The reader should also note how the aircraft that the 787 replaced, the highly successful 767, does not have the range to serve long trans-Pacific routes, as well as other routes that will be initiated, such as Tokyo-Berlin.

In April 2012, Boeing revealed that the second model of the Dreamliner, the 787-9, will have laminar flow horizontal and vertical stabilizers. The laminar flow concept is not new, but has seldom been incorporated in a large jet aircraft. At present, the concept is not being introduced in the wings. The system is passive and works off pressure gradients created by the speed of the aircraft to generate suction. Boeing believes that the application of laminar flow will further reduce fuel consumption. First flight of the -9 model is scheduled for Summer 2013 in Charleston, South Carolina, where it is being built.

As of April 2012, Boeing had seen the last of the 787-8 aircraft that had to go through "change incorporation" work at Everett. Not only did this mean quicker deliveries, but it also reduced the unit costs of future Dreamliners. The early ones were estimated by Wall Street to cost Boeing as much as $300 million each, but are now in the $190-200 million range, and the cost is estimated to be dropping around $10,000 each month.

May 2013 saw the 787 rate of production increase to seven per month, with the eventual goal ten per month. May 23, 2012, the first 787-8 airframe to be fabricated at the North Charleston, SC, plant had its initial flight, which constituted another milestone for Boeing. This 787-8 was the 46th to be built overall and is the first airplane for Air India. The Charleston plant is said to be on schedule to gradually increase production from the current rate to three three airplanes per month.

Passenger Reaction

Due to the small number of 787 deliveries to date (mid-2013), reaction from either carriers or passengers has been minimal. But in late June 2012, ANA released the results of a survey taken between March 22 and April 21, 2012. The survey was of 740 passengers who flew ANA 787s on the Tokyo-Frankfurt non-stop route. The results, as shown below, were highly encouraging. Furthermore, surveying passengers from such a long-haul flight was far more applicable than choosing passengers on some of the short-haul 787 flights that ANA operates, because the real benefits to Dreamliner passengers can only be identified on long-haul flights. Here are some of the results of the survey:

• 98% said they would like to fly on the Dreamliner again, while 25% said they would go out of their way to fly on it.

- 90% said their flight experience on the 787 met or exceeded expectations and expressed a strong preference for flying the Dreamliner.
- Over 80% said the higher cabin humidity, air quality, and cabin pressure met or exceeded expectations.
- 40% said the bigger windows exceeded expectations and an additional 50% were happy with the increased size.
- In other areas, such as headroom, personal space, window dimming, cabin lighting, cabin noise levels, lavatories, and smoothness of flight, passenger satisfaction ranged from 60% to 90%.

In general, frequent fliers were more likely to recognize and appreciate the unique and advanced features of the Dreamliner.

ANA also reported that fuel efficiency during the first six months of 787operation was 21%, higher than the 20% originally promised by Boeing.

This writer was recently able to obtain some additional input concerning the reaction of both flight crews and passengers to the 787. While staying at a hotel near Chicago O'Hare International Airport, I realized that Lot Polish Airlines crews stayed there, also. On two occasions while at breakfast, I queried them about their and the passengers' reactions. Both crews were extremely satisfied with the aircraft and indicated that passengers were also very satisfied. It is this writer's opinion, based in part on remembering initial problems with other new aircraft, that the Dreamliner will overcome any initial difficulties and go on to fulfill its promise.

2011-2013 Deliveries

In the period from September 2011 through December 2013, Boeing was able to deliver a total of 100 Dreamliners to different airlines. Seventeen of these went to All Nippon Airways, which, after all, had been the launch customer for the entire 787 program. Overall passengers, crews, and the airlines seemed very satisfied with the new airplane. While the monthly production was still low, it was gradually increasing. These deliveries were also important from a financial point of view, since it finally began putting money back into Boeing's coffers.

New Members of the Family and Additional Orders

In January 2013, American Airlines was finally able to consummate its original intent issued in October 2008 to purchase Dreamliners. The firm order was for 42 Dreamliners, with options for 58 more. It is not clearly defined which models American is ordering, but initial deliveries are to begin in November 2014. The order is worth $8.7 billion at current list prices.

The first outgrowth of the original 787-8 design, the -9 model, is to have its first flight in mid-2013 and its first delivery in 2014. The -9 is 20 feet longer than the -8 and the maximum gross take-off weight is increased by 55,000lbs over the -8. The additional fuselage length is achieved by adding two five-frame sections, one section each forward and one behind the wing. The maximum range of the -9 will be 8,500nm, or 300nm more than the -8. Seating capacity was increased to 250-290 passengers, or

50 more than the -8. The Everett, WA, facility will be assembling the -9 model in addition to the -8.

By 2012, Boeing was looking hard at a 787-10X model, a double-stretch version of the -8.

The 787-10 is 18 feet longer than the -9 model, and the extension is created by five frames forward and four frames aft of the wing. The net result is seating for 43 additional passengers in a three-class configuration. Overall, the -10 will carry 300-350 passengers and will have a maximum range of 6,500-6,750nm. Its maximum gross take-off weight is expected to be nearly 8,000lbs more than the -9. As in the other 787 models, power plants will be either the GE or RollsRoyce engines rated at 78,000lbs thrust. Based on the initial design specifications, Boeing believes that the -10 is 25% more efficient than airplanes of its size today and 10% more efficient than any aircraft currently being offered for future delivery. Boeing characterizes this model as being extremely efficient with a very low seat-mile cost. This would make for a very attractive airplane for the airlines. This view seems to be borne out by the fact that numerous potential customers have been pressuring Boeing for some time to introduce such a model. Unlike the -9 model, the -10 will require a considerable amount of redesign. One of the motivations for the -10 is Boeing's wish to outsell the Airbus A350 in all of its variants.

In mid-June 2013, Boeing formally announced the launch of the third member of the 787 family, the 787-10. Previously, the Boeing Board of Directors had given the company permission to begin offering the model to airlines. The launch was the result of a number of orders:

- Air Lease Corp. – 30
- GE Capital Aviation Services – 10
- International Airlines Group (IAG)/British Airways – 12
- Singapore Airlines – 30
- United Airlines – 20

These five orders total 102 787-10 airplanes. Boeing has scheduled final assembly and first flight test of the -10 for 2017, with first deliveries to begin 2018. The news was released at the 2013 Paris Air Show, where two 787-8 airplanes were flown in to be exhibited.

June 2013 saw the delivery of the first of 74 Dreamliners to International Lease Financial Corporation (ILFC), the largest single customer for the 787. This first delivery is actually for Norwegian, who is leasing the airplane. June also saw the first delivery of a Dreamliner to British Airways, the first of 24 on order. Additionally, British Airways will be leasing another 18 787s from the leasing firm IAG. In July, the first 787-8 was delivered to Hainan Airlines of China, the first of ten.

Some Other Events

April 2013 saw an event related to the 787 program which is a sign of the growing maturity of the program. April 3rd, Boeing opened its new and larger Everett Delivery Center (EDC). With 180,000 square feet of space, the new EDC has three times the area of the former site and will handle all wide-body delivery functions.

Also in April, Boeing's Flight Services unit began shifting two 787 flight simulators from the Seattle area to Miami International Airport. There, Flight Services is creating a new training site for flight crews of carriers from Europe and South America. Boeing also has flight crew training centers in London, Shangai, and Singapore. The Miami training center will expand to handle all Boeing commercial aircraft types by year's end of 2013. A 787 Full Flight Simulator costs around $20 million. The Flight Services unit has some 104 training pilots who split their time between training crews of airlines and delivering new aircraft to customers.

In June 2013, another event showed the continuing maturity of the 787 program, when the FAA approved the use of Required Navigation Performance - Authorization Required (RNP AR) for the 787 fleet. Using RNP AR operators can reduce fuel usage and fly precisely on prescribed routes using sophisticated on-board and satellite-based navigation systems.

Conclusion

With Dreamliners coming off the assembly lines from both the Everett and North Charleston plants, and with the monthly production rate steadily approaching the goal of ten per month, the 787 program is at last showing its true potential.

Chapter 16
Last Minute Problems

In January 2013, bad luck unexpectedly struck the 787 program, when two separate incidents marred the ongoing deliveries and service introduction of the Dreamliner. On Monday, January 8, 2013, a Japan Air Lines 787 on the ground at Boston Logan Airport had to disembark passengers and crew when smoke was smelled. Then, on Thursday, January 16th, an ANA Dreamliner was diverted to Takamatsu, Japan, when again smoke was smelled. All passengers and crew were evacuated without problem via the escape slides. In both cases, the problem was quickly traced to the two lithium-ion batteries on board, both manufactured by GS Yuasa of Japan.

The same day, the FAA grounded all fifty previously delivered 787s and prevented any further flying by any Dreamliner until the exact cause of the problem could be identified and solved. This move by the FAA surprised many and some in the aviation community considered it premature. In fact, it had been decades since an entire fleet of airplanes had been grounded by the FAA.

Meanwhile, Dreamliners continued to be completed, but could not fly. As a result, more and more 787s collected on the ramps at Paine Field.

Lithium-ion batteries have been known to be the cause of fires before on a number of aircraft. These batteries are made up of a stack of tightly-packed cells, with each cell having a layer of lithium separated from an oxidizer by a thin layer of ion-conductive polymer. Lithium-ion batteries are known for their outstanding performance. However, since lithium melts at 357 degrees Farenheit, as opposed to nickel batteries that melt at 2,800 degrees Farenheit, if the battery overheats for whatever reason, a fire will occur much more quickly. All of this was known to both Boeing and the FAA, and originally the latter evidently felt that the current design was safe.

After the compulsory grounding, Boeing and GS Yuasa put their heads together to determine both the cause of the problem and its solution. They immediately began a concerted effort to try and develop a fix for this overheating problem. The first issue was whether the higher temperatures were actually caused by the batteries themselves or by the electrical system. It was finally determined that the batteries themselves were most likely to have caused the overheating. Shortly after the grounding, Boeing convened a large group of engineers to determine the cause of the problem and design a fix. The exact cause appears to still be in question, but the team rather quickly developed a multi-layer fix.

Boeing was extremely proactive in developing a solution to its battery problem. It used both its own engineering resources and outside consultants to arrive at the final design changes. In the process, more than 100,000 man-hours were spent developing test plans, building test rigs, conducting tests, and analyzing test results.

The solution that Boeing and GS Yuasa arrived at was composed of a number of parts. First, the battery itself was redesigned. Insulating spacers made of phenolic-glass-laminate replaced the former spacers. These spacers are able to withstand temperatures more than three times as high as the former spacers. These were placed on either side of each cell. This resulted in each cell being better insulated from an adjacent cell. Second, more insulation was introduced on all sides of the battery. The wire harnesses that connected the individual cells to a Battery Monitoring Unit (BMU) were housed in heat and chafe-resistant sleeving, thus removing a potential source of short circuit. In addition, the voltage range of the BMU was reduced so as to prevent the possibility of voltage surges creating heat and possibly fires. Titanium vent tubes were installed that lead from each battery to drain moisture, heat, and, if it ever occurred, smoke outside the airframe. Finally, a 1/8" thick stainless steel sealed enclosure was designed which prevents any heat and smoke from escaping the battery, and more importantly, prevents oxygen from entering the battery, thus preventing any fires. But it should be understood that overall, the basic solution was containment, rather than actual removal of any potential problems, the reason being that no one had actually been able to discover the true reason for the overheating of the batteries.

February 9, 2013, Boeing, using one of the original test aircraft (ZA005), flew a 2 hour 19 minute test flight of the new battery configuration. Special test equipment installed for the test sampled battery readings 500,000 times per second. The flight was considered a success. Then, on February 11th, ZA005 flew an additional 1 hour 29 minute flight which again was successful. Documentation of the redesign and the test flights was collected and forwarded to the FAA. Boeing also carried out laboratory testing to validate the various changes in the battery design. Chief among these was the new enclosure, which was shown to totally eliminate any chance of smoke and heat escaping if battery overheating occurred.

March saw more flight testing of the new batteries as part of other test flights. April 19th, the FAA gave formal approval to the design changes for preventing thermal runaways. It is interesting to note that before formal FAA approval, Boeing had already given GS Yuasa in Japan authorization to begin manufacture of the redesigned batteries. At this time, a team of 300 engineers began the process of putting the 50 grounded 787s back into service: Ethiopian Airlines restarted service April 27th, Qatar Airways May 2nd, United Airlines May 20th, ANA June 1st, and LOT Polish Airlines June 5th.

The media coverage of these events was unfortunate. In the prior months, little had been written or said about the very successful entry into service and the initial services of the Dreamliner. But once this electrical problem came to light, the media went into a feeding frenzy which was simply not justified. Looking at this problem in the context of other new commercial aircraft first entering service, it becomes obvious that initial problems are quite common. Many times in the past, such problems were much more serious than what the 787 program faced. Unfortunately, this occurrence cost Boeing money and tainted an otherwise highly successful entry into service for the Dreamliner.

In mid-May 2013, Boeing was able to resume regular deliveries of 787-8 airplanes, with ANA receiving its 18th Dreamliner. Other carriers were also receiving 787-8 Dreamliners coming off the assembly lines.

July 12, 2013, an Ethiopian Airlines 787-8 experienced a transmitter fire while on the ground at London's Heathrow Airport. The transmitter in question was an Emergency Locator Transmitter (ELT) located near the tail. Once again, it turns out that the ELT, of which there are two, is powered by a lithium-ion battery, and once again, there is a question as to whether the fire originated within the battery or was caused by some so far undiscovered unknown electric overload. The fuselage crown near the tail section was badly burned, but observers pointed out that the composite fuselage was far more resistant to excessive heat than an aluminum one would have been.

Simultaneously with the battery, other lesser problems were also discovered. Electrical system power panels have had a string of failures and Boeing has been working with the manufacturer to resolve the issue. A somewhat more serious problem relates to the Auxiliary Power Unit (APU) manufactured by Pratt & Whitney. It was discovered that after landing, when the APU is shut down and the inlet door is closed heat builds up in the tail compartment. After 20 minutes on the ground, the heat causes the rotor shaft to bow and it takes up to two hours before the shaft straightens out again. If the APU is not restarted in short order, damage to the turbine can occur. An interim solution has been to change the operating procedure so that the inlet door is kept open and heat is allowed to dissipate. A long-term fix is being worked on.

Conclusion

These early problems that affected the 787 program were, to be sure, of a serious nature. But taken within the context of a new airplane full of innovations and compared with the problems of other start-up aircraft, they tend to shrink considerably. In fact, both Japanese operators of the 787 (ANA and JAL) reported that after their Dreamliners went back into regular service, the customer demand for seats showed no reduction, except for the normal month-to-month fluctuations.

CHAPTER 17
The Future of the Dreamliner

The Dreamliner's career as a premier commercial jet transport is in its infancy as of this publication, and the future is always hard to foresee clearly, if at all. Nevertheless, there are some indices which can only be interpreted as being very positive signs for the future. Total 787 sales as of this publication stand at 931 orders, by far the largest backlog of orders ever accumulated by a jet transport so early in its life. The Airbus A380, while not a direct competitor, has orders for 259 aircraft, a sign that very possibly Boeing's marketing people had a better grasp of the future than those of Airbus. The real competitor is the Airbus A350, which has accumulated 814 orders to date. Some of the A350 sales may be due to the long delays that new customers must accept to receive deliveries of the Dreamliner. There are also questions yet to be answered as to whether the A350 will encounter any problems during flight testing, as well as whether Airbus will be able to produce the airplane at the desired rate.

Another indication of the success of the 787 can be found in some recent remarks made by Steven Udvar-Hazy, Chairman and CEO of Air Lease Corp, a big 787 customer. Udvar-Hazy, a man that the aviation industry listens to carefully, had made some interesting comments during the 787's long gestation period, indicating that he thought Boeing might have to wait a long time to reach the break-even point in sales because of its production problems. But at the 2013 Paris Air Show, Udvar-Hazy said that he believed that the latest addition to the 787 family (the 787-10) would be such an economical aircraft to operate that it would greatly enhance the future of the entire Dreamliner family. Coming from a man who is known for having a very realistic outlook on the future, this was high praise indeed.

Another sales area for the 787 lies with a number of the major world airlines. Because of the 2008 world-wide economic recession, many of these airlines postponed any major aircraft purchases. In many cases, their wide-body jet fleets are due for replacement. For that reason, the next 12-18 months could see Boeing receiving some large additional orders for one or more of the 787 models.

Also promising have been the generally enthusiastic reactions of both executives and passengers of those carriers that have already placed Dreamliners in service; this in spite of some of the recent start-up problems that the 787 fleet has experienced.

One problem that Boeing will have to continue to address is the ability of the supply line to perform at the level demanded by the market and to do so while meeting the necessary quality standards. Boeing appears to be totally aware of this challenge, and in fact, has moved to bring some of the outsourcing back into the U.S.

Another challenge for Boeing relates to the need for capital financing. One has to keep in mind that in the next few years, the company will be simultaneously developing the 737 MAX, 777X, and the 787-10. All of this design and development, together with such associated functions as product and flight testing, will likely stretch the resources of the company to a large extent.

Given Boeing's long track record of success, it seems reasonable to predict that the 787 Dreamliner family will at the very least take its place as one of Boeing's very successful jet transports, and twenty years from now may even find it as the reigning product of all its wide-body transport designs.

A Look Back

Looking back at the history of the Dreamliner to date, it is striking to see both the great achievements and the infrequent, but nevertheless painful, errors. Initially, under the very capable leadership of Mike Bair, the design and development team achieved a truly memorable advance in jet transport design, doing so within the set timetable and cost parameters. The real problems arose from the upper level management decision to outsource production to the extent that Boeing did so. In theory, it was a reasonable business decision, but it was not accompanied by the sufficient oversight necessary

to protect the company from the start-up problems that ensued. Then Boeing compounded the problem by refusing to face reality and forcing the manufacturing completion of the initial aircraft, ZA 001, instead of leap-frogging to a later aircraft. This alone caused a very long delay that could have been avoided.

As far as the problems encountered to date during initial revenue service, this author considers them to be far less serious than the problems encountered by passenger aircraft, both reciprocating and jet, in the past.

Conclusion

Barring totally unforeseen future problems occurring with either the 787 program or with the world economy and the many airlines, the future of the Dreamliner seems to shine truly bright. The outlook is for a family of passenger aircraft that will remain in production for decades, providing large financial returns for Boeing, profits for the airlines operating them, and many trouble-free hours of comfortable flying for the passengers flying in them.

APPENDIX I

Chronology of 787 Dreamliner Problems

Part A

- **October 30, 2006** Boeing's chief executive officer, James McNerney, releases a statement promising that the 787 program will not face the same delays as did the Airbus A380. In an effort to back up this promise, Boeing commits more funds and personnel to the program, especially engineers and technicians to assist Tier 1 partners.
- **November 2006** Boeing reveals that the current weight of the 787-8 appears to be 5,000 pounds over its 340,000-pound maximum zero-fuel design weight.
- **January 16, 2007** A Boeing *Dreamlifter* delivers the first assemblies for the 787.
- **March 20, 2007** Vought makes progress on the fuselage production units for the 787.
- **May 8, 2007** Vought completes and delivers the first aft fuselage for the 787.
- **May 14, 2007** The first wing box is shipped by Mitsubishi Heavy Industries.
- **May 15, 2007** Global Aeronautica delivers the first assembled mid-fuselage.
- **June 25, 2007** The fastener shortage is first revealed. Boeing also indicates major assemblies for number 1 airplane arrived in Everett not fully completed, resulting in workarounds.
- **July 7, 2007** Number 1 airplane is rolled out for static display on the date promised, but with non-aerospace fasteners and an empty fuselage.
- **July 16, 2007** Boeing indicates that in spite of initial delays, it has taken steps to maintain delivery commitments to airlines. One way it is accomplishing this is by pre-certifying much of the airplane. This includes demonstrating compliance with a hundred areas of specific concern detailed by the FAA. Boeing hopes to achieve type certification three months faster than it did with the 777-200 in 1995.
- **July 30, 2007** Boeing announces it will invest $300 million in additional funding for research and development (R&D) work on the 787. This amount constitutes a nine percent increase in the R&D budget. To date, R&D spending has been increased by $1.4 billion. The first flight is still scheduled for late September 2007.
- **August 10, 2007** Boeing said its date for first the flight might slip because of delays in final assembly, avionics integration, and completion of software, hydraulic, electronic, and other systems.
- **August 20, 2007** Boeing admits that it is facing a very tight schedule and indicates that its three major challenges are (1) software and system integration, (2) structural testing, and (3) *travel work*. This latter term refers to work that should have been completed by Tier 1 companies. When it wasn't, Boeing had to scramble to complete this work in house.
- **September 5, 2007** A three-month delay in first flight is announced, and is said to have been caused by fastener and rivet shortages and incomplete software.

- **September 6, 2007** Boeing management has been hearing, much to its surprise, that its paperless VELOCITY system, which tracks the assembly process, is less efficient than its older system. Engineers maintain that the system is in fact causing them more work and slowing the assembly process at a time when Boeing can ill afford it.
- **September 10, 2007** Boeing's top management maintains that the three-month delay will not harm future shipments and that no further delays will occur. Further, Boeing is planning on a greatly compressed flight test program so as to not lose more time.
- **October 1, 2007** Alenia Aeronautica of Italy reveals that it is planning to increase production rates of its barrel sections to ten a month. To that end, the company is spending an additional $707 million to upgrade its facilities.
- **October 10, 2007** Boeing executives indicate that deliveries to its first fifteen customers will be delayed and admits the first flight will be six months late. They also indicate that production rates will reach the original schedule by aircraft number 28.
- **October 11, 2007** Boeing admits that the 787 delays are longer than anticipated and the first flight is now set for March 2008. This is the third consecutive delay announced by Boeing. The company also indicates that no managerial changes are contemplated as a result of the delay.
- **October 17, 2007** Boeing replaces Mike Bair as 787 program manager with Pat Shanahan, formerly Vice President and General Manager of Boeing Missile Defense Systems.
- **October 24, 2007** Boeing management is uncertain of the date of the first flight for the number 1 airplane.

- **November 5, 2007** Boeing managers admit to being surprised that Tier 1 companies had subcontracted design work. This disclosure may cause Boeing to structure future outsourcing differently, giving contractors less authority. In a related item, former 787 Program Manager Mike Bair, in comments made before local area business and political leaders, comments that Boeing's experience with the 787 program outsourcing may result in a changed future business plan. Bair also mentioned that the basic problem with the first airplane was that instead of the plant dealing with 1,200 parts, it had to try to deal with 30,000, which caused the system to be totally overwhelmed.
- **November 10, 2007** The chief executive officer of Vought, a Tier 1 company, acknowledges that the company performed poorly in its logistics, but that things were looking up.
- **November 19, 2007** Shanahan shores up 787 production by assigning four vice-presidents to various manufacturing and logistical positions in an effort to improve the production schedule of the 787.
- **December 17, 2007** In a new twist, it has been shown that the delays to the 787 program have also delayed the retirement of older 767s that the 787 is designed to replace. This in turn has caused a further ripple effect, since those older 767s would have been converted for the growing airfreight market.
- **December 17, 2007** Shanahan, 787 program manager, announces that "power on" should occur in January 2008 and first flight by the end of March. He also indicates that the design of the 787 is now 100 percent complete and that the aircraft is overweight but gives no specifics.

Shanahan realigns the duties of many of the program's managers, changes some of their duties, and in general instills a sense of urgency in the entire program. He also reveals at this time:
- Alenia took the horizontal stabilizer to design limit loads.
- The first flight test aircraft has already had 91% of its hardware qualified.
- The second flight test airplane is due to have assemblies arrive at Everett in November.
- Tier 1 companies are working on airplane number 7, the first due for delivery to All Nippon Airlines.
- Boeing test pilots are training in the simulator.
- **January 7, 2008** Photos just released of Boeing's 787 assembly line show three airplanes under construction. They also show a large number of support structures and assembly workers swarming over the airplanes, a clear indication these early deliveries had a great deal of travel work.
- **January 10, 2008** In response to questions from large financial concerns, Boeing neither confirms nor denies whether January would in fact see "power on" of the number 1 airplane.
- **January 14, 2008** Delivery of assemblies for airplane number 4, the second flight test aircraft, originally scheduled for late December, is now expected in late January. No specific delivery dates are announced for the other four flight test airplanes.
- **January 16, 2008** Boeing announces that first flight for the number 1 airplane has been postponed from the end of the first quarter to the end of the second quarter. Deliveries to customers are also expected to be delayed.
- **January 21, 2008** Boeing is unclear on when the first flight will occur. It admits the global supply

chain system has created a major problem, the dimensions of which Boeing underestimated. While trying to play catch-up, Boeing has had to deal with an assembly line system that failed to foresee this kind of detail work, as well as a problem in trying to maintain proper and necessary documentation.

- **February 15, 2008** Assembly begins on the second flight test airplane. This is actually airplane number 4 and follows two static test airframes.
- **February 18, 2008** Boeing insists the number 1 airplane will be the first 787 to fly and refutes reports that a later aircraft will be the first off the ground. It appears that these reports were prompted in part by the fact that the assembly of airplane number 2 is progressing much faster and with far less travel work.
- **February 25, 2008** A new controversy arises, with reports that Boeing might cancel the 787-3 short-range versions of the 787 family. This model had accumulated fifty-six orders to date. Boeing insists it will produce the airplane, but admits some engineering resources have been diverted in an attempt to speed up work on the -8 model.
- **March 10, 2008** General Electric, the maker of the GEnx-1B turbo fan engine that will power the 787, announces it will recertify the engine with improvements. The delay in the 787 program has given GE the chance to implement these changes. A key change is the introduction of more durable fuel nozzles in the twin-annular pre-swirl combustor (TAPS), which gives this engine substantially lower nitrogen oxide emissions than the Rolls-Royce Trent 1000, the other engine available to 787 customers. As of March, the GEnx-1B has completed required certification testing based on its original design.

All Nippon Airways, the Japanese airline that was the launch order for the 787, is having to consider strategic changes in its fleet make-up because of the late delivery of the 787, as well as the training for its flight and maintenance personnel. The airline feels that Boeing has not been candid in admitting program delays sooner.

- **March 24, 2008** A problem is revealed that was discovered in the all-important composite center wing box manufactured by Fuji Heavy Industries. During validation and certification testing carried out in 2007, this critical component showed structural weaknesses. The solution to the problem was a redesign that includes the addition of two hundred clips and brackets, plus an additional five hundred fasteners. The first six airplanes off the production line will be retrofitted with stiffener plates, while the seventh airplane (ZA007), which will be the first delivery to ANA, will receive a redesigned center wing box.
- **April 7, 2008** The first casualty in the Boeing global supply chain has occurred. Boeing has applied to acquire Vought's 50 percent share of Global Aeronautica, a company co-owned with Alenia Aeronautica of Italy. Located in North Charleston, South Carolina, the company has had the role of airframe and systems integrator, a role that Vought managers found difficult. Now the main Vought plant can concentrate on building aft fuselage sections 47 and 48. In the meantime, Boeing maintains that the first flight is still set for the end of the second quarter of 2008. Global Aeronautica's assignment is to assemble seven composite fuselage sections into two major assemblies. These are supposed to arrive in Everett, Washington, stuffed with wiring, hydraulics, floors, and systems. The lack of this stuffing has been the major contributor to the long program delays.
- **April 9, 2008** Boeing releases a new and revised schedule for the 787. First flight is now set for the fourth quarter 2008, and deliveries are to begin third quarter 2009, with twenty-five 787s scheduled to be delivered in 2009. While this places the program a full fifteen months behind the original schedule, the new schedule has sufficient built-in padding that Boeing fully expects to be able to adhere to it. Boeing also indicates that the 787-9, originally to be the third model delivered, will instead be the second, ahead of the -3 model.
- **April 14, 2008** All Nippon Airlines reacts negatively to the new schedule and requests that a complete list of delivery dates for its fifty airplanes be issued. Since the previous September, Boeing has had to postpone first delivery three times, and first flight four times. In spite of all these delays, the order book for the 787 has grown to 892 airplanes for fifty-seven customers.
- **April 21, 2008** In an interview with *Aviation Week and Space Technology*, Hamilton Sunstrand president David P. Hess makes some revealing comments. He feels Boeing's global supply chain approach is still entirely valid, but notes that when Boeing pushed the supply chain in order to fulfill its July 8, 2007, rollout promise, it caused severe problems that ricocheted all the way down the supply chain.
- **April 25, 2008** Boeing moves the number 4 airplane, the first static test airframe, from the

assembly line to the testing rig, making room for assembly of the number 5 airplane to begin, the third flight test aircraft.

- **May 1, 2008** Assembly begins on the third flight test aircraft, the first 787 to be fitted with interiors. To date, there are twenty-five 787s in various stages of production throughout the global supply chain.
- **May 5, 2008** Vought finishes fabricating thirty-five fuselage barrels at its Forth Worth, Texas, plant.
- **May 5, 2008** Boeing chief executive officer McNerney indicates he is convinced there will not be any more delays in the 787 program.
- **May 19, 2008** A survey of original equipment manufacturers (OEMs) shows that the type of outsourcing initiated at a global level by Boeing on the 787 program is gathering more converts all the time. According to the survey, however, the problems encountered by Boeing are likely to bedevil these same OEMs, unless more oversight and management throughout the entire supply chain is installed. For example, the delays suffered on the 787 because of the lack of a newly-designed titanium fastener could, in part, be traced to its manufacturer, Alcoa, not having allowed enough lead time in the procurement of the titanium for the fastener.
- **May 26, 2008** While Boeing's 787 production line appears to be smoothing out, new problems have surfaced. Brake control monitors furnished by Crane Aerospace are late owing to supplier problems. Additionally, Hamilton Sunstrand's power systems are also being delivered later than forecasted. These two problems could delay the promised June "power on" of airplane number 1.

Financial analysts continue to express doubts that the fifteen-month delay that Boeing announced won't stretch out.

- **May 26, 2008** Boeing announces that a rough plan for a 787 freighter version has been drawn up.
- **June 9, 2008** Hamilton Sunstrand delivers the electrical power system software, clearing the way for "power on" to be initiated on the number 1 airplane.
- **June 11, 2008** Boeing reaches the critical power-on phase on the number 1 airplane for the first time. This indicates the beginning of an eight-day segment, during which all electrical and electronic systems are checked and approved.
- **June 23, 2008** Major sections for the number 4 airplane begin arriving at the Everett plant. These sections arrive in a condition much closer to completion, and in fact, the nose section is 100 percent complete.
- **June 30, 2008** The number 1 airplane is towed to the ramp and the installation of the Rolls-Royce Trent 1000 engines begins.
- **June, July, and August 2008** Ground testing of aircraft ZA001 continues with no major problems surfacing. At this point, the reader might assume that the "bump in the road" has been pretty well overcome and that the next phase, flight testing, may begin shortly.

Part B

- **July 2008** *Aviation Week and Space Technology* reports that the flow of assemblies from the various Tier 1 partners is not only much better, but the assemblies are arriving at the Everett plant almost 100 percent complete. One factor that is new to Boeing and its partners is that the Tier 1 partners are now responsible for system integration. This additional responsibility may have further contributed to the early problems encountered by the partners with resulting delays.
- **September 6, 2008** The International Machinists and Aerospace Workers Union at Boeing goes on strike when they and Boeing cannot reach a contract agreement. Twenty-seven thousand workers in Kansas, Oregon, and Washington State stop working, thus effectively shutting down the Boeing Commercial Airplane Company. Naturally, this is bad news not only for the 787 program, but for Boeing as a whole.
- **September 29, 2008** Qantas Airlines indicates it is so upset over Boeing's refusal to commit to the 787-10 model that it may opt to buy the Airbus A350-1000, in spite of a projected 2015 delivery date for the latter. Boeing's offer of 777-300ERs instead of the 787-10 is being met with disinterest by Qantas.
- **October 6, 2008** Boeing announces that August 2009 is the new delivery date for the first 787 to All Nippon Airways, as well as a stretched-out delivery of all fifty of its aircraft, thus confirming the fifteen-month delay for initial deliveries. As a result, ANA orders nine 767-300ERs for delivery in 2010-2011 to compensate for the late 787 delivery. Engineers are planning to run the tests on the 787 data system over the next few days. Two more static tests are also to be completed before the first flight: one on the leading edges of the wings and one on the trailing edges.

- **October 20, 2008** A major Intent to Purchase agreement by American Airlines for the 787 is revealed. The agreement calls for forty-two 787-9 airplanes to be delivered in the 2012-2018 period. American would also have the right to order an additional fifty-eight airplanes for delivery between 2015 and 2020.
- **October 27, 2008** The union votes in favor of returning to work after further concessions are made by Boeing. It is estimated that the nearly two-month-long strike cost Boeing $100 million a day.

  Some interesting facts surface that relate back to the beginning of the *Sonic Cruiser* program and to the origins of the large-scale outsourcing initiated for the 787 program. Back in 2000, the Boeing board of directors had questioned the cost of a new airplane design, this in part because of a number of false starts on a replacement for the venerable 747 jumbo. The *Sonic Cruiser* design failed because of high fuel costs, and its advanced technology was passed on to the 787. In an effort to reduce manufacturing costs, as well as to spread its risks, Boeing develops the global supply chain business model.
- **November 3, 2008** With the machinists strike finally ended November 1st, the outsourcing of most of the 787 airframe shows up as the leading concern of Boeing factory workers, who point to major worries over additional future outsourcing, with more job cutbacks as a result.
- **November 5, 2008** Boeing reveals a new and serious problem. Three percent of the rivets on the initial six test airplanes were improperly installed. All the Boeing 787 team can do is grit its collective teeth and hope for the best.

- **November 10, 2008** Boeing announces that a revised delivery schedule is being developed for the 787. The two main causes for this step are the fifty-seven-day strike and the problem of the improperly installed fasteners.
- **November 17, 2008** The credit crunch of fourth quarter 2008 is causing changes in the entire supply chain of the 787. While customer airlines are not canceling orders, they are deferring deliveries. This in turn is causing suppliers all along the supply line to also slow down their production. As long as this slowdown does not become extreme, experts believe that none of the companies involved will be financially affected to any great extent.
- **November 24, 2008** An interview of Boeing Commercial Airplane President and Chief Executive Officer Scott Carson by *Aviation Week and Space Technology* reveals some illuminating information. With many of the 787 orders coming from foreign countries, 70 to 80 percent of the value of those orders are eligible to be financed by the Export-Import Bank of the United States. Major airplane leasing companies, such as ILFC and GE Commercial Aviation Services, are actively seeking additional financing. Carson admitted that some of the outsourcing contracts written are not realistic, as a result of which Boeing plans to pull some of the necessary engineering back inside Boeing.

  With the increasing delays in 787 deliveries, these same airlines are ordering 767s as a backstop to fill their near-term capacity needs. Boeing has currently accumulated a backlog of seventy-one orders for 767s. This translates to six years of production for the 767 production line. It also

means that while Boeing will receive profits from its 787 orders later than originally planned, it can make up some of that shortfall through increased 767 production, something which had not originally been foreseen.
- **December 11, 2008** In what some observers consider a surprise move, Boeing headquarters restructures the top organization of the 787 program. Shanahan, who has been the 787 program manager since October 2007, is upgraded to head the New Airplane Programs organization, which includes both the 787 and 747-8 programs. Scott Fancher, who had previously headed Boeing's missile defense program, is now the general manager for the 787.

  Boeing admits the first flight date for the 787 has now moved to the second quarter of 2009. This latest delay is the fifth since the original first flight date was announced and puts the 787 two years behind that original date. The latest delay represents a five- to six-month slip and is because of the double whammy of the machinists strike and the problem of incorrectly installed fasteners that has affected all the test aircraft. First delivery to ANA is planned for the first quarter of 2010.
- **December 22, 2008** The 787's scheduled maintenance program is approved by the FAA. As one of the required approvals for final certification, this FAA approval constitutes attainment of an important goal.
- **February 9, 2009** Boeing reveals that more 787 order cancellations have been received. Previously, Azerbaijan Airlines had cancelled its order for one 787 and S7 Airlines had cancelled fifteen of the model. Now LCAL of Dubai cancels sixteen orders for the 787 of the twenty-one originally

ordered. This brings the total number of cancellations to thirty-two.

• **July 6, 2009** Reports have been swirling around Wall Street that Boeing plans to purchase the Vought Aircraft Industry 787 assembly plant in North Charleston, South Carolina. This latest report seems to confirm that Boeing continues to be dissatisfied with Vought's performance on the 787. Proof is that in 2008, Boeing bought out Vought's share of the fuselage integration plant jointly owned with Alenia of Italy. This plant is adjacent to the Vought plant now under discussion.

• **July 7, 2009** The first test aircraft (ZA001) begins low-speed taxi tests at Paine Field, adjacent to Boeing's Everett plant.

• **July 13, 2009** Boeing confirms that it is purchasing Vought's North Charleston, South Carolina, plant for $1 billion.

• **July 27, 2009** More information on the 787 wing problem is finally filtering out of Boeing's offices. It turns out that the stringers near the wing-body joint were delaminating under stress testing at a point below the required 150 percent of the extreme load limit required by the FAA. This is in addition to the fact that the problem was not predicted by computer models. The 787 supply line is estimated to have forty airplanes in process, and at least twenty-five wing sets are in production at Mitsubishi. Until the proper fix for the problem is determined, the entire production complex is likely to be slowed.

• **August 24, 2009** A new problem has been disclosed in the 787 all-composite airframe barrels manufactured by Alenia in Italy. Skin "wrinkles" have been found in the skin close to the area where the barrels are joined. Investigation reveals that the problem was caused by a stringer trim machine that bonded edges that are slightly too large. The solution developed is to use small patches on the early barrels already produced. Future barrels will have additional ties applied to take care of the problem. While the problem causes a production line shutdown for a few weeks, it does not affect total 787 production. Furthermore, the problem is not considered to be a safety issue.

• **August 27, 2009** Boeing announces that the first flight is now scheduled to take place by the end of 2009. First deliveries of the 787-8 to customers will take place in the first quarter of 2010, while first deliveries of the larger 787-9 will begin in the fourth quarter of 2013. The company also indicates that by 2013, it expects to produce ten airplanes a month, although only seven will come from the Everett plant. The remainder will have to be assembled at a second assembly line whose location has yet to be determined. A full revised schedule is to be issued shortly.

• **September 7, 2009** The delays that accumulated on the 787 program appear to have resulted in still another top-level management casualty. Scott Carson, the chief executive officer and president of Boeing Commercial Airplanes (BCA), has stepped down from that position and will retire from Boeing at the end of the year. His replacement is James Albaugh, who had been chief executive officer and president of Boeing's Integrated Defense Systems (IDS) since 2002. Albaugh is the third top-level executive to have come over to BCA from IDS. This causes concern for customers, financial analysts, and other observers on two counts: why are BCA executives having difficulty managing the 787 program, and why are there not capable managers within BCA ready to move up?

It was also revealed that while seventy-plus orders for the 787 have been cancelled to date, it is clear that these were caused by the worldwide financial crisis, rather than by 787 delivery delays. In fact, in some cases, some customers are likely to have benefited from delivery delays in a market that has shown a marked downturn.

• **September 23, 2009** Boeing announces that necessary modifications to the number 1 test aircraft involving the wing-fuselage attachment have begun. The static aircraft is also to undergo the same modification. This work is expected to require thirty days, which would mean that the long postponed first flight could take place by late October or early November.

Boeing is also confirming that it will take a $2.5 billion write-off in the third quarter because of past problems of the 787 program. Interestingly, Wall Street shrugged off this piece of news and Boeing stock has been slowly appreciating.

• **October 5, 2009** Boeing has had to hire additional test flight personnel because testing of both the 787 and 747-8 prototypes will coincide. This was not part of the original plan, but 787 delays have put the two programs on parallel tracks. Ironically, while additional pilots are being hired, various administrative personnel assigned to the Boeing Flight Test Center have been terminated.

To train the new flight crews properly, Boeing leased a Continental 737-900ER to assist in preparing the new crews for the upcoming test programs.

• **October 26, 2009** Boeing president and chief executive officer McNerney says that the latest flight schedule for the first flight to be by the end of 2009 is on track and that he does not expect further delays. McNerney also indicates that Boeing is close to a final decision on a site for a second 787 assembly line.

- **October 28, 2009** After weeks of speculation on the part of industry and the media, Boeing finally confirms that it will build a new assembly plant adjacent to other 787 facilities in North Charleston, South Carolina. The plant, scheduled to begin operation in July 2011, is to assemble 787-9 airplanes.

As part of the deal with the state of South Carolina, Boeing has pledged to create 3,800 new jobs in return for $170 million in bonds for start-up capital. The number of jobs promised is said by analysts to be more than what is needed for the 787-9 program, thus indicating that Boeing may have other additional plans for this facility. A possible project is the assembly of the 787-10 double-stretch model, which has not yet been officially approved by Boeing.

In the meantime, unions that deal with Boeing in the Puget Sound area are up in arms over the expansion and fear that eventually Boeing may transfer much of its manufacturing out of the state of Washington.

- **November 12, 2009** Boeing announces completion of the side-of-body installation in the first 787 test airplane. The same modification is to be made to the static test airframe, which will then be retested.
- **November 16, 2009** Boeing announces completion of side-of-body installation on the number 2 and 3 test airplanes. The modification on the number 1 airplane is to begin verification testing shortly.

Boeing will break ground for its new 610,000-square-foot plant in North Charleston, South Carolina, November 20th. The 787 assembly plant is expected to cost as much as $1 billion, if not more. It will be located adjacent to the existing Boeing-Alenia Global Aeronautica building, which integrates fuselage sections, and is also adjacent to the former Vought building now owned by Boeing.

- **November 30, 2009** In a somewhat surprising announcement, an Airbus executive reveals that the long delays affecting the 787 may also have a negative effect on Airbus and its A350XWB program. This concern was caused by the fact that the Boeing delay has had an effect on many suppliers who also supply Airbus.

It is also rumored that first flight of the 787 may be very soon.

Meanwhile, the North Charleston site is seeing the beginning of site work. When completed, the site will include six separate buildings. Production of 787-8 airplanes is to begin in 2012.

- **December 12, 2009** Boeing completes all the ZA001 high-speed taxi tests necessary, including reaching Vr (rotating velocity) rotation speed and lifting the nose wheel off the ground. At that point, ZA001 reached a speed of 130 knots.
- **December 14, 2009** Boeing reveals that on December 15th, the first flight will take place, weather permitting. Finally, at long last, after twenty-eight months, the excruciating delays were finally over. Boeing was ready to begin flying the first 787.

Orders for January 2002 through December 2013

Aeroflot - Russian Airlines Russian Federation Europe	787-8	05-Sep-2007	22
Aeromexico Mexico Central America and Mexico	787-8 GE	15-Aug-2006	2
Aeromexico Mexico Central America and Mexico	787-9 GE	24-Dec-2012	6
Air Astana Kazakhstan Central Asia	787-8 RR	23-Feb-2012	3
Air Berlin Germany Europe	787-8 GE	07-Jul-2007	15
Air Canada Canada North America	787-8 GE	10-Nov-2005	10
Air Canada Canada North America	787-8 GE	23-Apr-2007	5
Air Canada Canada North America	787-9 GE	10-Nov-2005	4
Air Canada Canada North America	787-9 GE	23-Apr-2007	18
Air China China East Asia	787-9	22-Aug-2005	15
Air Europa Spain Europe	787-8 RR	30-Mar-2007	8
Air France-KLM Group France Europe	787-9	27-Dec-2011	25
Air India India South Asia	787-8 GE	30-Dec-2005	27
Air New Zealand New Zealand Oceania	787-9 RR	25-Aug-2004	2
Air New Zealand New Zealand Oceania	787-9 RR	26-Oct-2005	2
Air New Zealand New Zealand Oceania	787-9 RR	14-Feb-2007	4
Air New Zealand New Zealand Oceania	787-9 RR	23-Mar-2012	2
Air Niugini Papua New Guinea Oceania	787-8 RR	04-Dec-2007	1

ALAFCO Kuwait Middle East	787-8 GE	06-Jul-2007	8
ALC USA North America	787-10	13-Sep-2013	30
ALC USA North America	787-9	20-Dec-2007	8
ALC USA North America	787-9	06-Dec-2011	4
ALC USA North America	787-9	13-Sep-2013	3
All Nippon Airways Japan East Asia	787-8 RR	26-Jul-2004	33
All Nippon Airways Japan East Asia	787-8 RR	21-May-2009	3
All Nippon Airways Japan East Asia	787-9 RR	26-Jul-2004	17
All Nippon Airways Japan East Asia	787-9 RR	21-May-2009	2
All Nippon Airways Japan East Asia	787-9	21-Sep-2012	11
American Airlines USA North America	787-8 GE	01-Feb-2013	12
American Airlines USA North America	787-9 GE	01-Feb-2013	30
Arik Air Nigeria Africa	787-9 GE	30-Mar-2007	3
Arik Air Nigeria Africa	787-9 GE	11-Sep-2007	4
Avianca Colombia South America	787-8 RR	04-Oct-2006	10
Avianca Colombia South America	787-8 RR	23-Nov-2007	2
Avianca Colombia South America	787-8 RR	28-Sep-2012	3
Aviation Capital Group USA North America	787-9	30-Mar-2007	5
Azerbaijan Airlines Azerbaijan Central Asia	787-8 GE	22-Feb-2007	2
Biman Bangladesh Airlines Bangladesh South Asia	787-8	22-Apr-2008	4
British Airways United Kingdom Europe	787-10	05-Dec-2013	12
British Airways United Kingdom Europe	787-8 RR	24-Dec-2007	8
British Airways United Kingdom Europe	787-9 RR	24-Dec-2007	16
British Airways United Kingdom Europe	787-9 RR	05-Dec-2013	6
Business Jet / VIP Customer(s) USA North America	787-8 GE	27-Jun-2007	1
Business Jet / VIP Customer(s) USA North America	787-8	20-Dec-2007	1
Business Jet / VIP Customer(s) USA North America	787-8 GE	13-Nov-2012	1
Business Jet / VIP Customer(s) USA North America	787-9 GE	28-Jul-2006	2
Business Jet / VIP Customer(s) USA North America	787-9 GE	29-Sep-2006	1
China Southern Airlines China East Asia	787-8 GE	16-Dec-2005	10

CIT Leasing Corporation USA North America	787-8	19-Sep-2006	1
CIT Leasing Corporation USA North America	787-8 GE	19-Sep-2006	4
CIT Leasing Corporation USA North America	787-9	03-Jul-2007	5
Delta Air Lines USA North America	787-8 RR	06-May-2005	18
Ethiopian Airlines Ethiopia Africa	787-8 GE	30-Jun-2005	10
Etihad Airways United Arab Emirates Middle East	787-10	14-Nov-2013	30
Etihad Airways United Arab Emirates Middle East	787-9 GE	10-Mar-2008	31
Etihad Airways United Arab Emirates Middle East	787-9 GE	13-Dec-2011	10
GECAS USA North America	787-10 GE	13-Sep-2013	10
Gulf Air Bahrain Middle East	787-8	18-Jan-2008	8
Gulf Air Bahrain Middle East	787-8	14-Apr-2009	8
Hainan Airlines China East Asia	787-8 GE	28-Nov-2005	8
Hainan Airlines China East Asia	787-8 GE	18-Jan-2007	2
Icelandair Iceland Europe	787-8 RR	31-Mar-2006	1
ILFC USA North America	787-8 RR	07-Oct-2005	8
ILFC USA North America	787-8 GE	07-Oct-2005	8
ILFC USA North America	787-8 RR	19-Jul-2006	1
ILFC USA North America	787-8 GE	19-Jul-2006	1
ILFC USA North America	787-8 GE	24-Jan-2007	1
ILFC USA North America	787-8	18-Jun-2007	10
ILFC USA North America	787-8 GE	18-Jun-2007	2
ILFC USA North America	787-8 RR	18-Jun-2007	2
ILFC USA North America	787-9 RR	07-Oct-2005	4
ILFC USA North America	787-9	24-Jan-2007	1
ILFC USA North America	787-9 GE	18-Jun-2007	3
ILFC USA North America	787-9 RR	18-Jun-2007	4
ILFC USA North America	787-9	18-Jun-2007	29
Japan Airlines Japan East Asia	787-8 GE	10-May-2005	23
Japan Airlines Japan East Asia	787-8 GE	30-Mar-2007	2
Japan Airlines Japan East Asia	787-9 GE	10-May-2005	7

Japan Airlines Japan East Asia	787-9 GE	30-Mar-2007	3
Japan Airlines Japan East Asia	787-9 GE	09-Jan-2012	10
Jet Airways India South Asia	787-9	29-Dec-2006	10
Kenya Airways Kenya Africa	787-8 GE	06-Mar-2006	6
Kenya Airways Kenya Africa	787-8 GE	15-Dec-2006	3
Korean Air South Korea East Asia	787-8 GE	24-Oct-2013	1
Korean Air South Korea East Asia	787-9 GE	31-May-2005	10
LAN Airlines Chile South America	787-8 RR	31-Oct-2007	22
LAN Airlines Chile South America	787-9 RR	31-Oct-2007	4
Lion Air Indonesia Southeast Asia	787-8 RR	08-Jun-2012	5
LOT Polish Airlines Poland Europe	787-8 RR	08-Sep-2005	7
LOT Polish Airlines Poland Europe	787-8 RR	13-Feb-2007	1
MG Aviation Limited Israel Middle East	787-9 RR	01-Dec-2006	2
Norwegian Norway Europe	787-8 RR	28-Feb-2005	2
Norwegian Norway Europe	787-8 RR	31-Mar-2006	1
Oman Air Oman Middle East	787-8	17-Nov-2011	6
PrivatAir Switzerland Europe	787-8	14-Nov-2006	1
PrivatAir Switzerland Europe	787-8	15-Jan-2008	1
Qantas Australia Oceania	787-8 GE	30-Mar-2006	14
Qatar Airways Qatar Middle East	787-8 GE	05-Apr-2007	30
Republic of Iraq Iraq Middle East	787-8	22-Dec-2009	10
Royal Air Maroc Morocco Africa	787-8 GE	29-Nov-2005	4
Royal Brunei Airlines Brunei Darussalam Southeast Asia	787-8 RR	16-May-2005	5
Royal Jordanian Jordan Middle East	787-8 GE	30-Mar-2007	2
Royal Jordanian Jordan Middle East	787-8 GE	11-Nov-2007	2
Royal Jordanian Jordan Middle East	787-8 GE	17-Jun-2010	3
Saudi Arabian Airlines Saudi Arabia Middle East	787-9	04-Nov-2010	8
Scoot Pte Ltd Singapore Southeast Asia	787-8 RR	10-Oct-2006	10
Scoot Pte Ltd Singapore Southeast Asia	787-9 RR	10-Oct-2006	10
Singapore Airlines Singapore Southeast Asia	787-10	18-Jun-2013	30

Transaero Airlines Russian Federation Europe	787-8 RR	03-Apr-2012	4
TUI Travel PLC United Kingdom Europe	787-8 GE	17-Feb-2005	4
TUI Travel PLC United Kingdom Europe	787-8 GE	15-Sep-2006	5
TUI Travel PLC United Kingdom Europe	787-8 GE	25-Sep-2006	2
TUI Travel PLC United Kingdom Europe	787-8 GE	27-Feb-2007	2
TUI Travel PLC United Kingdom Europe	787-8 GE	31-Oct-2013	2
Unidentified Customer(s) Unidentified Unidentified	787-8	05-Dec-2008	2
Unidentified Customer(s) Unidentified Unidentified	787-8 GE	04-Jul-2013	1
Unidentified Customer(s) Unidentified Unidentified	787-9	05-Dec-2008	13
United Airlines USA North America	787-10	19-Feb-2010	10
United Airlines USA North America	787-10	18-Jun-2013	10
United Airlines USA North America	787-8 GE	30-Jun-2005	5
United Airlines USA North America	787-8 GE	31-Dec-2005	2
United Airlines USA North America	787-8 GE	06-Jun-2006	4
United Airlines USA North America	787-8	19-Feb-2010	7
United Airlines USA North America	787-8 GE	07-Nov-2012	1
United Airlines USA North America	787-9 GE	06-Jun-2006	9
United Airlines USA North America	787-9 GE	12-Mar-2007	5
United Airlines USA North America	787-9	19-Feb-2010	8
United Airlines USA North America	787-9 GE	07-Nov-2012	4
Uzbekistan Airways Uzbekistan Central Asia	787-8 GE	29-Jun-2007	2
Vietnam Airlines Viet Nam Southeast Asia	787-9 GE	16-Nov-2005	4
Vietnam Airlines Viet Nam Southeast Asia	787-9 GE	21-Dec-2007	4
Virgin Atlantic Airways United Kingdom Europe	787-9 RR	09-Mar-2007	15
Virgin Atlantic Airways United Kingdom Europe	787-9 RR	21-Dec-2009	1
Xiamen Airlines China East Asia	787-8 GE	22-Aug-2013	6

APPENDIX III:
Tail Art

ALL NIPPON	AEROFLOT	AEROMEXICO	AIR BERLIN	AIR CANADA	AIR CHINA
AIR EUROPA	AIR INDIA	AIR NEW ZEALAND	AIR NIUGINI	AIR PACIFIC	AIR SEYCHELLES
ALAFCO	ARIK AIR	ARKIA	AVIANCA	AVIATION CAPITAL GROUP	AZERBAIJAN AIRLINES
BIMAN AIRLINES	BOEING BUSINESS JETS	BRITISH AIRWAYS	CHINA EASTERN AIRLINES	CHINA SOUTHERN AIRLINES	CIT AEROSPACE

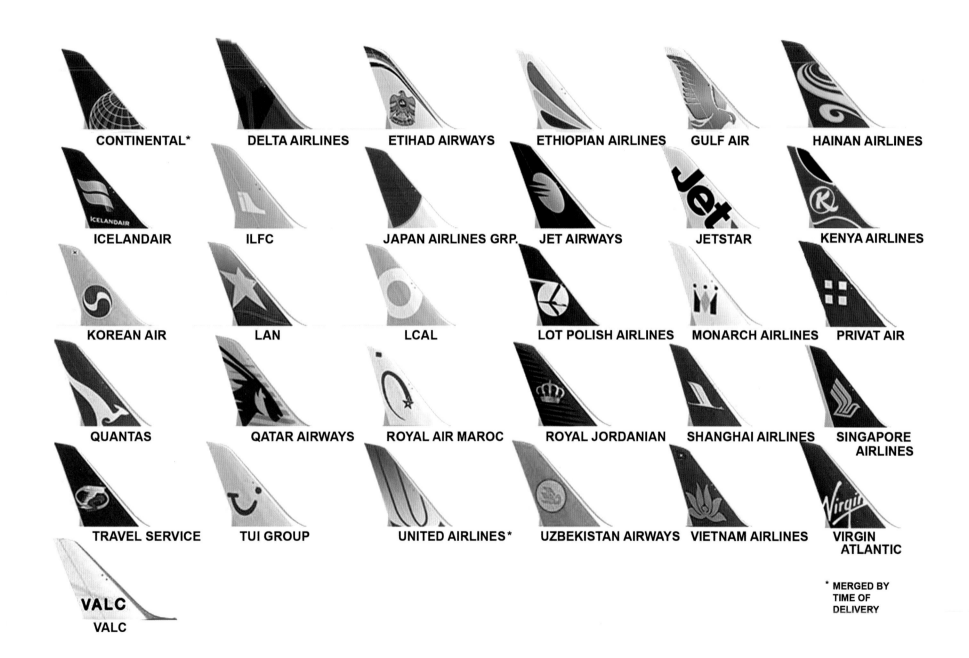

CONTINENTAL* DELTA AIRLINES ETIHAD AIRWAYS ETHIOPIAN AIRLINES GULF AIR HAINAN AIRLINES

ICELANDAIR ILFC JAPAN AIRLINES GRP. JET AIRWAYS JETSTAR KENYA AIRLINES

KOREAN AIR LAN LCAL LOT POLISH AIRLINES MONARCH AIRLINES PRIVAT AIR

QUANTAS QATAR AIRWAYS ROYAL AIR MAROC ROYAL JORDANIAN SHANGHAI AIRLINES SINGAPORE AIRLINES

TRAVEL SERVICE TUI GROUP UNITED AIRLINES* UZBEKISTAN AIRWAYS VIETNAM AIRLINES VIRGIN ATLANTIC

VALC

* MERGED BY TIME OF DELIVERY

Boeing 787-8 Operating Checklists

Before Startup Checklist
- Seat Belt Sign ON
- Fuel Quantity CHECK
- Engine Throttle IDLE
- Engines Area CLEAR
- Auto-brake Setting RTO
- Yaw Damper ON
- Fly-by-wire Setting CHECK
- Hydraulic ENG Pumps ON
- Hydraulic ELEC C1 Pump ON
- AC Packs 1 and 2 ON
- Equipment Cooling ON
- Fuel Pumps ON
- Startup Clearance REQUEST

Engines Startup Checklist
- APU Master Knob START > ON*
- APU Generator ON
- Engine EEC Modes ON
- Engine Starter Knob START
- Engine Fuel Controls RUN
- Engine Generators L1, R1 ON
- APU Master Knob OFF
- APU Generator OFF
- External Power OFF

Pre-Take-off Checklist
- Take Off Flaps SET
- Speed-brakes RETRACTED
- Instruments CHECK
- Landing Lights ON
- Strobe Lights ON
- Parking Brakes OFF

Take-off Checklist
- Centered on Runway CHECK
- Call our 80 knots CHECK

- V1 (Decision Speed) CHECK
- Vr (Rotation Speed) ROTATE
- V2 (Safety Speed) CHECK
- Positive Climb CHECK
- Landing Gears UP

Post-Take-off Checklist
- Auto-throttle (>200 KIAS) ON
- Taxi and Landing Lights OFF
- Flaps Lever AS REQ.
- Auto-pilot ON
- Route Manager ACTIVE

Climb-out Checklist (<FL100)
- Engine Instruments CHECK
- Hydraulic Systems CHECK

NOTE: Do NOT exceed 250 KIAS under FL100. If you do, the Fly-by-wire will reduce throttle to keep you under the limits.

Climb-out Checklist (FL100 to FL180)
- Max. Climb-rate 2500 fpm CHECK
- Auto-brake Setting OFF
- Seat Belts Sign AS REQ.
- Anti-Ice Controls AS REQ.
- Pressurization CHECK
- Engine Starters CHECK OFF
- APU Master Knob CHECK OFF
- Altimeter Setting SET 29.92

Climb-out Checklist (FL180 to Cruise)
- Approx. Climb Thrust 89% - 91% N1
- Max. Climb-rate (upto FL260) 1800 fpm CHECK
- Max. Airspeed (up FL260) 300 KIAS
- Max. Climb-rate (above FL260) 1000 fpm
- Mach Speed upto FL300 0.8 Mach SET
- Mach Speed above FL300 0.85 Mach SET

- Check N1 vs. N1 limit CHECK
- Fuel Quantity CHECK
- Equipment Temperatures CHECK

Descent Checklist
- Heads Up Display ON
- Seat Belt Sign ON
- Anti-Ice Controls AS REQ.
- Navigation Displays CHECK
- TCAS Instrument CHECK
- METAR and ATIS CHECK
- Engine Instruments CHECK
- Flight Displays CHECK
- Hydraulic Systems CHECK
- Air-Conditioning CHECK
- Pneumatic Systems CHECK
- Fuel Systems CHECK
- Window Heating CHECK

Check METAR with both ATIS and EFB Display. If there's a mismatch, reset the EFB. Also, load up the appropriate STAR (Standard Appraoch) or IAP (Instrument Appraoch) chart on the the Airport Charts page on the EFB.

Approach Checklist

NOTE: To get the runway's ILS frequency, either get it from ATIS or go to the EFB, Airport Information, Enter the Airport ICAO in the CDU's EFB INPUT page, go to the Runway Information page on the EFB, enter the Runway in the CDU's EFB INPUT page and click on SET NAV1 next to the ILS frequency on the EFB to set your NAV1 Radio.
- Landing Lights ON

- Altimeter Setting SET
- Navigation Radios TUNED
- Approach LOC (Localizer) ACTIVE
- Engine Instruments CHECK
- Maximum Speed 250 KIAS CHECK
- Flaps (<250 KIAS) SET 1 DEG
- Flaps (<230 KIAS) SET 5 DEG
- Flaps (<215 KIAS) SET 15 DEG
- Flaps (<200 KIAS) SET 25 DEG
- Flaps (<180 KIAS) SET 35 DEG
- Landing Gear (<2100 ft) DOWN
- Auto-brake Setting AS REQ.
- Speed Brakes CHECK RETRACTED, ARM

NOTE: Flaps requirement may vary with total aircraft weight. A flaps requirement calculator will be available on the CDU in the near future.

Landing Checklist
- Auto-throttle (500 AGL) OFF
- Auto-pilot (300 AGL) DISCONNECT

On Touchdown, (hope you do it smooooth)
- Reverse Thrust ENGAGE
- Speedbrakes UP, FULL

When slowed down to less than 70 KIAS
- Reverse Thrust DISENGAGE
- Auto-brake Setting OFF

To take over from the Auto-brake, apply manual brakes, and use manual brakes to slow down to taxi speed (max. 25 KIAS)

In case of a go-around, increase to full throttle, and confirm positive climb. Request further directions from ATC.